UNDERSTANDING
THOMAS BERGER

Understanding Contemporary American Literature
Matthew J. Bruccoli, Series Editor

Volumes on

Edward Albee • Sherman Alexie • Nicholson Baker • John Barth
Donald Barthelme • The Beats • Thomas Berger
The Black Mountain Poets • Robert Bly • T. C. Boyle • Raymond Carver
Fred Chappell • Chicano Literature • Contemporary American Drama
Contemporary American Horror Fiction
Contemporary American Literary Theory
Contemporary American Science Fiction, 1926–1970
Contemporary American Science Fiction, 1970–2000
Contemporary Chicana Literature • Robert Coover • Philip K. Dick
James Dickey • E. L. Doctorow • Rita Dove • John Gardner
George Garrett • Tim Gautreaux • John Hawkes • Joseph Heller
Lillian Hellman • Beth Henley • John Irving • Randall Jarrell
Charles Johnson • Adrienne Kennedy • William Kennedy • Jack Kerouac
Jamaica Kincaid • Tony Kushner • Ursula K. Le Guin • Denise Levertov
Bernard Malamud • Bobbie Ann Mason • Cormac McCarthy
Jill McCorkle • Carson McCullers • W. S. Merwin • Arthur Miller
Lorrie Moore • Toni Morrison's Fiction • Vladimir Nabokov
Gloria Naylor • Joyce Carol Oates • Tim O'Brien • Flannery O'Connor
Cynthia Ozick • Walker Percy • Katherine Anne Porter
Richard Powers • Reynolds Price • Annie Proulx
Thomas Pynchon • Theodore Roethke • Philip Roth
May Sarton • Hubert Selby, Jr. • Mary Lee Settle • Neil Simon
Isaac Bashevis Singer • Jane Smiley • Gary Snyder
William Stafford • Anne Tyler • Gerald Vizenor • Kurt Vonnegut
David Foster Wallace • Robert Penn Warren • James Welch
Eudora Welty • Tennessee Williams • August Wilson • Charles Wright

UNDERSTANDING THOMAS BERGER

Brooks Landon

The University of South Carolina Press

Published by the University of South Carolina Press
Columbia, South Carolina 29208

www.sc.edu/uscpress

Manufactured in the United States of America

19 18 17 16 15 14 13 12 11 10   10 9 8 7 6 5 4 3 2 1

Library of Congress Cataloging-in-Publication Data

Landon, Brooks.
Understanding Thomas Berger / Brooks Landon.
p. cm. — (Understanding contemporary American literature)
Includes bibliographical references and index.
ISBN 978-1-57003-828-0 (alk. paper)
1. Berger, Thomas, 1924– —Criticism and interpretation. I. Title.
PS3552.E719Z783 2009
813'.54—dc22
2009051099

For John Cofer Landon
and for Diane Bywaters Landon

Contents

Series Editor's Preface

The volumes of *Understanding Contemporary American Literature* have been planned as guides or companions for students as well as good nonacademic readers. The editor and publisher perceive a need for these volumes because much of the influential contemporary literature makes special demands. Uninitiated readers encounter difficulty in approaching works that depart from the traditional forms and techniques of prose and poetry. Literature relies on conventions, but the conventions keep evolving; new writers form their own conventions—which in time may become familiar. Put simply, UCAL provides instruction in how to read certain contemporary writers—identifying and explicating their material, themes, use of language, point of view, structures, symbolism, and responses to experience.

The word *understanding* in the titles was deliberately chosen. Many willing readers lack an adequate understanding of how contemporary literature works; that is, what the author is attempting to express and the means by which it is conveyed. Although the criticism and analysis in the series have been aimed at a level of general accessibility, these introductory volumes are meant to be applied in conjunction with the works they cover. They do not provide a substitute for the works and authors they introduce, but rather prepare the reader for more profitable literary experiences.

M. J. B.

Acknowledgments

For more than thirty years Thomas Berger has patiently and generously responded to my questions and sometimes far-fetched hypotheses about his writing. While scrupulously declining to comment on the "meaning" of his novels, Berger has frequently discussed their method and has been willing to answer questions about the sources and inspirations for his celebrations of language and of novel forms. Corresponding with Berger has been a privilege and a reward almost as great as has been reading his novels. I am grateful to him for permission to quote from his correspondence. I am also grateful to David W. Madden and to Jonathan Lethem for their efforts to introduce readers to the unique sensibility and style of Berger's fiction. Parts of this book were written at the Obermann Center for Advanced Studies at the University of Iowa, where director Jay Semel and Neda Barrett and Karla Tonella provide the kind of supportive environment scholars and writers dream of.

I have been writing about Thomas Berger for a long time now, so portions of this book have appeared in different form in a wide range of publications, most notably in *Thomas Berger* (Twayne, 1989). Portions of that book appear here by permission.

Finally I want to thank the late Matthew Bruccoli for his interest in adding a book on Thomas Berger to his Understanding Contemporary American Literature series and for his invaluable editorial guidance. Working with a legend was an honor.

CHAPTER 1

Understanding Thomas Berger

Career

Had the administrators of the Pulitzer Prize not overruled the recommendation of their judges' committee and given the 1984 Pulitzer Prize for fiction to Thomas Berger's *The Feud* rather than to William Kennedy's *Ironweed,* would Berger's place in American letters be significantly different? That is the kind of question suggested by Berger's 1989 novel, *Changing the Past,* but not the kind of question that Berger himself would ever dwell upon. After a writing career that spans fifty years and twenty-three novels, Berger knows that his reputation is assured by one of the most distinguished bodies of work in postwar American fiction. Having persisted throughout his career in the writing of novels that are aggressively intelligent and consistently resistant to the twin sentimentalities of idealism and despair, Berger easily ranks among the most accomplished novelists since the end of World War II, and his writing seems sure to earn him a lasting place in American letters. His novels have established him as not only one of the most energetic American writers but also one of the most unpredictable, since no two of his books seem, at first glance, to have much in common. The fact that each of his books seems to follow a different genre convention is further complicated by the fact that no established genres prepare his readers for what his novels quickly become, no matter what genre traditions they seem to start from.

Having read *Little Big Man,* readers and critics alike find it quite difficult to understand how *Regiment of Women* could come from the same writer. And the task is almost as difficult with any two of Berger's novels: little in *Arthur Rex* prepares readers for *Neighbors,* little in *Neighbors* prepares readers for *Reinhart's Women,* and nothing in *Reinhart's Women* prepares readers for *Adventures of the Artificial Woman.* Over a decade ago, Richard Schickel called Berger "one of the most radical sensibilities now writing novels in this country," and any careful examination of Berger's novels more than confirms Schickel's claim.[1] Berger's writing has always been just a bit too intelligent, a bit too unsentimental, a bit too hard to identify to garner him the number of readers and the popular acclaim easily granted to numerous contemporaries whose prose skills, narrative designs, and philosophical interrogations pale in comparison. For those readers long charmed and profoundly rewarded by Berger's indisputable genius, this is hard to understand. It just doesn't seem fair.[2]

Indeed, in his introduction to *Meeting Evil* (1992), Berger's eighteenth novel, when it was republished in paperback by Simon and Schuster in 2003, Jonathan Lethem, an award-winning novelist as hip as any America can offer, has once again raised the fiercely loyal battle cry of Berger's intensely loyal readers, many of nearly cultish devotion. "I'm grateful for the chance," writes Lethem, "to shout that Thomas Berger is one of America's three or four greatest living novelists."[3] It is important to remember that among Thomas Berger's twenty-three novels are at least two stunning sweeping classics, *Little Big Man* (1964) and *Arthur Rex* (1978); the celebrated sequel to Jack Crabb's fantastic adventures, *The Return of Little Big Man* (1999), *Neighbors* (1980), and *The Feud* (1983); and the four novels in the unique Reinhart series, the most recent of which is *Reinhart's Women* (1981).

For all their delightful complexity, Berger's novels are eminently accessible, just difficult to characterize in their insistent diversity. That the above catalog of Berger's best-known novels leaves out such widely differing rewarding reads as *Killing Time* (1967), *Regiment of Women* (1973), *Sneaky People* (1975), *Who Is Teddy Villanova?* (1977), *Meeting Evil* (1992), and *Suspects* (1996) reminds readers that Berger ranges far and wide for his literary models and honors antique forms just as surely as he gives them contemporary voice. And this now expanded catalog *still* does not mention five other Berger novels, *Being Invisible* (1987), *The Houseguest* (1988), *Orrie's Story* (1989), *Changing the Past* (1990), and *Robert Crews* (1994), books that if considered alone would mark an admirable and noteworthy oeuvre, if not the "career of quiet dazzle," marked by all twenty-three of his books.

That career has unfolded steadily since the appearance in 1958 of *Crazy in Berlin.* While most of Berger's novels have received critical acclaim, none has been a best seller, and his career has been marked more by the noteworthy roster of appreciative reviewers and critics who have been fascinated by Berger's unique fiction than by popular acclaim. However, Berger's third novel, *Little Big Man* (1964), is generally regarded as his masterpiece, that codified his spot in the ranks of important American novelists. *Little Big Man* did not gain widespread recognition when first published, but the success of Arthur Penn's film adaptation in 1970 redirected attention to the novel, as did numerous critical articles praising its unique voice and historical vision. Historians and critics of Western literature hailed *Little Big Man* as one of the great historical (and historically accurate) novels of postwar American fiction.

Berger's subsequent novels, particularly *Killing Time* (1967), *Who Is Teddy Villanova?* (1978), *Neighbors* (1980), and *The Feud* (1983), have been the subject of significant reviews and articles by a wide range of writers and academics.[4] In 1989 I authored *Thomas Berger,* the first critical book devoted entirely to Berger, and in 1995 David W. Madden edited *Critical Essays on Thomas Berger.*[5]

The most recent, and one of the most perceptive, celebrations of Berger's writing, comes from Jonathan Lethem, in "Uncertainty Principle: Berger's Ambivalent Usurpations," Lethem's introduction to the 2003 paperback edition of Berger's *Meeting Evil.* Berger has never become a critical cottage industry, but his champions are so numerous and so passionate that it would be misleading to call him neglected. Nevertheless, it remains an article of faith among Berger readers that he deserves recognition as one of the most important American novelists of the twentieth century.

As might be expected of a writer in the mold of Vladimir Nabokov—and one who has widely ranged his novels across genres and historical eras—only the most oblique and ultimately insignificant connections can be drawn between the circumstances of Berger's life and the particulars of his fiction. Nevertheless, a brief summary of Berger's background may be of interest, particularly since his desire for privacy has given him something of a reputation as a recluse. In a 1990 *Washington Post* interview with David Streitfeld, Berger commented on his reputation of being reclusive: "The plain truth is that I would shameless suck up to anybody who might further my career (which indeed seems to be precisely what I'm doing here), but in the far-off days when I went public in quest of self-aggrandizement, I encountered only other opportunists, *mes semblables et freres*, who expected to do to me what I had intended to do to them."[6]

As a man as well as a writer, Berger both invites and defies description. In his mideighties, he is a big man whose shaved head draws attention to penetrating eyes under eyebrows he once described as "arched in perpetual curiosity." His jacket photo, by Jerry Bauer, freezes his age at fifty and presents him as a magnificent head, gazing from shadows. The overall effect manages to be at once faintly monkish and vaguely Charles Adamsish—a distinct but indecipherable suggestion of what the Czech film director Milos Forman affectionately called Berger's "veerrdness."

Berger was born in Cincinnati, Ohio, in 1924 and grew up in the nearby suburban community of Lockland, where he attended the same public school from kindergarten through high school. His father was the school's business manager. Berger notes of his childhood, "Very early in life, I discovered that for me reality was too often either dull or obnoxious, and while I did play all the popular games that employ a ball, lower hooks into the water, and, especially fire guns, I preferred the pleasure of the imagination to those of experience, and I read incessantly."[7] When asked by David Madden what provoked him to write fiction, Berger elaborated:

> As a child I always loved to read and exercise my imagination. I have a vague memory of wanting to grow up to be a foreign correspondent, but that had to do almost entirely with wearing a trench coat, and I think that before I got too old I understood the difference between journalism and fiction and came to prefer the latter as being more likely to serve the truth: I mean of course, using Pascal's

> distinction, the truth of the heart and not of the reason, which is to say the serious truth as opposed to that of expedience and vulgarity. I regard myself as a teller of tales that are intended primarily to enchant or at least entertain myself. Only by living in the imagination can I successfully pretend I am a human being.[8]

When in high school, Berger worked part-time in a branch of the Cincinnati Public Library, and he also did library work when he was in college, experience that would later help him secure his first job in New York City.

The circumstances of Berger's childhood do not seem to have had much of a direct influence on his fiction (certainly little, if anything, in his writing could be termed autobiographical in any strict sense), but the *sounds* of his childhood—the speech he grew up listening to—have exercised an influence little short of profound. *Sneaky People, The Feud,* and *Reinhart in Love* were generated as much from his fascination with the language of his childhood as from conventional concerns with plot, theme, or story. While writing *The Feud,* Berger reported, "I'm having a splendid time recreating the speech I heard when a child" (28 January 1982), and he has identified *Sneaky People* as "my tribute to the American language of 1939—to be philologically precise, that of the lower-middle class in the eastern Middle West, on which I am an authority as on nothing else."[9] More recently he explained: "I have all my life listened to the radio regularly, beginning in its golden age, the 1930's. And I don't have to remind you of my interest in sound, particularly that of human speech. In fact a good many of my sentences take their pretext from the sound of a certain word" (23 May 1979). Readers familiar with the trademark deadpan humor of the radio duo of

Bob and Ray may also find echoes of their style in Berger's writing. He acknowledges that he has long been a fan of their brilliant humor, terming them "masters of American dialogue" and concluding, "I should say that it is very likely they have been an important influence on me" (24 September 1987). Perhaps even more important to Berger's writing were the now classic movies of the 1930s and 1940s, references to which appear again and again in his novels, usually suggesting that the worlds of those movies largely influenced the behaviors or attitudes of the characters in Berger's novels. Indeed, in some respects his fiction frequently aspires to the recognized artificiality of classic American cinema, his novels striving to create "alternative" worlds sharing many of the assumptions and codes valorized in the films of his youth. In more recent novels Berger also provides ample evidence that he is very well versed in the vagaries of American television.

Disenchanted after a short bout with higher education, first at Miami University in Ohio and then at the University of Cincinnati, Berger enlisted in the army and served from 1943 to 1946, his experiences giving him some of the background for his first novel, *Crazy in Berlin*. In 1948 he received his B.A. at the University of Cincinnati, and he was a graduate student in English at Columbia in the school year 1950–51. There he completed course work for an M.A., including a class with Lionel Trilling, and began a thesis on George Orwell, which he never completed. Berger not only abandoned that project, but left grad school altogether, although he acknowledges that "no doubt an Orwellian point of view can be seen in much of what I write."[10]

While it would be unwise to overestimate Trilling's influence on Berger's writing, it is important to note that many of Berger's statements about his fiction and many aspects of the fiction itself parallel Trilling's beliefs, particularly as represented in his essay "The Meaning of a Literary Idea." While Berger recalls that as a student in Trilling's course in modern American literature he "worshiped Trilling . . . and was much taken with his sort of sociocultural criticism" (28 January 1979), he downplays suggestion of lasting impact: "Make of Trilling's influence what you will. I don't see much of it in my fiction, in which I think my influences are other literary artists, not critics, and yes, the movies and TV" (11 June 1987). From academic graduate study, Berger turned his attention to the writers' workshop at the New School for Social Research. At the New School, Berger "studied classical Greek and philosophy for a while with refugee professors from the great universities of Germany, who had fled Hitler" (11 June 1987). Called "the University in Exile," this special faculty seems likely to have helped shape Berger's lifelong fascination with the parameters of freedom and victimization. In the New School writers' workshop, Berger's fellow students included William Styron, Jack Kerouac, and Mario Puzo. Since 1950 Berger has been married to Jeanne Redpath, an artist he met at the New School.

Under the aegis of the New School workshop director Charles Glicksberg, Berger, who explains he had always thought of himself as a writer, began to write short stories: "I produced one story a week for three months, most of them melancholy in tone, maudlin in spirit, and simple of mind, Hemingway then being my model. Graduating in time to the influence of Faulkner, I published a thing or two of little merit during the next five years in 'little' magazines, but I didn't begin my first novel and develop my own style, such as it is—and little did I know that it would be different in each successive novel—until I was within a few months of my thirtieth birthday."[11]

"Dependency of Day and Night," published in the spring 1952 *Western Review,* confirms the accuracy of this self-assessment, but suggests that the Hemingway influence was even then heavily tempered by Berger's sense of irony, as Berger's soldier protagonist suffers not from battle wounds but from dermatitis.

Of his short fiction Berger is distinctly unenamored. As he has explained, "the marathon is my event, and not the hundred-yard dash":

> My gift is not seen at advantage in short works of fiction. (Nor do I usually read short stories with much pleasure.) Perhaps this is because I do not have much room in a story to create my alternative reality—and I am not unusually eloquent as a mere commentator on the reality I must, being human, share with everyone else. To put it another way, in the novel I have before me the possibility of being Alexander or Caesar—or Genghis Khan: there is a land of some magnitude to conquer. But a story seems a kind of Liechtenstein or San Marino: what does one have when he has assaulted and taken it? A trade in postage stamps. (23 August 1977)

Despite this preference, Berger's short fiction has appeared in magazines ranging from the *Saturday Evening Post* to *Playboy* and the *North American Review.* He has written reviews and short satirical pieces for *Esquire,* where he also wrote a column on film from 1972 to 1973. Berger has written four plays, only two of which, *The Burglars: A Comedy in Two Acts* and *Other People,* have been published, the latter of which was also produced in 1970 at the Berkshire Theatre Festival in Massachusetts.[12] A Berger radio play, *At the Dentist's,* was produced by Vermont Public Radio in 1981.

From 1948 through 1951, Berger supported his writing by working as a librarian at the Rand School of Social Science. One cannot read the issues of the *Institute of Social Studies Bulletin,* in which some of Berger's early book reviews appeared, without realizing that his work at the Rand School immersed him in an exciting, intellectually and ideologically charged environment, quite a break, no doubt, from earlier life with Protestant, "right-wing Ohio Republican" parents, when Berger had himself been completely uninterested in politics. Even in those early reviews, however, Berger's interest clearly lay in ideas rather than in ideologies, a distinction rigorously maintained throughout his writing.

In 1951–52 he was a staff member of the *New York Times Index,* and in the following year he was a copy editor for *Popular Science Monthly.* During the early 1950s, Berger wrote a number of reviews, many of which were for *New Leader* and the *Institute of Social Studies Bulletin.* Of particular note are those of Orwell's *Shooting an Elephant,* Koestler's *Age of Longing,* and Arendt's *Origins of Totalitarianism* in *Intro* and those of the anonymously authored *A Woman in Berlin* and Poliakov's *Harvest of Hate* in the *Socialist Call.* In the former three, Berger discusses the limitations, opportunities, and responsibilities of the ideological novel, while in the latter two can be found part of the likely background for his first novel, *Crazy in Berlin.* These early reviews offer little promise of Berger's subsequent prose style, nor do they more than hint at the complicated sensibility seen in his novels.

Having lived in New York City from 1948 to 1953, Berger moved frequently during the next twenty-six years, moving first to "a little village on the Hudson River," then to London, then to the beach at Malibu, California, before moving back to another village on the Hudson, then returning to London, and then back to New York City, where he remained for another seven and a half years. Next came a year in the Hamptons on Long Island, followed by three years on Mount Desert Island in Maine. In 1979 he moved to his present location, once more in a small village on the Hudson riverbank. "I have lead a quiet life for the past quarter century," he notes, "writing novels, talking with my wife (now of 57 years) and whichever of her dachshunds is current, and going out only on the weekly trip to the supermarket" (10 June 2007).

Until 1964 and the publication of his third novel, *Little Big Man,* Berger did freelance editing to supplement the income from his writing. That writing won a Dial fellowship in 1962, the Western Heritage Award in 1965, and the Rosenthal Award that same year. In 1975–76 Berger was Distinguished Visiting Professor at Southampton College; a decade later he was awarded an honorary D.Litt. by its parent institution, Long Island University. For the first semesters of the 1981–82 and 1982–83 school years, Berger was visiting lecturer at Yale. In 1983 he declined an appointment to the American Institute of Arts and Letters, a quiet manifestation of his "fundamental lack of a feeling of community with most of my literary fellows: I am necessarily *with* them (chronologically), but I am not *of* them" (21 June 2007).

Little interested in teaching, lecturing, or participating in the literary community, Berger is first and last a novelist. "I never take a vacation," he has written, "because what would it be from? I became a novelist many years ago so that I might live in a continuum of make-believe in which there are no weekends and, more importantly, no Monday mornings" (6 September 1977). In 1980, he concluded a written interview with Richard

Schickel by stating a succinct personal credo: "I should like the reader to be aware that a book of mine is written in the English language, which I love with all my heart and write to the best of my ability and with the most honorable of intentions—which is to say, I am peddling no quackery, masking no intent to tyrannize, and asking nobody's pity. (I suspect that I am trying to save my own soul, but that's nobody else's business.)"[13]

Overview

Thomas Berger's devoted readers know how difficult a task it is to describe his writing—and any effort to do so with utility must alternate between general statements of Berger's method and specific analysis that is just as likely to challenge as it is to confirm those statements. His novels wear twenty-three different masks, cutting across so many convenient critical categories and defying so many well-fed expectations that only the most general descriptions can introduce new readers to Berger's writing, celebrating as it does the diversity of novel forms, the complexities of language, the paradoxes of the human condition, and the possibilities of prose style. Perhaps the one thing on which critics agree is that Berger's talent is unique. The variety of Berger's novels, a range with no equal in contemporary American literature, underlines the precision of his craft, while distracting readers from the steadiness and the seriousness of his purpose. And because Berger's central concerns are deeper and older than those associated with any particular culture in which his novels are set, they are particularly challenging to describe.

The goal of this book is to explain at once why Berger's novels are actually much more complicated than they at first seem and then to explain the radical implications of his writing. To understand the writing of Thomas Berger, a reader needs to recognize his primary allegiance to language and prose style, his celebrations of the artifices of fiction over the "facts" of reality, his rejection at once of both sentimentality and irony as unchallenged worldviews, and his embrace of the human in all its banality, weakness, and inexplicable optimism. Understanding Thomas Berger requires the reader to realize that the interpretation of Berger's novels *is* the study of his style and that the discussion of meaning really centers on the ways in which a reader experiences his writing. When Berger suggests that only the "selfish" reader will get the most out of his work, he explicitly spells out what his novels implicitly demand: far from encouraging readers to "lose" themselves in fiction, his novels challenge their readers to become conscious of themselves in the act of reading.[14]

Language and Style

The apparent diversity of genres, subjects, and themes in Thomas Berger's twenty-three novels is unified by his thoroughgoing fascination with the many dimensions of prose style, appearing as they do in the languages of life as well as those of literature. This fascination with language gives rise to all the fundamental patterns of Berger's fiction, informing the basic structure, themes, and character portrayals in his novels. As a result, his fiction challenges readers to recognize that they live more in a world of words than of things, a world where the mechanisms of language—the ways in which people think and talk about existence—determine the quality of experience more than do the "facts" of experience themselves. Indeed, as character after character encounters (but does not often learn) in Berger's novels, the very idea of a "fact" is a linguistic rather than sensory phenomenon, and as such it can be manipulated and distorted, usually to someone's specific ends, to the detriment of someone else. Readers can expect a series of recurring situations in Berger's novels in which language seems to war with "reality." Or, more properly, the situation reminds readers that whatever the physical, experiential terrain of "reality," they know that sensory terrain primarily from the map of language—a map continuously redrawn to suit the selfish interests of the mapmakers in all humans.

One way of summarizing this overriding concern is simply to say that for Berger, the novel's most profound subject must always be the power of language. The persistent goal of Berger's novels is to shift attention, from a purportedly real world of experience, to the ways in which that world is conventionally perceived as a construct of language. It is in this sense that Berger cheerfully warns that we should not confuse fiction with life, because "the latter is false," and it is in this spirit that he reminds the readers of *Killing Time* that his novel "is a construction of language and otherwise a lie." The magnificent "lie" of fiction, built upon the even more basic "lie" of language, where words are not the things they name, fascinates Berger and supplies one of the most prominent recurrent subjects in his novels.

Berger's sentences, frequently elaborately serpentine, twist syntax, display exotic diction, and sharpen his thoughts and images toward ever more precise edges. His mastery of his prose style, however, does not mean that his attitude toward language is that of a craftsman toward his tools. Instead, the larger effect of Berger's novels is to suggest that the novelist's manipulations of the prose surface of his book are those of momentary and isolated control rather than those of ultimate mastery, a state roughly akin to that of a bronco buster who often stays on, but never manages to break, a particular horse. Berger has said that language is "a morality and a politics and a religion" to him, and his novels suggest that indeed in language reside the roots and the power of all such abstract systems.[15] Accordingly his novels all address the workings of language, particularly the ways in which language determines the perception of reality.

A major assumption underlying Berger's writing would seem to be that understanding of the referential world is largely determined by the ways *it is talked about,* the linguistic codes and formulas people have evolved for shaping their lives and their literature. This may at least in part account for persistent reminders throughout Berger's fiction that "Nature" is the source of physical and physiological "facts" that defy the spin of language and sometimes awkwardly remind readers that some concepts of "normality" actually rise from the way things are, as opposed to the way one might wish them to be. Berger's novels strongly suggest that many of the problems of human existence stem from the reification of verbal constructs and from the consequent confusion of language with the referential world. A corollary implication is that this confusion arises in significant part from the fact that these verbal constructs—linguistic codes for discussing racism, patriotism, or sexuality, for instance—are born of efforts to manipulate perceptions of reality for the interest of a particular worldview.

Consider that Jack Crabb, in *Little Big Man,* bounces back and forth not just between white and Plains Indian cultures but between competing codes of conduct designed to legitimize all manner of cruelty. Berger shows how Jack's greatest problems are at bottom matters of *definition,* and the many different narrative codes Jack employs to tell his story reflect some of the major ways in which we have talked about the West, depending on the moment's perceived needs. Consequently Berger's novels focus not so much on ideas or themes (although they swell with both) as on the relationship between language and thought. Language *is* Berger's theme, and if his novels can be said to support a central thesis, it is roughly that the interaction of competing and conflicting language codes provides the most important constant of human existence.

Sneaky Celebrations of Genre

Because Berger's fiction never advertises its anomalies, seeming to follow conventional narrative patterns, linear time schemes, and standard syntax, its experimental or innovative dimension is often overlooked. In this respect, Berger's style somewhat resembles the broad pattern of deception best explained by Poe's Inspector Dupin in "The Purloined Letter," where he explains the advantages of hiding something in plain sight, where it escapes detection by being excessively obvious. Berger's literary experiments are of this kind, sneaky in their obviousness.

To recognize that this so-obvious-as-to-be-overlooked experimental aspect is a major feature of Berger's style, the reader must understand the nature of his celebrations of classic novel genres. The jacket note written by Berger for *Who Is Teddy Villanova?* reviews the general scheme of his career: "Each of Thomas Berger's novels celebrates another classic genre of fiction: the western *(Little Big Man)*, the childhood memoir *(Sneaky People)*, the anatomical romance *(Regiment of Women)*, the true-crime documentary *(Killing Time)*, and the Reinhart books (*Crazy in Berlin, Reinhart in Love,* and *Vital Parts)* together form a sociological epic."

Who Is Teddy Villanova? extends this pattern to the classic American hard-boiled detective story, and *Arthur Rex* to Arthurian romance; *Neighbors* traces its lineage to Kafka, Laclos, and Sade; and *Reinhart's Women* continues the sociological epic of the Reinhart series. Berger describes his twelfth novel, *The Feud,* as a "Dreiserian slice of life," while *Nowhere,* his thirteenth, clearly invokes the utopian/dystopian tradition of Swift and Butler. *Being Invisible,* Berger's fourteenth published novel, has ties to H. G. Wells's and Ralph Ellison's quite different invisible men, while *The Houseguest* presents a self-made hollow man in the tradition of *The Great Gatsby* (although Berger suggests that this novel may have had its origins in a John Belushi skit on "Saturday Night Live").

While *Changing the Past* (1989) does not seem to start from any specific novel tradition, it clearly shares assumptions with "Dr. Jekyll and Mr. Hyde," as well as with the "three wishes" tradition in folklore and fairy tales. *Orrie's Story* (1990) resets the *Oresteia* in postwar America, and *Robert Crews* (1994) celebrates one of the very starting points of the novel itself, DeFoe's *Robinson Crusoe.* Both *Changing the Past* and *Meeting Evil* (1992) can be read as parables with affinities to Kafka's "Before the Law," a reminder of the importance of Kafka to understanding Berger. *Suspects* (1996) reminds us of Berger's interest in police procedurals. *The Return of Little Big Man* (1999) extends the vanishing of Plains Indians life so carefully chronicled in *Little Big Man* to the final vanishing of the American West as it disappears into the simulations of the World's Columbian Exposition and the theatricalizations of Buffalo Bill's Wild West Show. *Best Friends* (2004) offers another example of the doubling and confusion of "kicker and kickee," long a feature of Berger's fiction, and *Adventures of the Artificial Woman* (2004), while characterized by Berger as more "literary conceit" than novel, can only remind us of the complicated educational trajectory of the creature in Mary Shelley's *Frankenstein.*

The notion that these books parody their genre forms has dogged Berger's career, appearing in most reviews of his work. However, the careful study of genre sources that has preceded the writing of these novels has been for Berger too much a labor of love to result only in parody. Unlike parody, Berger's novels start from, rather than aim toward, the traditions of literary formulas, a testing and broadening of possibilities rather than a burlesquing of limitations. Berger has explained: "I never think about form. The structure of any book of mine comes from the sequence of the words. My conscious intention is always to write as conventional an example (of whichever genre) as I can manage to do. Thus I never begin with the intention to deride a genre; my purpose is always to celebrate it, to identify and applaud its glories" (11 February 1977). While he goes on to admit, "I am usually hoodwinked by my imagination before I get far," that imagination looks far beyond the conventions of literary genres. In a 1980 interview with Richard Schickel, Berger expressed his impatience with those who mistake him "for a merry-andrew with an inflated pig's bladder," because such readers "can never understand that I adore whichever tradition I am striving to follow, and that what results is the best I can manage by way of joyful worship—not the worst in sneering derision."[16]

The novels of a protean writer as widely read as is Berger will inevitably contain echoes and invocations of the pantheon of great literature, and scrambling reviewers and critics have noted Berger's debt to or affinity with Shakespeare, Dante, Smollett, Goethe, Tolstoy, Dostoyevsky, Melville, Dickens, Proust, Kafka, Faulkner, and Nabokov (to name just a few). Include the Berger novels that obviously start from particular literary models, and this list must be expanded to include Aeschylus, Malory, Moore,

Defoe, Mary Shelley, H. G. Wells, Booth Tarkington, Dashiel Hammett, and Raymond Chandler (again to name just a few). To speak of Berger's literary influences, then, is to say as little and as much as to note the influences on Joyce's *Ulysses*. Suffice it to say that Berger's fiction is inspired and informed by the great traditions and works of literary history.

What makes Berger's experiments with literary traditions hard to detect is that he follows the rules of conventional literary arrangement, but he may do so through an unexpected and unsettling jumble of literary codes. This juxtaposing of incongruous—if not seemingly incompatible—aspects of prose and genre style results in an intensification of the "fictionality" of Berger's novels. This effect has been most effectively analyzed by Jonathan Lethem, who explains:

> I can think of no other American writer more invested in and trusting of the means and materials of fiction qua fiction: scenes and sentences, chapters and paragraphs, and, above all, characters—their voices and introspections, their predicaments in fictional worlds. He's cultivated this investment to the exclusion of all forms of topicality or sociology, autobiographical appeals to readerly interest, superficial "innovations," or controversialism. Berger's too interested in the mysteries of narrative to bother with metafiction, yet his world does possess a certain rubbery pleasure in its own artifice. He doesn't bother to disguise fiction's proscenium arch—his "realism," such as it is, resides in his assiduous scrutiny of daily existence, at levels both psychological and ontological. Berger adores novels too much to play at their destruction or to be embarrassed at his participation in a tradition.[17]

Berger's novels characteristically start from some recognizable literary tradition only to twist it in ways that call attention to the fact that it is indeed "a literary tradition," whose protocols, whether scrupulously observed or self-consciously subverted, construct an artificial world that can only remind readers of the ways in which "reality" is itself equally a construct. If readers can be sure of only one thing in his writing, it is that expectations are meant to be disproved. To this end, Berger tries to make of each novel an "independent existence," an alternative reality he hopes the reader will approach "without the luggage of received ideas, a priori assumptions, sociopolitical axes to grind, or feeble moralities in search of support" (8 November 1976). "If you want to know what I do," he has more recently suggested, "go look at *Neighbors,*" explaining that in its writing he had no idea what was coming next: "I had no idea, but I usually don't in my books. I don't plot, I don't make notes, I don't structure, I don't outline. That's why I say the style, the language, is so important, because once I get the style, the style writes the book. I never think of it consciously. I sit down at the typewriter, and I get into that style, that voice, and I begin to hear it or begin to see it."[18]

This technique is not without its consequences, however, as Zulfikar Ghose, Berger's friend and himself a novelist of unique sensibility speculates: "Novels whose subject matter is their greatest appeal are invariably vastly popular. . . . Novels which stand on their style alone win readers slowly, in little bands here and there, until the work becomes one of the layers which compose human consciousness."[19] Or, as Jonathan Lethem puts it, "Each time Berger writes he ventures out with only his style for courage."[20]

What Berger terms the "alternative reality" or "independent existence" of his novel is a verbal world that both owes its existence to a number of traditional and arbitrary conventions of representation and seeks to remind readers that the artificiality of these conventions is of interest and significance in itself—not just as a means to the representation of reality. Berger's persistent reminders throughout his novels "that a work of fiction is a construction of language and otherwise a lie" emerge primarily from some kind of unexpected juxtapositioning of incongruous units of narrative—whether at the level of the sentence or of the novel and its traditions. He does this time after time, juxtaposing seemingly incongruous sentence styles, narrative codes, and other forms or concepts within the text of his novels.

The most obvious example of Berger's use of this technique is probably *Who Is Teddy Villanova?*, in which he places side by side the landmarks of the American hard-boiled private-detective story and a protagonist who speaks (as another character pointedly observes!) "as though quoting Macaulay." The unexpected juxtapositions in that novel exist in the disparate literary formulas it invokes, as well as at the level of its sentences, which wildly swing back and forth from street vernacular to an ornateness and intricacy so refined as to make an English professor blush.

Much more subtle and conceptual forms of this phenomenon can be found in Berger's other novels and form one of the significant continuities of his style, serving to turn familiar literary patterns into unexpected means to self-reflexive ends, denying or inverting attendant expectations about what those literary patterns usually mean. Accordingly readers quickly recognize familiar formula landmarks—say of the historical novel in *Little Big Man* or of the hard-boiled detective story in *Who Is*

Teddy Villanova?—in Berger's novels, but that recognition comes with significant differences, like seeing an old friend suddenly gone cheerfully insane or an old insane friend cheerfully restored to reason. The effect of Berger's "strange-making" is to pursue formula conventions past the point of their emblematic meaning to the point where they must assume a fresh, particular meaning within the context of his novel only. In creating these unexpected juxtapositions at every level of his writing, Berger redirects concern from the story told by his fiction to the story that *is* his fiction itself.

For example *Little Big Man* combined formula elements from the traditional western with those from Nabokovian tour de force, presenting the stereotype of the frontier hero but undercutting that stereotype with the sophisticated self-consciousness of his narration: just as much as or more than it is *about* the "Old West," *Little Big Man* is *about* the ways in which the "Old West" has been constructed by the ways in which we talk and write about it. In the same manner, *Regiment of Women* so mixed sexual stereotyping with linguistic and literary codes that it managed to miff readers on both sides of the women's rights issue, blinding many readers and reviewers alike to the fact that Berger's real concern in that novel was with the vagaries of language rather than with those of sexuality. In each case, Berger constructed his novels in unexpected ways from unexpected combinations of literary, linguistic, and cultural codes, ever reminding his readers of the insidious determinism of expectations. One of the results of this technique is that Berger's writing simply does not seem to fit existing critical categories—or, more perversely, it seems to fit several antithetical ones at once. His fiction swells with paradoxes, seeming to embrace what it exposes as delusion, celebrating what it seems to parody, absolutely refusing to subscribe to any codified philosophy, whether romantic, existentialist, or absurdist, modernist, metafictional, postmodernist, or deconstructive.

Berger's Characters

Any Berger character, no matter how minor or how despicable, is capable of advancing propositions about reality that deserve serious consideration, a condition complicated by the fact that not only do the propositions of different characters clearly contradict each other, but also by the equally clear case that the propositions advanced by a single character almost always exist in contradiction with each other. Indeed, that all Berger's characters have something to say worth thinking about and that none of them speaks with uniform moral reason, much less authority, makes reading his fiction both a challenge and a frustration to the reader who expects fiction to have some fairly consistent normative "message." Even a cursory review of Berger's novels reveals that his characters usually find themselves in conflicts that largely result from the vagaries of language: the lives of his characters are affected more by words than by actions, and insofar as true freedom might be defined by Berger as "the ability to be consistent with oneself," his characters are enslaved by language. They are victimized by definitions that exclude or threaten them, by rhetoric that makes them lose sight of physical facts, and by language designed more to preclude than to encourage clear thinking. For this reason the plot of a Berger novel typically chronicles the efforts of protagonists to free themselves from someone else's verbal version of reality. In this sense Berger's novels have all explored the processes of *victimization,* with Berger approaching his subject much as a jeweler might examine all the facets of some bright and terrible diamond.

From Carlo Reinhart in *Crazy in Berlin* to Lydia Graves in *The Houseguest* to the animatronic Phyllis in *Adventures of the Artificial Woman,* Berger's characters live blurring lives in which they oscillate between being victims and victimizers, between manipulating and being manipulated by the kinds of rhetoric or language codes that organize human life. Reinhart, for instance, knows that his true quest is for "freedom" but also realizes that he cannot "define the nature of his captivity, let alone identify the chief warden, though naturally he knew as well as anybody that we are our own jailors" (172). Berger's protagonists struggle, whether consciously or unconsciously, to free themselves from the inexorable tendency to think of themselves as victims of outrages and impositions, both humorously small and tragically large. Almost never in control of the situation around them, these characters consistently find themselves outmaneuvered, outsmarted, insulted, and imposed upon. Their victimization is usually funny but always serious, often seemingly trivial but always with an underlying pattern that falls little short of an old-fashioned naturalistic determinism. While all his main characters seem on the verge of some momentous discovery that language is all that really matters, that to control their lives they must first learn to control the codes that define and evaluate their existence, only Joe Detweiler of *Killing Time,* Georgie Cornell of *Regiment of Women,* and John Felton of *Meeting Evil* seem finally able to break through the fictions of their verbally determined environments: Detweiler does so through insanity, Cornell does so through an inadvertent return to nature, and

Felton ultimately recognizes that truly meeting evil demands action rather than language.

Berger's central, and particularly his peripheral, characters are a string of outrageously impossible but hauntingly plausible individuals who seem, in Berger's words, to be "persistent liars" and "monsters of one persuasion or another."[21] Never brandable as good or evil (with the noteworthy exception of Richie, in *Meeting Evil*), his characters appear to the reader as appealing in their often-bizarre excesses as they are sadly humorous in their deficiencies. Most important, as Reinhart finally understands of a wife who leaves him and of a son who taunts and despises him, all Berger's characters, whether for good or ill, *do their best.* They may trick, abuse, betray, and even murder one another, but in a world where understanding seems full of drawbacks and the irresponsible have, as Reinhart notes, "a permanent one up on those who feel obligations," they are no more and no less than normal.

All observing Ishmaels, acted upon more than they act, Berger's characters are generally content not so much to try to change or even judge the world around them as to survive and understand it. Even when granted what might seem to be fantastic power, as is Fred Wagner in *Being Invisible* or as is Walter Hunsicker in *Changing the Past,* Berger's characters discover that—even when realized—fantasies of wish fulfillment can't really change the nature of their lives. Nevertheless, almost all of them consistently engage in desperate fantasies when faced with disaster, only to find their dream-logic shattered by real-life humiliation. But even in the midst of their desperate fantasies, Berger's characters display a penchant for serious concept spinning or for advancing philosophical propositions.

Whether educated or illiterate, young or old, privileged or imposed upon, male or female, his characters are uniformly contemplative, musing about general lessons and principles even when in desperate circumstances. For a Berger character, the attempt to understand experience involves the continuous formation of propositions. These propositions cover aspects of human life both small and large, banal and profound, and often seem a kind of collaboration between Berger's narrators (quite different from book to book) and characters, the former precisely articulating the more vague intuitions, perceptions, and suppositions of the latter. For example, in *The Houseguest,* Bobby Graves's point of view considers the proposition that "the concept of civilized behavior would seem to include a least a sense of balance, if not justice in the narrowest of legalistic senses" (195), while his wife, Lydia, who recognizes Bobby's lack of moral strength, feels he may nevertheless make an effective lawyer because "it may well be that the ideal advocate for others is someone who cannot speak effectively for himself—he has no distractions" (8). Indeed a more or less steady stream of such propositions identifies its initiating point of view *as* that of a Berger character, but further discriminations are next to impossible: propositional thinking is what Berger characters have in common, and distinctions among characters rarely emerge from their specific reflections.

In the courtroom of his novels, Berger is neither judge nor advocate, feeling that his job is to maintain his characters in equilibrium, a concern of "art and not politics or sociology."[22] Accordingly his novels brim with characters of wildly opposing viewpoints, none of whom ever has the last word, since Berger never presents a character whose testimony can be totally believed or who can be totally discounted. Indeed, those of his characters who most closely approach straw-man caricature, such as Splendor Mainwaring and Claude Humbold, prove so consistently outrageous that they are "so chicane as to achieve finally a kind of integrity."[23] Even an ostensible villain such as General Custer in *Little Big Man* is not denied the dignity of his conception of self, even though events reveal the obvious flaws in that conception.

All Berger's characters reflect a fascination with people much like that ascribed to Reinhart. "Vile they might well be, but it happens that vileness is fascinating—to a degree of course. For example, he said to himself now, you will never find a transvestite bear" (338). In many ways, Reinhart remains the prototypical Berger character, even if Jack Crabb is the best known. For, while Jack addresses the audience of his expected with narrative gusto and vernacular eloquence, he does not engage most of the "actual" acquaintances mentioned in his tales with Reinhart's love of argument and repartee. And Jack, while he must try to make sense of the cultural and consequently moral divide between white and Indian, is not the connoisseur of ever-finer moral distinctions we find in Reinhart—and indeed in most of Berger's characters. Only Reinhart, the prototypical Berger moralist, would consider whether the greater moral opprobrium attaches to an American soldier who fails to repay a monetary debt to a survivor of Auschwitz or to an American soldier who has sex with a sixteen-year-old German girl in his employ ("Owing money to an alumnus of Auschwitz was a good deal rottener than any sexual transgression" [CIB, 272]).

If Reinhart learns any singly most important lesson during his life, it would seem to be that he must jettison "the ballast of moral judgment," as he finally realizes that "he had been burdened with it, made lead-footed, hunchbacked, his life long"

(VP, 392). But, like almost all of Berger's main characters, jettisoning the ballast of moral judgment is the act of which Reinhart is most singly incapable. While Reinhart's theory only infrequently coincides with his practice, his controlling belief is a simple pragmatism that applies to the characters in all Berger's novels: "make no mistake, people use us as we ask them to: this is life's fundamental, and often the only, justice" (CIB, 310).

What critics have been largely unable to see is that Berger characteristically uses familiar figures in his novels—the chicane businessman, the crooked politician, the bumbling existential hero—without making them a part of the familiar assault on the culture of middle America. That his novels are often described as satires on society perplexes Berger as much as does the notion that they are parodies of classic literary forms: "The naive invariably believe that I strive, and fail, to write social criticism for the delectation of the illiterates who take the daily newspapers seriously and for the semiliterates who make up their staffs. They assume there is a consensus of men of good will and believe that I am trying to associate myself with it" (2 April 1977).

Put off by what he refers to as the "platitudes of social meliorism," Berger concerns his fiction more with the perceptual and spiritual foundations of civilization than with its articulation into specific cultures and specific systems of belief. A perversely philosophical, blind, German Jewish, Nazi doctor in *Crazy in Berlin* may suggest Berger's attitude when he warns Reinhart: "If you think I shall tell you what is right or wrong, my friend, you are mistaken. That is your own affair. I care only for practical matters" (341). Above all, in crafting his characters, Berger refuses to become another person who *knows better.* Berger has explained his own moral reticence, and by extension that of his characters, simply: "The older I get the more reluctant I am to make judgments of that kind about other people's lives or about all of life. I am happy to say that life continues to exceed my capacity to define it. And, as Reinhart might say, it isn't as if one has an alternative."[24] Accordingly Berger's characters neither represent nor call to mind worthy causes. Instead, they learn, or their lives suggest to the reader, that the very idea of a cause—even one as noble as the code of chivalry Arthur gave to his knights—ultimately works against the best interests of true individuality.

Comic Moralist, Moralistic Comic, Both and Neither

A constant in Berger's otherwise genial and generous response to critics and reviewers with whom he disagrees or agrees alike has been his bridling at being termed a comic novelist. As he patiently explained to David W. Madden in an interview: "On the subject of whether my work is comic or not, I can only say that my intention is to tell a straightforward story for my own entertainment. Surely there are funny passages, but my purpose is not to inspire laughter except incidentally. What I dislike about being called a 'comic novelist' is that reviewers who don't like my books find it too convenient to condemn them for not being funny enough."[25] Somewhat less patiently, Berger told Laurel Graeber on the occasion of the 1992 publication of *Meeting Evil:* "I think some people dismiss me as a clown who makes fun of serious things. . . . I've been trying in recent years to be grimmer and grimmer and grimmer. . . . I wanted to write a book no one could call comic."[26]

A year earlier, on the occasion of the publication of *Orrie's Story,* Berger had expressed an even more exasperated view in an interview with B. A. Nilsson: "I made an intentional effort to avoid anything that could be called comedy. . . . I have never intended to be funny and have always disliked the label of 'comic Novelist,' which has been applied to me by the humorless half-literates who read only to confirm received ideas. *Orrie's Story* goes out of its way to be grim. Nevertheless, the anonymous buffoon who wrote the prepublication review for *Publishers Weekly* denounced it as an example of unsuccessful black comedy."[27]

While reasonable enough and certainly pragmatic, this longstanding protest against being identified as a comic writer may be precisely correct, but is also misleading insofar as Berger's fiction consistently celebrates incongruities, which, if not comic, are undeniably funny. After all, as the book jacket illustration for *The Feud* reminds us, that novel featured, among many delightfully humorous moments, one when young Tony Beeler escapes a malicious small-town cop by hitting him in the face with a lemon meringue pie—a signature slapstick moment even when put to serious use.

Michael Malone distinguishes Berger as "a writer of comedy (as opposed to comic writer)" and suggests a number of ways in which responses to Berger's writing confirms Malone's observation that "terms for comedy have long been a hodgepodge of jumbled misuse, tossed about as loose synonyms for tone."[28] Perhaps it is Jonathan Lethem who, in his introduction to *Meeting Evil,* has most diplomatically and most authoritatively addressed Berger's aversion to being associated with the comic:

> As a favor to my friend I have avoided the word which has dogged his years on this planet: I have not called him *comic*. But I would fail here if I didn't report that his books have made me laugh harder, over *my* years on the planet,

> than any others on my shelves. I predict that you will laugh too, and that you will find, as I have, that this laughter sustains itself even after the contemplation, inevitable after absorbing more than one or two of Berger's books, of the vast distress at the universal human plight (though it is an even-keeled, contemplative distress, as in the way of the Buddha) which necessitated their writing. Berger isn't comic. He, like life, is merely, and hugely, fucking funny.[29]

Somewhat paradoxically, while Berger has balked at accepting the label of being a comic writer because of the misleading connotations of that term, he has readily accepted the label of being a moralist, even while insisting that he lacks what is generally understood to be the moralist's reforming agenda. When asked by David W. Madden to respond to the characterization of *Being Invisible, The Houseguest,* and *Changing the Past* as modern morality tales, Berger denied that he preaches morality, but noted that he is "interested almost exclusively in moral situations."[30] When, later in that interview, Berger is asked to comment on the claim that he is a writer of "stringent moral parables," he acknowledges that he could "reasonably" be called a writer of parables and continues: "I am happy to be called a moralist, which by the way does not conflict at all with my stated intention of writing only to amuse myself. What amuses me are tales of moral significance: my own are always personal inventions, even when I use history or established legend, but hardly ever self-regarding."[31]

All Berger's novels again and again identify and investigate the complexity of moral issues, whether of the capital "M" Morality of matters of life and death or of the little "m" morality of politeness and everyday responsibility. What his fiction generally does *not* offer is answers to the questions it raises about morality. Explaining why his "tales of moral significance" do not propose solutions to moral problems, Berger recalls in a letter to Zulfikar Ghose a conversation with Arthur Koestler in which Koestler admitted to Berger he could not help trying to save the world:

> He said this wryly, of course, and then asked me whether I felt the same urge. I said no, that I wouldn't walk across the street to save the world, because I did not see it as a problem to which there was a solution. . . . Existence seems to me to be simply there. It is certainly basically painful, but the true pain, beneath the inconveniences that can be dealt with, is not the kind of thing that can be eradicated by scientists or economists or politicians or mass religious movements; although to individuals involved in these, life may be more gratifying than it would be without a cause.[32]

Citing his belief in a "fundamental reciprocity, which maintains the principle of constant damage in the universe," Berger concluded simply that he did "not see life as responsive to any 'cure.'" Which is to say that Berger does not usually moralize in his fiction or does so only superficially and incidentally on what may at first seem to be trivial issues, but that he takes morality deadly seriously.

The insistent message of Berger's fiction is that *every* decision has a moral implication and every human interchange involves some moral dimension or calculus, whether large or incredibly small. Indeed, permutations of the word "moral" appear again and again in Berger's novels, frequently attached to situations that seem more phatic than occasion for moral reflection—as when Robert Crews considers it "morally degrading" to stay out in the rain rather than entering a cave that might be occupied by an unknown human or when Roy, in *Best Friends,* contemplates a possible humiliation which he accords "the moral equivalent of vomiting or diarrhea." In Berger's worlds, moral issues involve ever-finer distinctions and can be measured only by complicated calculations, as Roy also illustrates when he attempts to evaluate his moral culpability for blurting out to his best friend's wife that he loved her: "He had neither lied nor exaggerated when he admitted that he was in love with her, but he should never have done so. Hypocrisy requires more moral courage than candor, for truth is a destructive element, more dangerous to retain than release, whereas confession is a rude display of bad taste. He might not have distinguished himself by achievement, but he had always before been at pains to avoid gracelessness" (127). While Berger involves his characters in too many moral equations to number or describe, the above passage suggests some of the complex of words, terms, and concepts that structure his moral situations: "lied," "hypocrisy," "truth," "rude," "gracelessness." Similarly Berger's relentless moral calculus addresses situations that factor in words such as "responsibility," "propriety," "obligation," "ethical," "decency," "fault," "blame," "guilt," "betrayal," "loyalty," "humiliation." One of the clear implications of his approach is to suggest that, at some level of understanding, *all* moral decisions are of great importance, whether their consequences involve matters of life and death or only pride or embarrassment.

This seeming absence of a sense of proportion or hierarchy in moral issues is one source of what has repeatedly been identified as the Kafkaesque in Berger's fiction, and it is worth noting that Berger's view of Kafka centers on the importance of maintaining a moral stance even in the face of impossible situations. As Berger explained to David W. Madden: "What has always struck me most forcefully in Kafka is the hero's being not only totally without power but also having not even a vague idea of what's happening to him, yet trying with all his strength to maintain his standards nevertheless: just because the effort is hopeless, utterly doomed, is not an acceptable reason for quitting, even if he knew to quit, which he doesn't, but that doesn't matter, because he wouldn't!"[33]

This seems to particularly be the case in Berger's more recent novels. For example, although a castaway from human society, Robert Crews retains an equally acute moral sensibility. Even in the wild, completely separated from other humans, Crews worries "about behaving improperly in a milieu of plants and animals." He considers a range of moral issues raised by his being thrown entirely into the world of nature, seeing the irony in a morality "founded on inches and ounces" that attaches moral value to the relative size of creatures he kills, but he also comes to understand the moral imperative of survival. Berger's most recent novel, *Adventures of the Artificial Woman,* is also one of his most interesting in terms of its interrogation of morality, as its animatronic woman, Phyllis, is *moral by design,* as she is programmed to be logical, to tell the truth, to obey all laws of which she is aware, and to have making sense as her only cause. And yet, as her creator realizes, being programmed to be moral can only make Phyllis morally neutral, although it does establish her as an interesting judge of human morality. Phyllis quickly concludes that humans are better at technology than at morality, and her moral status as a machine, particularly as one involved in the sex industry and politics, focuses her creator,

Ellery Pierce, on the moral choices facing him and his creator, Thomas Berger, on the larger nature of morality itself.

While one reviewer accurately observed that Berger's *Changing the Past* "reads like a cross between a medieval morality play and an episode from *The Twilight Zone,*" and while that novel does contain what may be Berger's ultimate moral comment when a character realizes that "life is taking your medicine," it is *The Houseguest* that seems to contain Berger's most sustained consideration of moral issues as they relate to individual choices in matters usually seen as mundane.[34] Here, as is true elsewhere in Berger's novels, moral issues present themselves in a range of situations involving personal responsibility, honor, motive, justice, the law, virtue, vice, and various structures of power. One of the clear suggestions of *The Houseguest* is that "morality" is a phenomenon manifesting itself along a continuum from manners to the law and that questions and outcomes at every stage of that continuum should be taken seriously. Indeed, the plot of this novel might be characterized as a tutorial in the ways in which moral distinctions undergird relations of power, a constant concern in Berger's fiction.

The Inspiration of Nietzsche

If Berger, despite his disavowals, can be said to present a moral philosophy in his fiction, it is because his novels have much in common with the general view advanced by Nietzsche, particularly in his *Beyond Good and Evil* and *The Genealogy of Morals.* To note this similarity, however, is far from accounting for the complicated relationship between Nietzsche's view of the world and the world of Berger's fiction. What makes the relationship between Berger and Nietzsche so complicated is that

Berger's novels tend to be set in worlds that support Nietzsche's theories of human interchange but do not necessarily lend themselves to Nietzschean solutions. What Nietzsche describes in a tone always approaching exasperation, Berger portrays with a resigned and often gentle equanimity: the general tenor of his novels is of acceptance rather than of criticism. As the young Reinhart somewhat fatuously announces to a cynical Berliner: "I accept life. Some things in it are by nature hateful" (CIB, 378).

Berger approvingly cites Nietzsche's claim in *Beyond Good and Evil* that "there are higher problems than the problems of pleasure and pain and sympathy; and all systems of philosophy which deal only with these are naivetes," a reference that helps to explain Berger's dissatisfaction with the platitudes of social meliorism, although nowhere in Berger's fiction can be found the championing of suffering with which Nietzsche concludes this discussion.[35] In a letter to Zulfikar Ghose, Berger has glossed Nietzsche's easily misunderstood philosophy: "His vision is utterly original and one cannot understand him unless one puts aside such assumptions as that the poor are necessarily morally superior to the rich or that victims are necessarily heroes. He plunges through such surfaces, rejects such false disjunction."[36]

Nietzsche's belief that the will to power is the most basic of human motivations and that this will to power has necessarily created morality for selfish reasons and pursued it by immoral ends would seem to be the starting assumption for the world of any Berger novel. "Life," Nietzsche claims, "is *essentially* appropriation, injury, conquest of the strange and weak, suppression, severity, obtrusion of peculiar forms, and at the least, putting it mildest, exploitation," and a better description of life in the world of Berger's fiction would be hard to find.[37]

And yet, for all the correspondences between Berger's fiction and Nietzsche's philosophy and for all the respect Berger holds for Nietzsche, significant differences appear in the ways in which they proceed from shared assumptions. Perhaps most significant is the disparity between Nietzsche's implication that knowledge can only advance the will to power and Berger's depiction of knowledge as a kind of insidious torment. For Nietzsche knowledge serves to abolish the concept of guilt, but for Berger it is the leading cause of guilt and the necessary precondition for most kinds of suffering—most masochistically, from nothing more than banality. The energy that informs so much of Nietzsche's writing can only be seen as ultimately optimistic, while Berger's energy is almost always ironic. One of Reinhart's many epiphanies is that "you can't afford irony if you are seriously interested in acquiring power," and in Berger's novels what Nietzsche would identify as the will to power is always frustrated by a kind of "will to irony," which both enlightens and paralyzes his protagonists.

Berger's sensibility may often coincide with Nietzsche's, but it is not necessarily derived from it.[38] Rather, it seems to be the case that Berger's thinking bears a natural affinity to the antimoralistic, antipietistic stance represented by a number of writers and thinkers—including Nietzsche, Laclos, and Sade—who insist that the official accounts of existence are at best myopic and at worst cynically hypocritical. While continuing to insist that he has no conscious philosophical intent in his novels, Berger did offer David W. Madden this complicated specification: "My own philosophy is an amalgam of Nietzsche and Simone Weil, who may superficially be seen as impossibly divergent but come together in a stern *amor fati:* one must 'not merely bear what is necessary, still less conceal it . . . but *love it'* (Nietzsche). 'I saw it (the love of fate) as a duty we cannot fail in without dishonoring ourselves' (Weil). But my conscious purpose in writing novels is not to promote my beliefs or even to suggest or reflect upon them: it is rather, as I have continued to insist, only to amuse myself."[39]

And what must be remembered is that the art of Berger's novels mediates any ideas it may concern itself with. For instance, a Berger character may implicitly or explicitly accept the validity of Nietzsche's account of human interchange without being able to act upon that knowledge. As Reinhart laments, "the mere formulation of a principle has absolutely no effect on existence *in re;* which, for example, is why you'll look forever to find a good Christian" (RIL, 87–88). In one ironic sense, the character who understands but cannot profit from Nietzschean thought may be the ultimate victim, the true antithesis to the *Übermensch,* and it is precisely in irony of this sort that Berger most revels. "I never think consciously in a Nietzschean fashion when writing fiction. If I did, I should not be at all Nietzschean. For me any hint of tendentiousness breaks the fictional trance and one is left with only hateful reality" (26 July 1983).

Like Nietzsche, Berger implicates his reader in the text; like Nietzsche, he views life in dialectical terms (although resistant to synthesis); like Nietzsche, he suspects the self-serving pieties of conventional morality; and like Nietzsche, he sees the dangers inherent in the reifying, hypostatizing nature of language. But in Berger's hands these concerns undergo celebration and transformation just as surely as does literary form. In the world of Thomas Berger's fiction, not even Nietzsche has the last word.

CHAPTER 2

Legendary Landscapes

Little Big Man, The Return of Little Big Man, Arthur Rex

All Thomas Berger's novels can be thought of as captivity narratives, his characters all incarcerated in the prison house of language. Yet three of Berger's most celebrated novels, *Little Big Man, The Return of Little Big Man,* and *Arthur Rex,* are captivity narratives in a much more literal sense, the first written in the well-codified frontier description of life in the captivity of Indians; the second zeroing in on Jack Crabb's enthrallment by his idealization of women; the third reflecting, as does its primary source, the fact that the great telling of the Arthurian legend was by a prisoner, Sir Thomas Malory—and that Arthur was in many ways a prisoner to his own ideals. *Little Big Man* is Berger's response to the great American myth of the frontier, representing as it does most of the central traditions of American literature. *The Return of Little Big Man* shifts its emphasis from the clash between white and Indian on the frontier to the equally one-sided clash between the Old West and the steamroller of progress. With *Arthur Rex,* Berger takes on the Arthurian legend, the Matter of Britain, one of the great traditions in British literary history and no less a vital national myth.

The Achievement of *Little Big Man*

"You must understand that I did not write *Little Big Man* as an exercise in social criticism," Thomas Berger said in an interview.

"It was not intended as an indictment of the white man. I wrote it for the same motive that informs all my fiction: to amuse myself."[1] Had Berger never written anything other than *Little Big Man,* he would have earned a respected place in American literary history.[2] *Little Big Man* has by now been almost universally recognized as a great American novel. As L. L. Lee accurately observed in one of the first articles to give careful consideration to *Little Big Man:* "This is a most American novel. Not just in its subject, its setting, its story (these are common matters), but in its thematic structures, in its dialectic: savagery and civilization, indeed, but also the virgin land and the city, nature and the machine, individualism and community, democracy and hierarchy, innocence and knowledge, all the divisive and unifying themes of the American experience, or, more precisely, of the American 'myth.'"[3]

Frederick Turner was correct when he concluded in his 1977 reassessment of *Little Big Man* for the *Nation* that "few creative works of post–Civil War America have had as much of the fiber and blood of the national experience in them."[4] Just as certainly, it is now safe to say that *Little Big Man,* the novel, will more than match its survival skills against those of Jack Crabb, its 111-year-old protagonist. And in some ways *Little Big Man* must be acknowledged as Berger's greatest novel—not necessarily his best, but the one in which he took on the sweeping matter of his American literary and mythological heritage and made a lasting contribution to both.

Little Big Man seems at once the most accessible and the most singular of Berger's novels. By invoking the figure of Gen. George Armstrong Custer and offering a version of America's most fascinating military defeat, Berger's novel risks assimilation into the cottage industry of "last stand" literature. By developing Jack Crabb's wondering vision and wonderfully witty vernacular voice, the novel obviously invites comparison with *Huckleberry Finn.* And because the fictional character of Crabb shares so many aspects with the traditional picaro, notwithstanding the fact that it also shares those aspects with many a "real" character in the Old West, Berger's novel represents a literary tradition older and broader than any American literature could produce for itself.

A Story about Storytelling

Little Big Man is a story purporting to tell the truth about the old American West. It is ostensibly transcribed from the tape-recorded reminiscences of "the late Jack Crabb—frontiersman, Indian scout, gunfighter, buffalo hunter, adopted Cheyenne—in his final days upon this earth." That Jack's final days come some 111 years after his first and that he claims to have been the sole white survivor of the Battle of the Little Bighorn put this "truth" in some doubt. Equally strong and contradictory evidence exists that the last of the old-timers is hopelessly senile and that he is a conscious craftsman of fiction as concerned with developing his own story *as a narrative to be read* as he is with relating the incidents of his life. Furthermore, Jack's narrative takes shape through the patently unreliable editorship of one Ralph Fielding Snell, a fatuously gullible and weak-minded self-professed "man of letters," who not so incidentally reveals parallels between his life and that of his narrator. Snell, who does admit to some doubts about Crabb's story, concedes that he passes on its claims only after his own emotional collapse of some ten years, and his foreword and epilogue contain numerous hints that this emotional condition persists. Yet against all this self-reflexivity stands the disarming realism of Jack's tale, the authority and credibility of his voice. The action in *Little Big Man* is episodic, its story a macaronic of historical events and personages, its atmosphere the swirling myths that transformed people and events into America's defining epoch: the West. What unites the disparate threads of the novel's action and its swings between the antithetical worldviews of white and Indian culture is the voice and vision of Jack Crabb, one of Berger's greatest achievements, blending as it does conflicting styles and sources into a stunning synthesis.

Jack's description of his Cheyenne upbringing illustrates his unique ability to combine a child's uncritical (or, on occasion, cynical) acceptance with the cultural insights of an anthropologist:

> It ain't bad to be a boy among the Cheyenne. You never get whipped for doing wrong, but rather told: "That is not the way of the Human Beings." One time Coyote started to laugh while he was lighting his father's pipe, because a horsefly was crawling on his belly. This was a serious failure of manners on his part, comparable to a white boy's farting loud in church. His Pa laid away the pipe and said: "On account of your lack of self-control I can't smoke all day without disgusting certain Persons in the other world. I wonder if you aren't a Pawnee instead of a Human Being." Coyote went out upon the prairie and stayed there alone all night to hide his shame.
>
> You have got to *do things right* when you're a Cheyenne. (67)

Whatever else may be said of Jack, let there be no doubt that *he gets things right* whenever he speaks of Indian ways. Indeed

Jack's description of Cheyenne life draws heavily from anthropological studies such as E. Adamson Hoebel's *Cheyennes: Indians of the Great Plains* (1960) and George Bird Grinnell's *Fighting Cheyennes* (1956). In like fashion almost all of Jack's major experiences with the Cheyenne derive from historical or anthropological fact. Likewise, when Jack speaks of Custer or the cavalry, the fine points and drawbacks of specific handguns, the growth of frontier cities, or other matters of white culture, he is equally accurate and often equally insightful.

Jack's experiences and impressions are woven from a mad mélange of histories, memoirs, biographies, legends, novels, and even movies about the West; and it is a mark of Berger's pervasive irony that most of these sources are put by him to uses antithetical to the intent or bias of the original authors. There is simply no way of knowing how many of Jack's experiences, in matters both small and large, Berger directly or indirectly drew from other sources. In acknowledging and specifying many of those sources, Berger has said of his research, "After reading some seventy books about the Old West I went into a creative trance in which it seemed as though I were listening to Jack Crabb's narrative" (18 December 1984). The genius of *Little Big Man,* however, has much more to do with Berger's principles of selection, combination, and comment than with facticity.

Jack Crabb's Critical Voice

Although the accuracy of Jack's details has been noted by numerous critics, most notably Leo E. Oliva, what has been overlooked is that Jack also offers a folksy-sounding but astute critical commentary on the literature of the West.[5] Indeed, one of the wonderful ironies inherent in Berger's structure of *Little Big Man* is that Jack, the ostensible man of action, reveals much more knowledge about narrative tradition and strategy than does Snell, the ostensible man of letters. In a most subtle fashion, Berger has so crafted Jack's voice as to make it at once a part of, and a comment on, the process through which the Old West has been created by language. On one level, Jack's manipulations of language serve to characterize him as a self-styled teller of tall tales in the best tradition of both white and Indian cultures. First and foremost, Jack is a storyteller, with his primary allegiance to language rather than history.

Actually, as Berger would no doubt specify, what we call history *is* language, and perhaps nowhere is this truer than in the case of the "history" of the American frontier. One of the singularly most appropriate ways in which Berger designed *Little Big Man* as the "Western to end all Westerns" was to make Jack's voice and character such an obvious pastiche of fact and fantasy, of literary myths and received truths. From Cooper onward, the literature of the frontier has been filled with seemingly crude and unlettered characters who ultimately drop their rough personas to reveal either noble birth or genteel background and education (a continuation of the "mysterious stranger" tradition that Fielding devised for *Tom Jones*). Berger plays against this specific convention in western literature by keeping Jack's persona scrupulously democratic and unprivileged, while allowing just enough narrative sophistication to show through to call Jack's true nature into question.

Even more significant in Jack's literary ancestry is the long tradition of so mythologizing frontier and western personages as to make virtually impossible the separation of man from myth. Henry Nash Smith's *Virgin Land* chronicles this phenomenon from the time of Daniel Boone (some of whose experiences were woven by Cooper into the life of Natty Bumppo) to manufactured heroes such as Kit Carson and Buffalo Bill. William Cody, notes Smith, was practically transformed into the persona of Buffalo Bill by the power of dime novelist Ned Buntline's fictions.[6] Against such a background in which *the literature of the West* in many ways managed to become its operating reality, the character of Jack Crabb assumes an ironic realism in its own right: the more impossible or implausible Berger makes Jack, the more he has in common with the legendary personages of western "history."

Jack himself comments on this phenomenon as it affected Wild Bill Hickok and also as it operated in the Cheyenne mythologizing of Little Big Man. Called out by Hickok, Jack notes that the gunfighter "referred to himself like he was an institution: personally, he didn't care so much about these supposed outrages of mine, but he could not let the noble firm of Wild Bill Hickok, Inc., be loosely dealt with" (320). Showing a remarkable resemblance to white practice in at least this one respect, the Cheyenne so convince themselves that Jack fought bravely then turned into a swallow at the rout at Solomon's Fork that they almost kill him because his existence does not seem to square with their myth. Again Jack astutely notes the mechanics of myth-making: "If you'll look again at the myth they had built around Little Big Man, you'll see what I mean. It hadn't aught to do with me personally, and insofar as I was to be identified with it, I had to live up to it rather than vice versa. If I did something that would not jibe with the legend, that meant I was not Little Big Man. By this means Indians kept their concepts straight and their heroes untarnished, and did not have to lie" (184–85).

Yet Jack never sounds too objective or too analytical or too self-referential to maintain his crude persona. Never does his insight obscure his own blindnesses, never do his observations and opinions become completely trustworthy. Rather than actually possessing the wondering vision of a child, Jack merely employs it as a convenient narrative technique, always reserving and usually exercising the right to respond to what he relates. His dilemma is that Jack is too accepting to succeed in white society, but not accepting enough to be really comfortable with Indian life. The deeper acceptance shown by Old Lodge Skins, the acceptance at the heart of Cheyenne philosophy, always remains just beyond Jack's grasp. And while he effectively conveys to his audience the idealistic appeal of that philosophy, he also scrupulously chronicles its drawbacks, the greatest of which is simply that it cannot prevail against the white man. The best Jack can achieve is a kind of fragmentary rationalization that victory is not necessarily the true test of a worldview. Having heard Old Lodge Skins tell of the massacre at Sand Creek, noting that the Cheyenne killed there are now on the Other Side, "where there are no white men," Jack draws a distinction between losing and not winning: "The latter designation he pronounced nowadays in a special way: not exactly hateful, for Old Lodge Skins was too much a man to sit about and revile his enemies. That was for a loser, like the Rebs what lost the Civil War. And he wasn't a loser. He wasn't a winner, maybe, but neither was he a failure. You couldn't call the Cheyenne flops unless they had had a railroad engine of their own which never worked as well as the U. P.'s or had invented a gun that didn't shoot straight" (227).

What is perhaps most interesting in Jack's voice, however, is not its cultural relativism but its ability to transcend cultural issues in pursuit of larger truths. While critics have noted Jack's insight into the workings of the specialized epistemologies of

Indians, white settlers, gunfighters, and cavalrymen, his ability to synthesize the vagaries of his experience into larger propositions about reality has not been remarked. This ability does not make Jack wise, as the pattern of his recurrent personal disasters starkly attests, but it does align him with Berger's other protagonists, all of whom pursue the grail of understanding, usually at considerable personal cost. Reflecting on the ironies of frontier conflict, in which missions of apology and revenge were always uncoordinated and matters of life and death often turned on complicated misunderstandings, Jack sighs that "it would have been ridiculous except it was mortal."

Inevitably critics have likened Jack's voice to that of Huck Finn. However, this comparison is misleading. Unlike Huck, Jack's wondering vision is mostly a pose, one frequently belied by his shrewd analysis of motives and meanings in the situations of his life. While readers frequently understand more about Jack than he is able to realize himself, their knowledge of those he encounters is limited to, but rarely narrowed by, his insights. What is significant here is that Jack routinely advances opinions, explanations, and insights infinitely more complex than those Huck Finn could ever dream of.

One of Berger's most significant stylistic accomplishments in *Little Big Man* is the creation of a voice for Jack that dramatically captures the simple essence of the vernacular but escapes its intellectual limitations. The vernacular ring to Jack's voice arises primarily from a smattering of well-codified colloquialisms: "commenced to," "a deal of," "what had" (in place of "that had"), "they was," "knowed," "them" (in place of "those"), and so on. Combined with Jack's use of natural, historically appropriate metaphors and the accuracy and specificity of his details, this technique more than masks the sophistication of

Jack's narrative technique. Berger achieves great economy in his use of these colloquial code words, which, although relatively few, are well placed and impart backwoods credibility to Jack's narration without limiting the precision of either his syntax or his diction.

In addition Jack's narration derives much of its credibility and sensory impact from its earthy figures of speech. For example, the description of the "massacre" of Jack's father's wagon train has an Indian grimacing "like he smells something stinking" and howling "like a coyote under a full moon." One of Jack's last sights of his mother has her looking "like one of them little dolls you can make out of a hollyhock blossom with a bud for its head," and Jack crosses a river on his way to Old Lodge Skins's camp holding on to the tail of a swimming pony, "spinning behind like a lure on a fishline." Other period metaphors include references to "sparks when you throw a horseshoe in the forge," to muscles that hum "like plucked bowstrings," to a sound "like when you throw a stone against a keg," and to Indians swarming across the Greasy Grass River "like bees out of a shaken hive."

What is so remarkable is that Jack's voice rings so true, while also containing so many unexpected signs of sophistication. Included in his vocabulary are such unlikely terms as: *disjunction, recumbent, quandary, signification, obdurate, circumferentially, phenomenon, equable, cognizance, egress, colloquy, exemplify, predilection, surfeit,* and *stentorian.* His command of prepositions and adverbs alone, the careful use of directional terms such as *therewith, henceforward, thereunder, heretofore, hitherto, henceforth,* and *forthwith,* reveals considerable lexical polish. And more significant than this erudite vocabulary is the precision and rhetorical craft of many of Jack's sentences.

Consider the sophisticated, efficient, and suspensive syntax of but one of Jack's many precisely crafted and elaborately extended observations:

> As I say, none of us understood the situation, but me and Caroline was considerably better off than the chief, because we only looked to him for our upkeep in the foreseeable future, whereas he at last decided we was demons and only waiting for dark to steal the wits from his head; and while riding along he muttered prayers and incantations to bring us bad medicine, but so ran his luck that he never saw any of the animal brothers that assisted his magic—such as Rattlesnake or Prairie Dog—but rather only Jackrabbit, who had a grudge against him of longstanding because he once had kept a prairie fire off his camp by exhorting it to burn the hares' home instead. (46)

Even Ralph Fielding Snell calls attention to this phenomenon, noting that "Mr. Crabb is astonishingly circumspect as to language" and offering a strained rationale for the presence in Jack's vocabulary of such a word as "apprehension." In fact, Snell invites his readers to consider a number of specific apparent inconsistencies in Jack's narration, including the fact that while Jack's own voice is often ungrammatical, his representation of Custer's speech or of Indian discourse is always impeccable, only to conclude that "your garageman or bootblack" is equally capable of civilized rhetoric if he only wishes to do so (22–23). Berger's game here is a complicated one: by having Snell point out the surprising flashes of apparent sophistication in Jack's narration, he puts readers on guard to the possibility that the entire narrative is a hoax; by calling attention to this verbal phenomenon, however, Snell both diverts attention from even more unlikely aspects of Jack's voice and confirms readers' suspicion of his own weakness of perception. The overall effect is to bolster Jack's credibility.

Just as surely as the interplay between the editor Snell and the narrator Crabb can only remind us of that between the editor John Ray, Jr., and the narrator Humbert Humbert in *Lolita,* the literature of the West swells with first-person narratives of astonishing sophistication. Indeed, Jack's voice and character can only remind us of his possible ties to Cooper's Natty Bumppo, and to possible connections with Melville's *Life of Israel Potter* and *Moby-Dick.* Perhaps Berger himself best suggested the inherently American literary core of his own novel in his discussion of *The Pathfinder:*

> Whenever you wish to stir up the heirs of Western civilization, put on a coonskin cap and pick up a flintlock. More than anyone else, Cooper is responsible for this image, which may be sentimental and only too easy to burlesque, as in the legend of Davy Crockett, but then all the great themes of American literature—gigantism (Melville), hysteria (Hawthorne), vulgarity (James)—are already halfway toward parody at their conception. America is that sort of place as well as the home of the wisecrack. But we must remember, too, that Crockett, for all his lies and boasts, actually did lose his life defending the Alamo. America is also the place where real life, if only in the form of real death, eventually overtakes and legitimizes invention.[7]

The Pursuit of Freedom

Jack's voice may be Berger's greatest achievement in *Little Big Man,* but he crafts that voice to important purpose. Although in many ways the story of Jack's narrative is itself as fascinating as, or more fascinating than, the story of his life, Berger means to direct our attention to his constant concern with the crucial relationship between language and freedom. It is in this light that *Little Big Man,* a literal model of a "captivity narrative," most directly dramatizes Berger's fascination with the ways in which language serves to make captives of its users. And, in this one fundamental respect, Berger's contribution to the literature of the frontier strikes a radically new note.

Whether by virtue of a noble primitivism, as in the case of Cooper's Leatherstocking, or by virtue of an opportunistic amorality, as in the case of most of the frontier characters of the southwestern humorists and the "wild and woolly" heroes of the Beadle dime novels, the western hero has been at bottom the very exemplar of individual freedom—often of anarchic freedom. Deadwood Dick, for example, is beyond the reach of almost all obligations because he has survived hanging as a thief. "I was cut down and resuscitated by a friend," he explains, "and thus, while I hung and paid my debt to nature and justice, I came back to life a free man whom no law in the universe could molest for past offenses."[8] In surviving the Battle of the Little Bighorn, Jack strikingly parallels Deadwood Dick's remarkable resiliency but certainly gains no sense of freedom or relief from responsibility through his escape.

However, what finally distinguishes Jack from his literary predecessors is that *he is not free:* he may escape the trappings of captivity, whether at the hands of the Indians, the Pendrakes, or commercial creditors, but Jack remains the slave of his own standards—his haunting sense of obligation to definitions. As he diagnoses his own problem when he runs away from the Pendrakes, intending to return to the Cheyenne, "God knows I thought enough about it and kept telling myself I was basically an Indian, just as when among Indians I kept seeing how I was really white to the core" (160). He may claim that "you can't get away from the fact that failure gives you a great liberty" (192) or advise, "just fall to rock bottom and you'll be a happy man" (164), but he reveals a much greater truth about his own life when he complains that "most all troubles come from having standards" (164). Jack does have standards, no matter how low his situation, but cannot reconcile the competing claims of the Cheyenne standards, which he understands and respects, with white standards—which he simply cannot keep from measuring himself against, no matter how unjustified or contradictory he knows them to be. When Jack opens his narrative with the claim, "I am a white man and never forgot it," he refers to his personal curse as much as, or more than, to a matter of racial pride.

The problem is that Jack's sense of himself always looks beyond the concrete satisfaction of his very real accomplishments to the impossibly abstract ideal of civilization; Jack judges himself, not as a man, but as a *white* man. Hard-nosed pragmatist or cynic in so many things, Jack is a sucker for the ideal of civilization and progress, even though he finds the reality inexorably disappointing. For him Mrs. Pendrake emblemizes civilization, even when her actual conduct profoundly disillusions him: "She always knowed the *right thing* so far *as* civilization went, like an Indian knows it for savagery. . . . I figured to have got the idea of white life, right then. It hadn't ought to do with the steam engine or arithmetic or even Mr. Pope's verse. Its aim was to turn out a Mrs. Pendrake" (134). The point of all this is that while Jack's sensibility is "beyond sentimentality" in most matters—and thus frequently a kind of wisdom as useful as, or more useful than, that of Old Lodge Skins—at heart it is hopelessly romantic in its acceptance of the myth of progress and civilization, the myth of white culture that steamrolled the West.[9] Intellectually Jack is all for the Indian concern with what is, as opposed to the white preoccupation with how things *should be,* but his commitment never grows firm enough to afford him any satisfaction. He simply knows too much to remain happy as an Indian, resignedly acknowledging that their way of life is perfect only "if you been born in a tent and carried on your Ma's back and lived with hocus-pocus since the day you was born and never invented the wheel" (371–72).

The one seeming exception in Jack's life proves the rule of his misery. On the night of his Indian son's birth, the night before Custer's attack on the Cheyennes camped along the Washita, Jack achieves his greatest moment of personal freedom, overcoming his white sense of morality to fulfill his Cheyenne obligation to his wife's sisters. Before making love to the three sisters, Jack faces his usual dilemma ("As usual, trouble lay in deciding whether I was finally white or Indian"), but for once manages to suppress his "white" standards: "There could be no doubt that I had once and for all turned 100 percent Cheyenne insofar as that was possible by the actions of the body. . . . No, all seemed right to me at that moment. It was one of the few times I felt: this is the way things are and should be. I had medicine then, that's the only word for it. *I knew where the center of the world was*" (253).

Once but not for all. The key phrase in Jack's revery is "insofar as that was possible by the actions of body," and what he fails to achieve is liberation through the actions of the mind. Custer's attack shatters his peace, destroys the world whose center he has just found, and throws him back into the clutches of white standards and expectations. Appropriately enough, the only real and lasting triumph in Jack's life must be created and measured in accordance with those standards. The triumph is his uncorrupting of the young whore, Amelia, the one hoax in his life that really succeeds, based as it is almost completely in the abstract ideals of white society and carried off almost entirely through the medium of language. Embedded within a structural framework that must remind readers, at least in passing, of that of *Lolita* is a delightful inversion of Lolita's story: here, the older man *uncorrupts* the nymphet, making her life the measure of his devotion to bourgeois morality. Tellingly enough, when Jack records his satisfaction at Amelia's success, he measures his pride in cultural rather than personal terms: "If respectability was always denied me personally, at least in this instance I was able to arrange it, so to speak, for another. That's about as high as a white man can aspire" (344).

Jack's *achievements* are Cheyenne, his *aspirations* are white, and therein lies a kind of captivity against which his shiftiness has no power. What may be the most significant of the many levels of meaning in *Little Big Man* is, not that Jack survives, but that he suffers—ever-victimized by his own hypostatization of "white" ideals. Like all Berger's major characters, Jack displays many of the afflictions of Nietzsche's man of ressentiment, fighting and scheming for physical freedom but always hobbled by his own sense of impossible obligations.

The Return of Little Big Man

In *The Return of Little Big Man,* Berger allows his best-known character to take up his story where he left off, following the Battle of the Little Bighorn. Berger deftly resurrects Jack's inimitable voice and wondering vision, and turns both toward chronicling the birth of a new century in which simulacra such as Buffalo Bill's Wild West Show replace the Old West; the 1893 Chicago World's Fair offers glimpses of America's technology future; and an indomitable New Woman captures Jack's heart and his story. This is not to say, however, that Berger did not face some daunting challenges in writing this novel, nor that all those challenges could be completely overcome.

First there is the problem of sequels in general, which rarely seem as effective as their precursors and almost never seem necessary. However, when Berger cut off Jack Crabb's narrative at the Battle of the Little Bighorn, there really was a lot left for him say—about the closing of the West, the "domestication" of America's Native Americans, the coming of a new century with a markedly different ethos, and about Jack's continuing efforts to find personal freedom that would also give him peace of mind. For 1876, the year in which Custer and his men died at the Little Bighorn, was also the year of the American Centennial Exposition, held in Philadelphia, the first of a series of memorable expositions or World's Fairs that introduced millions of American visitors to the idea that the future would be different—that the era of the pioneer, the cowboy, the settler, and their Indian antagonists was about to give way to the era of the engineer and the inventor.

Most sequels follow hard on the heels of some original, and Jack resumes his narrative having aged only a year since the end of the events in *Little Big Man*. But, for Berger and for readers of *Little Big Man,* an amazing thirty-five years have intervened, thirty-five years which, as one reviewer noted, have made 1964 feel "about 111 years ago."[10] During those thirty-five years, a noteworthy and very popular movie has been made of *Little Big Man,* Berger has published seventeen more novels, and original readers of *Little Big Man* have been treated to a cascade of texts in a range of media, all of which seemed to support the authoritative vision if not the exact veracity of Jack's narrative.[11] Of course, for many of Berger's readers of *Little Big Man,* Jack's voice might sound more than a little like that of Dustin Hoffman, who so memorably portrayed Jack in Arthur Penn's celebrated 1970 movie of his story. Whatever its divergences from Berger's novel—and there were many, some of great significance—Penn's movie almost certainly meant for many of Berger's readers that *The Return of Little Big Man* appeared in a context quite different from that in which its literary ancestor first appeared.

Moreover, in the years since 1964, Berger's audience had been treated to or assaulted by numerous other big budget "new" western movies, movies that almost always shared and frequently made a hash of the self-reflexive and revisionist ethos pioneered by *Little Big Man,* not to mention a raft of books, both fictional and nonfictional, published since 1964, which spoke directly to subject matter and an ethos Berger formerly had pretty much to himself as far as shaping it for popular audiences. Just to name a few, these films, television programs, and books (and frequently one title refers to productions in several media) that focused on American Indians now include familiar titles such as *Bury My Heart at Wounded Knee, Son of the Morning Star, Custer Died for Your Sins, The Court-Martial of General George Armstrong Custer, Buffalo Bill and the Indians, or, Sitting Bull's History Lesson, Dances With Wolves, A Man Called Horse, Soldier Blue, I Will Fight No More Forever,* and *Geronimo: An American Legend.* Indeed, Evan Connell's award-winning study *Son of the Morning Star: Custer and the Little Bighorn* (also made into a film) lists over one hundred and fifty books and articles published since 1964 in its bibliography—and Connell's book was published some fifteen years before *The Return of Little Big Man.*

Possibly even more telling of the sea change in public awareness since 1964 of our history of *images* of American Indians, there now exists a stunning number of books and articles devoted not to the history of American Indians but to media constructions and misconstructions of that history.[12] And gunfighters in the Old West had by 1999 also become the subject of numerous revisionist studies such as Allen Barra's *Inventing Wyatt Earp* and numerous "new" western movies, purporting or implying that they were closer to historical "truth" than the westerns of "old" Hollywood.[13] Consequently, in writing *The Return of Little Big Man,* Berger, no matter the approach he took in his sequel, could not regain the pioneering effect or cultural impact of *Little Big Man.*

This time out, Berger turned his attention to Jack Crabb's participation in events and stories less dramatic but no less important than those recorded in *Little Big Man.* To this end, while still relying on Jack's perspective on legendary events such as the death of Wild Bill Hickok, the Gunfight at the OK Corral, and the death of Sitting Bull, Berger makes it clear that the more important keys to our understanding the end of the nineteenth century had to do with the coming of a new order in which Bat Masterson's *aura* becomes more important than his actual record in gunfights, in which the Gunfight at the OK Corral is revealed to be anything but exciting—much less heroic, in which show business simulacra of the Old West—emblemized by Buffalo Bill's Wild West Show—become more compelling than its actuality, and in which the 1893 World's Columbian

Exposition (another celebration of simulacra) marked not only the closing of the frontier but the coming of a new century of new attitudes toward the place of both Indians and women in a society driven by the increasing valuation of appearance over reality just as surely as it was by technology and business.[14]

Still a Story about Storytelling, Still the Story of Jack's Critical Voice

The Return of Little Big Man opens in Jack Crabb's voice. Ralph Fielding Snell is gone, Jack having escaped him by faking his death, and as a consequence, Jack's narrative now escapes the self-reflexive note Snell provided *Little Big Man,* as Jack speaks directly to his readers. That a simulated death saves Jack this time not from perishing at the hands of Indian warriors, as it did at the Battle of the Little Bighorn, but from the clutches of Snell and his lawyers, sets the tone of this narrative in which stark violence more and more cedes center stage to complexity, particularly the complexity of simulation, in the drama of progress. What is new in Jack's account is a glimpse into the "pacification" and "domestication" of Plains Indians both in the harshly normative education offered by Indian mission schools and in the simulation-centered show-business world of Buffalo Bill's Wild West Show. What is even more radically new in Jack's experience is the strong-willed and fiercely independent Amanda Teasdale, a New Woman, along lines associated with the reformist efforts of Jane Addams. Addams joins Bat Masterson, William F. Cody, and Sitting Bull (who Jack says "would of come to the top of any races he belonged to") as the most valorized historical personages in Jack's tale, which is also noteworthy for the attention it devotes to women in the Old West, including several "calico queens" (celebrated whores and madams), Allie Earp, Custer's widow, and Annie Oakley. And what is new for everyone is the splendor of Chicago's White City, the World's Columbian Exposition, where, for all of its sensational simulations, the future it represented was inexorably replacing the world so brilliantly evoked by Jack in *Little Big Man.*

Few, if any, readers would miss Ralph Fielding Snell, but also now gone is Old Lodge Skins, the one stabilizing and centering influence in Jack's life. Also now gone is the conflict between white and Indian worldviews that so consistently haunted Jack in his previous narrative; Jack knows the Indian way of life is inexorably over, a passing emblemized by the murder of Sitting Bull by other Indians carrying out white orders. Now the conflict is much more between the nineteenth and the twentieth centuries—with Jack once more in the middle, one foot in either world. Odd as it may sound, the magnificent presence and mentorship provided by Old Lodge Skins is displaced in this telling to Jack's dog, Pard—pragmatism with a tail—and to Jack's growing love interest, Amanda Teasdale, whose seemingly wild-eyed idealism almost always proves grounded in some acceptance of the real. Faithful dog and maddeningly idealistic New Woman can't match the wisdom of Old Lodge Skins, but, like him, they provide motivation, direction, and new perspectives to Jack's life.

What is familiar in Jack's narrative is his conscious fascination with language and his no doubt unconscious allusions to or invocations of other works of literature. Jack, who has learned the hard way that "words can mean anything" (106), reflects both on the changing connotations of words such as "cowboy" (174, 238) and on the inherent confusion in news accounts of the Old West due to the vagaries of similar-sounding names, multiple appearances of the same nicknames and honorifics, and to sloppy or inaccurate reporting (391–92). Almost in smiling response to those who have characterized his voice as much like that of Huck Finn's, Jack now assumes the guise of an anti-Huck, declaring not that it is time for him to light out for the territories, but declaring "it was time I got civilized" (303). Indeed, Jack remains a *most literate* vernacular narrator whose sentences can occasionally give Henry James a run for his money, as in the following syntactic marvel describing Jack's dog, the inimitable Pard:

> Now if you know only the kind of pets ladies keep indoors, or even sporting hounds, and so on, you might expect old Pard to make a greater display than he done when he seen me for the first time in more than three years, having tracked me over hundreds of miles, but just as he weren't the type to bear a grudge, thank goodness, he had lived the sort of life in which the interests of survival tended to hold down emotional demonstrations, in which he reminded me of myself, so we never hugged or anything, but I was real glad to see him, a feeling which alternated with amazement at his feat, which exceeded anything I had heard of at the time, though in the many years since, now and again dogs have somehow followed their families at greater distances on foot while the humans used the motorcar, so when I tell about Pard it might be easier to believe than the experiences I relate concerning historical personages, though all are equally true. (145)

In *The Return of Little Big Man,* Jack's narration often seems more concerned with perceptual issues than with historical events. As he puts it "in general not being taken altogether serious give me freedom to say things others might not" (278). Or, as he elaborates, "If you want to know what I consider most valuable of all the things I learned from the Cheyenne, beyond the practical matters like riding, hunting, et cetera, I'd have to say how to look at life from other angles than the obvious" (220). And, while Jack may not be sure of his purpose in life, he seems confident that the purpose of his narrative is "to look at life from other angles than the obvious," and the most rewarding target of his parallax here, as it was in *Little Big Man,* is the at once otherworldly and rock-solidly pragmatic worldview of the Indian mind. When, as usual, Sitting Bull, a magnificent man in Jack's telling, undercuts one of Jack's hypothetical arguments with the eminently practical rejoinder that "it is a waste of time to talk about the impossible," Jack acknowledges the limits of his understanding: "Now, see, that's another Indian thing: you could speak about dreams, visions, and the like all you wanted, but they figured it pointless to mess with reality. I don't know as how any white person, including even me, can understand the distinction altogether, but there is one. I can't tell you often enough that while talking to an Indian was sometimes exasperating, it seldom failed to refresh my mind" (227).

Indeed Jack does a good job of balancing his exasperation with Indian thinking against his respect for it. Exasperation shows when he notes their stubbornness: "Show them railroads, electric light, New York City, steamboats, St. Paul's cathedral, Buckingham Palace, these folks who never found the wheel on their own and lived in hide tents, and they still insisted on staying Indians" (279). Approaching this trait from another angle, however, Jack faults Indians for not seeing things "in the long run," as when they "kept thinking they could stay completely Indian despite all the evidence to the contrary," but acknowledges: “That was what was both great and hopeless about them” (108). Similarly, when Jack reflects on the invulnerable pride of the Cheyenne, despite the fact that their “successes were momentary whereas their catastrophes had all but brung them to extinction,” he concludes: “if you still believe yourself best after all that, it’s mighty damned impressive for my money, and I ain’t going to try to talk you out of it, for you might be right on some higher level” (221).

That Indians will not let external circumstances affect their essential identities, however, is not to say that they have not reached certain accommodations with the reality of white dominance. Their way of life is over, and they know it, as is possibly best exemplified in their acceptance of the education of their children at white missionary schools. Although dismayed by the rigidity and cultural insensitivity of the school at which he works, and never as ready as is Amanda to agree that Indians should abandon their old ways, Jack declines to condemn the enterprise, noting the “success” stories of some Indian students and reassuring his readers: “I don’t want you to think the place was an absolute flop by any means” (124). Jack regretfully understands that while the values and cultural assumptions of the mission school may be as barbarous in their own way as many practices whites have ascribed to savages, some of the school’s practices, such as attempting to deny their students use of their own language, may be necessary: “But I did see the point that them young Indians ought to learn as much English as they could if they was going to prosper or even survive in the coming years now the Plains tribes had no immediate means of keeping body and soul together except on the basis of learning white ways, and you’d never do that talking only in Cheyenne” (102–3).

If Indian epistemology remains one of Jack's narrative preoccupations in *The Return of Little Big Man,* his interest in white thinking seems to narrow to a new concern with theory—theory having to do primarily with reform movements aimed at Indians and women and theory having to do with simulation that Jack experiences as show business in the guise of Buffalo Bill's Wild West Show but senses as an attribute of the onrushing future exemplified in the spectacle of White City, at once a sham and a very real harbinger of progress. In the genius of Buffalo Bill's showmanship Jack sees one of the only happy outcomes for American Indians at the end of the nineteenth century as his Wild West Show treated them fairly, offering them employment playing themselves in terms less demeaning and more enjoyable than were most of the alternatives open to them. And Jack sees in Cody a kind of New Man, one particularly well suited to a future in which simulation would more and more compete with the real: "If he were not the inventor of a new style then he perfected it, and of course by now it is a pretty standard mix in which the true and the false are so intimately intertwined as probably never to be told apart, and anybody tries to figure them out will get thrown so off balance as to fear for his reason. I expected it's only owing to this state of affairs that anybody ever gets elected to public office in this country" (205). In contrast with Cody, Wild Bill Hickok cannot adjust to the new world of simulation, and is uncomfortable playing himself in one of Cody's shows. Hickok complains that "the hardest thing I ever tried to do was to be a make-believe Wild Bill Hickok," explaining: "It got to be too much for me to be the real myself pretending to be the fake Wild Bill" (17).

One of the reasons Jack is so impressed by Bat Masterson is that he, like Cody, seems to have grasped intuitively the emerging ethos of simulation to the point that he may never have actually killed anyone in a gunfight, but nevertheless maintained a fear-inspiring reputation as a gunfighter. "Bat Masterson, as Crabb sees him," Berger explains, "is invulnerable, almost imperturbable, maintaining an authority over his fellow men by mere presence, seldom even drawing a gun."[15] In this respect, Masterson, Cody, and the Columbian Exposition all share some of the attributes Jack associates with storytelling, a connection Berger has spelled out: "As for Cody and his red performers, they were real, having in many cases actually spilled the blood of each other's race, but were impersonating themselves in make-believe, adjacent to imitations of the Eiffel Tower, cannibal villages of the South Seas, Middle European beer gardens, and majestic white palaces, the last made of plaster of Paris. It was as near as they could come in those days to virtual reality, in which all is pretense. But given my profession, I can scarcely knock it."[16]

While it is clear that in his thinking about Buffalo Bill's Wild West Show and about the World's Columbian Exposition Jack is playing on the margins of simulation theory, he associates "theory" with France in general ("I found there was nobody like a Frenchman for taking nothing for what it appeared to be and reserving judgment till he decided if he was being made a fool of or not" [318]) and with social reformers in particular, maintaining a healthy skepticism toward both. "Looking at things according to a theory is done only by educated people," Jack tells Amanda, not so innocently adding, "on account of only they know how" (300). More pointedly and sounding distinctly like Nietzsche (whom Jack may have run into while touring France with the Wild West Show), Jack briefly critiques her general condemnation of men as being symptomatic of a "way of the world that them who don't run it find fault with them who do: it's a way of getting even" (302).

At only a small remove from theorists are idealistic social reformers, particularly Amanda Teasdale ("Like most people with a cause she heard only herself giving her own side" [290]), who constantly challenges Jack's willingness to rationalize injustice as inevitable and who eventually captures both his heart and his mind, and her associate and role model, Jane Addams, founder of Hull House. Amanda and Jane Addams challenge Jack's conception of himself and understanding of his identity just as surely as did the competing worldviews of whites and Indians in *Little Big Man:*

> In short, Jane Addams was a troublemaking do-gooder after Amanda's heart, a fellow ex-college girl reared genteelly, and in Miss Addams's case with quite a lot of money, who figured they had it easy enough in a life that was real mean for many others, to whom it would be nice to lend a hand. You could see them as a pain in the arse, which I expect they could be, and doing what they did on account of guilt at their own good fortune instead of accepting it as coming from God, and maybe that could be so, and you could doubt what they did made much difference in the long run and instead blow up everything and start over, if you, as the saying went, regarded the right thing as a big omelet and individuals like so many eggs. (411)

Only Amanda's and Jane Addams's "pain in the arse" idealism and occasionally maddeningly unrealistic activism turns Jack's thoughts to his own lack of purpose:

> I begun to total up my own contribution to the human race, at the age of better than half a century, as nil, and I seen most of the individuals I had frequented as worthless in the greater scheme of things: gamblers and harlots, most of them, leaving aside the entertainers such as Buffalo Bill and Annie Oakley, who I guess did bring pleasure to many folks, and nothing wrong with that, but it didn't feed the hungry or rescue poor women from sweatshops or do anything for the freed slaves come north to live worse than before Emancipation. You name the dirty deal and Jane Addams was trying to correct it while I had been looking in the opposite direction. (412)

Once again Jack has defined himself into a hopeless situation: while his specific actions, both in *Little Big Man* and in *The Return of Little Big Man* have been consistently aimed at helping those in need, whether white or Indian, his principles have never been those he now associates with "do-gooders." His motivation may not always have been unselfish, but his actions have rarely, if ever, worked to the malicious harm of anyone in situations other than those threatening his own survival. Lack of certainty whether provided by religion, education, a sense of racial superiority, or any other guiding story about his life continues to haunt Jack. "There has been little of my own motives I was ever sure of, and still less of my deeds," he complains. "Looking from one angle, my existence has consisted of a series of regrets." Once again, Jack has found the angle from which he can never find satisfaction or peace with himself.

Individual Purpose and National Destiny

All Jack's familiar subjects come together at the 1893 World's Columbian Exposition, which happily marks the success of his own quest for the love of Amanda Teasdale and his discovery, through Amanda's example, of a guiding purpose for his life. More important, the Columbian Exposition marks the "official closing" of the frontier and the redirection of American expansiveness, as announced by Frederick Jackson Turner in his "The Significance of the Frontier in American History" speech to the American Historical Association meeting held in conjunction with the great fair. And perhaps no better sign of the closing of the frontier could be found than the appropriation and commodification of its conflict between whites and Indians by Buffalo Bill's Wild West Show, whose spectacular staged reenactments were not officially part of the Columbian Exposition but were located just outside the fair's Midway Plaisance and was probably mistaken by most tourists as part of the fair itself. Cody's "solution" to the Indian problem was simply to transform it into entertainment, a co-optive strategy as futuristic in its implications as any of the great exhibits at the fair.

By the time Jack finds himself in Chicago working in Buffalo Bill's Wild West Show he has bounced around the West, spending time in Deadwood and Tombstone and Dodge City, usually working as a bartender; toured Europe with Cody, where he met Queen Victoria and attended a party thrown by the Prince of Wales; and survived time in the mean streets of New York City. He has traveled, and he has experienced countless marvels, but he has not found a purpose for his life. Vaguely he would like to be a better person, and vaguely he suspects it will take a woman to make him better, which possibly explains the series of impossible crushes he has had on "respectable" and quite unattainable women. In the person of Amanda Teasdale Jack finally finds both the "real romance" he has never before experienced and the reason for being or purpose he has been seeking. Unlike his previous infatuations with Mrs. Pendrake, Dora Hand, Libbie Custer, and Annie Oakley, this time Jack grows into love based on respect for Amanda's will and values, on her status as his practical equal and moral superior rather than as an object of adoration. Jack has always been searching for the center of the universe, and Amanda, he realizes, is already there and may point the way for him as well. "If she had created men," Jack gushes, "they would have been nicer than the ones turned out by God" (112). Although Amanda scares Jack "in that region of the heart where you feel you just ain't up to the job" (404), he finds her arguments as hard to counter as those of Indians, and he recognizes that she is a "durable woman" who never loses her class no matter what the situation.

From the outset of their relationship, Amanda challenges Jack's laissez-faire pragmatism concerning Indian welfare with her activist pragmatism. When Jack declares he would like to help Indians, but he is sorry he "ain't got the power to give them back all their home grounds," Amanda introduces him to her brand of practical idealism: "You're wasting time, Mr. Crabb. What is needed is not sniveling about the past, which is dead and gone. The Indian must face the present and the future. He can no longer be a hunter and warrior. But he is capable as any other person of any race. That his ways are now obsolete should not reflect adversely on him. He can learn new ones. For all, reading and writing, doing sums. How to plant and harvest crops for the men. For the women, the domestic sciences as practiced by the civilized race, which it cannot be emphasized enough is nevertheless not morally superior" (87–88). Of course, as Jack eventually realizes, he's been wasting time in his own life, and Amanda's determination to find ways to act effectively on her beliefs, offers him a guide to his future, just as Old

Lodge Skins had guided him through his youth. And, in yet another self-reflexive turn in his life, Jack's most promising venue for action is to join Amanda in writing a book about her and his knowledge of Indian life, though—and here readers must imagine Jack's and Berger's tongues firmly in cheek—Jack avers, "How that might be done I had no idea, being as you know barely literate" (414).

Jack discovers purpose through his recognition and acceptance of Amanda as "a real modern woman, advanced beyond her time," and Berger uses the always instructive arguments Jack has with Amanda to suggest a larger view of the history of American progress celebrated by the Columbian Exposition. Noting that Amanda intends her book about the history of the West to be harder on whites than his view of that history would be, Jack sums up: "For while I certainly agreed that much of it was fairly rotten, I couldn't help being impressed by what happened since Chris Columbus had the guts to cross the Atlantic in that eggshell boat and find a whole new world for the Europeans to corrupt, if you want to put it that way, but also to build some remarkable things and establish principles that if ever carried out in full really might offer a better life for many, in fact had already done so" (417). When Jack and Amanda turn one last time to this argument, Berger seems to offer through another of Jack's magnificently crafted sentences both a wish for better public discourse and a final assessment of the world Jack and his creator have so compellingly created in both *Little Big Man* and its worthy sequel: "As I say, we didn't ever argue with bad personal feeling, like the other person was a fool or scoundrel, but nevertheless always held to our own positions, hers being that the mischief resulting from Columbus coming to the New World probably outweighed the good, whereas mine held that somebody was sure to of done it sooner or later with the same results, for such was the natural itch of mankind to go to wild places and tame them, and of all the examples of such throughout the world, America was by far the best result even if not yet perfect" (429).

Arthur Rex

Aptly described by one reviewer of *Arthur Rex* as "the Green Knight of American fiction: a mysterious, protean outsider whose pose of destructiveness masks a fierce reverence for form and meaning," Berger has jokingly remarked that "the most difficult thing in life is to maintain one's belief in one's own hoax" (6 September 1977). This most difficult of tasks constantly falls to almost all of Berger's protagonists and, of his twenty-three novels, *Arthur Rex* most systematically explores the difficulties, dangers, and rewards of sustaining belief in the hoaxes both of the self and of culture.[17] In this exploration, Berger's presentation of Camelot has much in common with his earlier presentation of the old American West. At bottom, Jack Crabb's most serious problems in *Little Big Man* stem precisely from his inability to hold securely to his own hoax in the midst of so many others, both white and Cheyenne. If Jack is Berger's most basely democratic character, King Arthur is certainly his most nobly aristocratic, but substitute *myth* or *legend* for *hoax* and it becomes clear that in the world of Berger's writing, Jack and Arthur, king and mule skinner, share exactly the same problem: for all the events and epistemologies that roil their lives, both men are finally defined by the complex intersections of the concept of freedom with the concept of power. Appearing by turns—and often as one—in his novels as Holy Grail and *fata morgana,* these two most complicated hypostatizations obviously intrigue Berger, and he delights in casting them anew in his fiction.

Arthur Rex is obviously Berger's homage to Sir Thomas Malory and to the line of tellers who have made the Arthurian legend the "Matter of Britain." In it Berger inevitably brings modern scrutiny and his sense of humor to the legend of King Arthur, but he does so in keeping with his self-professed "genuine hunger for gallantry and a passion for panache." And just as surely as his characters struggle to meet their own self-perceived responsibilities, this—like all Berger's novels—reveals his own sense of responsibility to literary tradition. Indeed, Michael Malone has recorded Berger's resentment at coming across an Arthurian screenplay written by someone who had apparently read "none of Malory, Chretien de Troyes, Wolfram von Eschenbach, Alf Tennyson, Dick Wagner's *Tristan* and *Parsifal* and the many other forerunners whose works I ransacked (including two books for children which were my principal sources). . . . This unbelievable trashy practitioner," Berger exclaimed, "had *invented* his own Arthurian narrative!"[18]

That a king may not be free, constrained by the dictates of his self-proclaimed code of chivalry, and that doing good may have evil consequences are but two of the many ironies of the Arthurian story, and it is those ironic notes that Berger's novel sounds again and again. Complexity finally overwhelms Arthur and even the wicked who oppose him, uniting both good and evil in the crucible of irony. Berger's narrator specifies that the tragedy of the Round Table lay, not in its dissolution, but in the cause of its fall, "for this was the only time that a king had set out to rule on principles of absolute virtue, and to fight evil and to champion the good, and though it was not the first time that a king fell out with his followers, it was unique in happening not by wicked design but rather by the helpless accidents of fine men who meant well and who loved one another dearly" (447). Only when engaged in mortal combat with his fellow knight and respected friend Gawaine does Launcelot reflect "on the differences amongst men, and how though a company of them might hold the same principles, each member might honestly interpret these in another way" (462).

Berger's retelling of the Arthurian legend has a double focus, at once true to the heroic essence of the myth and searching for the deeper truths beneath that heroism and its tragic end. He has indicated the complicated nature of this double focus with the observation: "We now know that greatness, wisdom, and courage are necessarily conjoined with selfishness, childishness, and petulance—had not Winston Churchill been an egomaniac, Britain would have fallen to Hitler, to give a political example. What is 'old' in the Arthurian myth is that God loves the knights of the Round Table and hates their enemies" (11 February 1977). Or as Berger has put this dichotomy another way, "The Arthurian legend is essentially infantile: and you must understand that I believe children are naturally vicious" (2 April 1977).[19] One of Berger's most compelling characters, Gawaine, the most human and ultimately the wisest of Arthur's knights, suggests some of the effects of Berger's belief when, late in his life, he is asked by a brother if he does not long for the old days of action: "'Nay,' said Sir Gawaine. 'I am happy to have had them in my proper time, but of a life of adventure it can be said that there is no abiding satisfaction, for when one adventure is done, a knight liveth in expectation of another, and if the next come not soon enough he falleth in love, in the sort of love that is an adventure, for what he seeketh be the adventure and not the lovingness. And methinks this sequence is finally infantile, and beyond a certain age one can no longer be interested in games'" (361).

Complexity in Camelot

In pursuing some of the adult and ironic implications of the Arthurian legend, Berger's retelling in no way diminishes the glory of Arthur's attempt or the measure of his achievement, but it does devote greater attention to the cause of the legend's final tragedy. In one sense, that tragedy centers, not on the dissolution of the Round Table nor on the estrangement of Arthur, Guinevere, and Launcelot, but on the erosion of the innocently idealistic belief that life can be governed by the simple principle of opposing good to evil. A typically perverse problem Berger poses for both Arthur and his knights arises from the pride with which they define themselves precisely by the evil they oppose: in ridding the land of that evil, they call their own existence into question more than they affirm it. When the young Percival's mother challenges his wish to become a knight, she observes that "for all the brave men in the world who fight for the good, there is no less of evil anywhere" (378). He can only wanly answer, "If there were no evil, then what would become of bravery?" And when Sir Percival, the most naive of knights, searches for the Holy Grail, he encounters a kind of relativity that Arthur's rule cannot assimilate. "And some of the men he met were fairly good, and some were very evil, but most were a mixture of virtues and vices whether they wore silk or rags, or lived in a palace or a hut or a cave, and taking them all in all, all were corrupt to a great degree, but none was without some small virtue, and all were equal in that they lived in Time" (419).

Nor does complexity spare the evil, even when they try to reform. Berger's Sir Meliagrant captures and imprisons Guinevere, only to be so confounded by that "metaphysical lady" that he reluctantly renounces his evil métier in hope of winning her love. But "whereas he had been fearsome when vile, he was but a booby when he did other than ill," and his decision to reform leads in quick succession to his being robbed and wounded by a beggar, then killed in a fight with Launcelot that he knew he could not win. "This honor," muses Sir Meliagrant before his death, "can be a taxing thing" (175). In somewhat similar fashion, having had little success in her schemes against Arthur, the crafty Morgan la Fey finally enters a nunnery, "for after a long career in the service of evil she had come to believe that corruption were sooner brought amongst humankind by the forces of virtue, and from this moment on she was notable for her piety" (453).

What dawns too slowly on Arthur and some of his knights is the realization that the code of chivalry, like any system of abstract definitions and principles, comes into conflict with itself if pursued too blindly. "To have a purpose is good," counsels the Lady of the Lake, "but to be so intent upon it as to see only its end is folly. Never to be distracted is ultimately to serve nothing but Vanity" (105). Ultimately Gawaine's honor—as defined by the code—demands that he avenge his father's death, which was at the hand of another knight, even though that death is itself justified by the requirements of honor. Arthur sadly notes that the code's guidance begins to blur because "distinctions are sometimes hard to draw, for our obligations do oft war each on each." To Launcelot, Arthur resignedly admits that "evil doing hath got more subtle, perhaps even to the point at which it can not properly be encountered with the sword" (392).

It is the warring of obligations to equally compelling rationales for action that finally leads the two greatest of Arthur's knights, Launcelot and Gawaine, to fight each other. During that sad fight, Launcelot suddenly understands that "if Gawaine's morality were complex, it was because chivalry in general was more complicated than it seemed, for it is not easy always to know what is the noble thing, or what is brave and generous or even simply decent" (461). In Berger's hands, Arthur's most anguishing discovery is not that he has been betrayed by his queen and his most trusted knight, but that his philosophy has been shallow. Too late comes his tragic epiphany that "to the profound vision there is no virtue and no vice, and what is justice to one, is injustice to another," a sentiment strikingly similar to Nietzsche's conceptual formula for Aeschylus's Prometheus, "All that exists is just and unjust and equally justified in both."

Despite this central flaw in Arthur's great dream, Berger makes it clear that Arthur's legend is not to be judged or reevaluated by the dream's success or failure. Nor in this or any other Berger novel should irony be mistaken for absurdity. The Lady of the Lake assures the dying Arthur that he could not have done better in his life than he did, and the ghost of Sir Gawaine offers to his king the Round Table's poignant epitaph: "We sought no easy victories, nor won any. And perhaps for that we will be remembered" (484).

The Telling of the Tale

As with all tellers of the story of King Arthur, Berger's central concern is with reminding his readers that while the matter of myth and the matter of history may not be the same, both may be equally true or equally false. The final words of Berger's narrator specify that King Arthur "was never historical, but everything he did was true," a distinction maintained in Berger's subtitling his own work *A Legendary Novel.* In Berger's view of things, the legendary should not be confused with the spurious, particularly since, as his narrator wryly observes, "it is only in the historical world that a reputation can be gained by talk alone, and in the realm of legend only deeds are counted" (427).

Berger's agent provocateur subtly redirecting our attention toward newly understandable aspects of the Arthurian legend is, of course, his unnamed narrator—certainly Berger's most original character. It is through this narrator that Berger pays homage to Malory while refusing to make his own the limits of Malory's vision, and it is through this narrator that Berger creates, not just another version of the Arthurian story, but a comment on the traditions of its telling.

The narrator of *Arthur Rex* uniquely mirrors the dilemma of the characters in his story in that his obligations to various narrative traditions "do oft war each on each." His telling celebrates Malory and strives to be true to Malory's spirit, as well as to the larger tradition of Arthurian legend, but Berger's narrator differs from his master's in important respects. Perhaps most obvious, Berger's narrator pays lip service to Christian piety, as Malory took great pains to do, but undercuts that phatic piety with much pragmatic assessment and critique of Christianity as a system of belief. Similarly the narrator ever redirects our attention from the norms of knightly conduct to the realities of power and, while respecting the conventions of the age's depiction of women, even more consistently portrays the women in the Arthurian legend as the only characters deep enough and realistic enough to understand its meanings. Finally Berger so draws his narrator as to use him, both implicitly and explicitly, as a commentator on the language and the literature of the Arthurian story.

One of the clearest results of these subtle shifts of emphasis is that for all the pro forma declarations of the primacy of Launcelot, Gawaine emerges as Berger's "best" knight. In the Arthurian catalog of superlative qualities, Gawaine appears to offer a kind of golden mean. As the Green Knight explains to Gawaine, "To be greater than you is to be tragic; to be less, farcical" (214). And it is one of Berger's characteristic ironies that his version of the Arthurian legend has the two greatest knights fight to the death, Launcelot prevailing in arms even as he begins to understand that Gawaine has bettered him in understanding. Similarly Berger's narrator distances himself from Malory's tale by presenting Merlin as more Nietzschean than Machiavellian and using him to analyze Christian belief. Amused by Arthur's persistent deflation of the myth surrounding Excalibur, Merlin cautions: "I am a wizard and not a logician, as you are a king and not a philosopher. Any effort to compound these offices is inadvisable" (38).

Central to the problem of hierarchical thinking, which is itself central to the events in Berger's telling, is the blindness of Arthurian men to the wisdom of Arthurian women, "for not even Merlin, with all his arts, could divine the ways of women." One of the most poignantly revealing moments in the novel comes when Arthur grumbles to Launcelot about the inscrutability of the Lady of the Lake, referred to by the king as "that woman." "Tell me, Launcelot, art thou truly at ease with any female?" "Sire, I am not," said Sir Launcelot. "Dost understand them at all?" asked King Arthur. And Launcelot said, "Nay, I do not" (304). Berger has claimed that in *Arthur Rex*, "perhaps for the first time since Marie de France, the queens and princesses are permitted their due in the tales, of which they are the traditional survivors; and as Launcelot, invincible on the field, must defer to Guinevere in the boudoir, so must Tristram be shown as the helpless sex-object of two Isolds."

Even more significant in this respect is the emphasis Berger gives to the tutoring of Gawaine by the Lady of the Lake, which culminates in his finest and most philosophical act—his marriage to, and subsequent acknowledgment of the free will of, Lady Ragnell. "Thou art not an object which I possess like unto a suit of armor," reasons Gawaine. "Thou art one of God's creatures, and in all fundamental matters thou must answer only to Him" (325). Her enchantment broken precisely by his refusal to exercise a power over her that is clearly granted him by the hierarchical schema of their time, Lady Ragnell calls attention to one of the many ironies implicit in Berger's presentation, explaining to Gawaine, "And in allowing me mine own choice, thou hast liberated me in more ways than one" (326). In embedding "The Wedding of Sir Gawaine and Dame Ragnell" in his Arthurian story, Berger most clearly rejects Malory's depiction of Gawaine and the simple chauvinism of most medieval narratives, for despite the perfunctory condescension of his narrator ("And so with females, of whom the wise man saith, *Turn them upside down, they do look much the same*"), Berger's women are by far the most interesting characters in *Arthur Rex,* and his most wise.

CHAPTER 3

The Midwestern Novels

Sneaky People, The Feud, Orrie's Story

Given the diversity of models and motives that shape Berger's fiction, any attempt at grouping his novels by theme, setting, or even recurrent characters runs immediately into problems, as apparent similarities frequently mask more important differences. For instance, *Who Is Teddy Villanova?* and *Nowhere* both have Russel Wren as their protagonist, but these two novels represent dramatically different literary traditions and prose styles. Nevertheless, readers may find it useful to think of the similarities that tie together *Sneaky People, The Feud,* and *Orrie's Story.* Berger has identified his celebration of the language of the Midwest as of great importance in *Sneaky People* and *The Feud,* and, while the geographical setting of *Orrie's Story* is not specified, the language of its characters, while neither as vernacular nor as colorful as that in the other two books, does not identify itself with the dialogue of any other Berger novel. Notwithstanding its different approach to reproducing the language of a specific period and place, however, much about *Orrie's Story* suggests more connections with *The Feud* and *Sneaky People* than with any other Berger novels.

All three novels are set in small towns, *Sneaky People* in 1939, *The Feud* in the mid- to late 1930s, *Orrie's Story* just after the end of World War II. More important, each of these novels prominently features boys on the cusp of manhood, who, although in quite different ways, confront questions about what it means to be a man, including the vagaries of male/female relationships and complicated by significant differences between them and their fathers. In Berger's hands, *Orrie's Story* becomes much more a coming-of-age story than is the *Oresteia,* and, in that respect, it takes its place in the company of the coming-of-age stories at the center of *The Feud* and *Sneaky People.* Moreover, each involves the death of a father, while *The Feud* and *Orrie's Story,* weave a narrative of revenge around those deaths. Indeed, while they do so in incredibly different ways, *The Feud* often verging on slapstick comedy, *Orrie's Story* verging on tragedy, these two novels most explicitly interrogate the mechanisms and meanings of revenge, a constant dynamic in the world of Berger's fiction.

Sneaky People

Sneaky People is Berger's seventh and, with the possible exception of *Reinhart's Women,* his gentlest novel, notwithstanding the fact that much of its action concerns plans for a murder. The novel chronicles the coming of age of a fifteen-year-old boy, Ralph Sandifer, in a dreamy small-town world where nothing is nearly as bucolic as it seems and all situations are heavily ironic. Given the scheme of Berger's novels as "celebrations" of classic genres, *Sneaky People* almost has to be a tribute to Booth Tarkington's *Penrod* or *Seventeen.* But this is a story of several different kinds of initiations, and its focus is divided among five adult characters in addition to Ralph. Ralph's father, Buddy, owns a used-car lot and plans to have one of his employees murder Ralph's mother. Naomi, the drab, mousy-seeming mother, secretly writes and sells pornography, trading on her knowledge that "because sexual congress was ludicrous in life, its depiction must necessarily follow suit, nay, go it more than one better if interest were to be provoked from the reader, who having come into the world with genitals was himself a born clown" (279). Contrasted with Naomi's imagination of preposterous sex is the considerable experience of Laverne, Buddy's mistress, a good-natured sometime whore and full-time pragmatist. It is Laverne who sexually initiates Buddy's fifteen-year-old son, Ralph, into manhood, but his more important discovery is the sneaky truth that "manliness was sometimes mere folly" (254). Another of Buddy's employees, Leo Kirsch, knows women only through his long-suffering submission to a domineering and hypochondriac mother ("You missed it, Leo. . . . You missed my hemorrhage") and through his fantasy letters to young girls pictured in the newspaper.

In fact *Sneaky People* presents quite a catalog of possible male-female relationships, almost all of which are primarily structured by misunderstanding—both of the self and of others. Consequently most of the humor of the novel arises from situations that deflate the hypostatized rhetorical worlds that each character has come up with to make sense of, or to mask, the reality of his or her life. Finally Berger's characters are "sneaky" simply because they are human, and their secrets are nothing more or less than the inherent condition of their existence. As D. Keith Mano so aptly noted in his review of *Sneaky People,* Berger "prefers the padded bra in all of us."[1]

Apart from the humor of its situations, this book creates a steady background of genial vernacular banter, a world of familiar but now-neglected colloquial commonplaces, exclamations, and retorts. As much as, or more than, even *Little Big Man,* this book reveals that Berger should be acclaimed for his ear as well as his vision. He has described *Sneaky People* as his tribute to the Midwest language of his youth. Characteristically Berger concluded his description of this celebration of language by saying, "I can think of no pretext more serious, morally or aesthetically, for the writing of a novel."[2] He explains: "American English had its great flowering in the 1920s and 30s, lay dormant during World War II except in the military forces—he who has never been under arms *never* learns authentically to curse—and has degenerated badly since the advent of the television news broadcast, in which speech has become the sniveling lackey to impulses of light. . . . The possibilities for wit—and thus for life—decline with the language."[3]

Certainly the language of *Sneaky People* is anything *but* homogenized and is the source of the great majority of the book's wit and energy. Ralph's mother, for example, strikes even her son as speaking a bit oddly ("almost English, sometimes reminding him of Merle Oberon"), and her writing style under the name Mary Joy is even more noteworthy, as in the following: "New Year's Day, 8 A.M.—Lying here upon my pink satin sheets, my black-lace nightie drawn up above the twin swellings of my creamy-white breasts, tipped with erect rubicund nipples surrounded by large roseate aureolae, I greet the fresh new year with an exploratory finger in the deepest recess of the warm, moist grotto between my heaving ivory thighs, and think of another Jan. 1 on which, like the year, I was too a virgin" (252–53).

Berger's narration in this novel subtly approaches tour de force in its combination of vernacular diction and rhythm with serpentine syntax, as sentence after sentence winds toward increasingly specific images. When Ralph hears a friend revile the woman he has just become infatuated with, his reaction is described in typically humorous specificity:

> That Hauser referred to Laverne Linda Lorraine; that drunkenly they had been heading for her staircase on Saturday night; that his kind friend on the one hand was on the other a stinking, vile, obscene criminal whose filthy tongue should be ripped out—all this was clear.
>
> But it could also be regarded as an established truth that, except in movies and ancient narratives such *as* the series about Frank Merriwell, a normal modern individual did not commit violence in response to verbal attacks on a woman's honor, especially those made in ignorance by an imbecile who no doubt had been home all afternoon playing with himself while perusing the little eight-page fuckbook the edges of which could be seen protruding from his back pocket as he climbed the steps. (178)

Sentences such as these are the norm in *Sneaky People,* supplying a kind of syntactic joy all their own, in addition to giving readers humorous insights into the thinking of Berger's characters.

The Feud

Berger's twelfth novel, *The Feud,* written some seven years after the publication of *Sneaky People,* resurrects both the mid-1930s small-town semblance of the earlier work and its fascination with the spoken language of that time. "*The Feud* is my most modest work," Berger has written, "a little memoir of the place and time of my youth, more or less the same *mise en scene* as that of *Sneaky People,* but the characters are of a lower class"

(7 December 1982). In another note, the author indicated that he thought of *The Feud* "as a kind of Dreiserian slice of life" (25 April 1982). Berger's descriptions are accurate to a point, but this "most modest work" was judged best novel of 1984 by the judges' panel for the Pulitizer Prize (a decision administratively overruled in favor of William Kennedy's *Ironweed*).[4] A paragon of prose efficiency even in Berger's exquisitely precise canon, *The Feud* posits a richly textured semblance with a perfectly controlled minimum of exposition and limns its features in record time. Almost devoid of time-marking brand-name identifications, Berger's narration is at once generic and precise, as when specifying that a rake "was not the implement made specifically for leaves, but rather the iron-spiked rake used to scratch the ground for gardening," and the most extended physical description in the novel is of a carefully detailed basement.

This novel's apparent Dreiserian simplicity masks one of Berger's most sophisticated narrative voices, one with a point of view at once Olympian and warmly understanding of the fourteen characters whose sensibilities it so clearly establishes. At times historically omniscient ("Jack suspected he had made a mistake that day in the garage, and he still regretted it, as men do, many years later, though by then he was filing dispatches from the other side of the world"), this narrative voice smoothly segues in and out of the more limited points of view of selected characters, as in describing a boy's thoughts in a moment of ardor: "She had a sweet, damp smell, like the bathtub after it had been used by his sister, who had left home by now and worked in the city as a cashier in a moviehouse, and therefore he hadn't smelled that in a while: it was not perfume as such" (31).

The Feud walks a tightrope between presenting information in the idiom readers would expect from the character on whom the narrative is focused at that moment and between offering a kind of editorial observation beyond the capabilities and concerns of the point-of-view character. A fairly obvious example of narrative voice tied to a character would be: "It was tempting to take him at face value, but having had experience with our dusky friends, Walt was aware they were none too reliable with the names of white men" (87). An example of the latter, less likely point-of-view character-grounded voice would be: "But defective sight in daytime does not improve in the dark" (30); or "Plunkett and Hines, who ordinarily would have hooted derisively as he returned to them, had been cautious now, owing to the earlier foot-in-the-mouth (feet, if you counted Plunkett's coarse announcement of Eva's approach), and they received his explanation impassively" (39); or "Tony felt like punching someone—not his brother, who was totally innocent, but something inanimate that could represent the face of the god of Chance" (97). From the wide range of its narrative stances, and particularly from the restrained wisdom of its disembodied narrator, Berger's novel derives a quiet, timeless authority and offers one of the best examples of his employment and mastery of free indirect discourse, or as he prefers to identify the technique, *style indirect libre*. Most important, however, *The Feud* presents not a slice of life so much as a model of a thoroughly contingent world, one much more consonant with the propositions of systems theory than with the morally pegged determinism of Dreiser.

In place of Dreiser's selectively punitive determinism, Berger presents a world uniformly described in terms of consequences rather than intentions. In the world of *The Feud* almost anything may happen, and everything that does occur impinges upon everything else: change any aspect of the system, and all aspects will be affected. Try to refinish an old piece of furniture, and you start a feud; start a feud, and your family ricochets off its events in wildly new directions. Chaotic in normative or moral terms, such a fictional world is simply an unexpectedly realistic model of the "real" world when understood in terms of systems mechanics. Of course, the important point here is, not that Berger understands or could possibly care about systems theory, but that it offers a clear explanation for the way he presents life in his fiction. And once again it turns out that the conventional-seeming surface of Berger's celebration of a novel form (this time the Dreiserian slice of life) masks a radical substructure that is uniquely Berger's.

In its most narrow sense, Berger's title refers to the sudden eruption and three-day playing out of an intense feud between the family of Dolf Beeler, a resident of Hornbeck, and the family of Bud Bullard, who lives in neighboring Millville. Fueled by misunderstanding, misplaced pride, pathological insecurity, small-town xenophobia, self-serving interpretations of events, and the convergence of an incredible sequence of coincidences, this feud is finally remarkable for nothing quite so much as its representation of the *way things actually happen* in life—a sign of its realism rather than of its adherence to realistic literary conventions. The action of this novel and the thoughts of its characters quickly reveal that the dynamics of feuding, quaint though the term may sound, is one of the received structures of human experience, a mold just waiting to be filled, whether by Montagnes and Capulets, Hatfields and McCoys, or Beelers and Bullards. *Inimicare humanun est* (to feud is human). As will be seen again in *Orrie's Story,* revenge is a phenomenon that Berger examines from a number of perspectives, ranging from the comic to the tragic.

This focus on revenge isolates Berger's fascination with discerning the subtle distinctions between actors he identifies as "kickers and kickees," in a reciprocal system guaranteeing that those labels will alternate as the feud progresses. In many ways, feuding is the perfect dynamic for all Berger's primary concerns, as not only do feuds posit a process in which kickers and kickees—victims and victimizers—are continuously being redefined but the feuds are themselves also inevitably structured by language and inevitably question our understanding of freedom.

When the middle-aged plant foreman Dolf Beeler decides to make good on a longstanding promise to his wife to refinish an old piece of furniture, he goes to Bud Bullard's hardware store in the adjoining small town to buy the necessary paint remover. Told by Bullard's son that he must throw away his cigar, Dolf replies that it is not lit, occasioning a rapidly escalating series of conflicts that culminates in Bullard's cousin Reverton pulling a gun on Dolf, handcuffing him, and forcing him to kneel on the floor and apologize. Freed moments later, Dolf remains mentally paralyzed: "He could not understand what had happened to him, how on a normal Saturday morning he could have had such a terrible experience" (7). Dolf can't, but readers soon understand that in the semblance of Berger's novel, radical contingency is norm rather than exception.

Had the owner of the hardware store in Dolf's town not recently committed suicide, Dolf would never have gone to Bud's store in Millville in the first place. Had he not been waited on by Bud's more or less rotten son, because Bud was busy talking to his cousin Reverton, the dispute about his unlit cigar would probably not have arisen. Had not Dolf initially mistaken Reverton first for a minister (reverend/Reverton), then for a policeman, the trajectory of the dispute would have been entirely different. Had cousin Reverton not been at the store and not been a classic paranoid who carried an unloaded track starter's pistol to give him an edge in disputes, then the initial disagreement could never have led to the kind of public humiliation that turns him against the entire Bullard family. All this is precipitated on this particular day because Dolf decided to honor a promise made to his wife years before. And the feud is further escalated when Bullard's hardware store burns down that night, the fire actually started accidentally by Bullard's son but seen by the paranoid Reverton as an act of cowardly revenge by Dolf Beeler. Indeed, Berger's semblance is so complicated, and the sequence of its seemingly unconnected events so perversely woven together, that just to outline them takes great effort, the only accurate overview being that *what happens, happens.*

Of course within two days Dolf gratuitously picks a fight with a coworker distantly related to the Bullard family and seems to win it only to suffer an eventually fatal heart attack, which might be reckoned a far more terrible experience, but one equally unbelievable—in life as in fiction—before it occurs. Moreover, this quiet-seeming novel swells with crucial and unexpected changes within the three days of its action. One of Dolf's sons, Tony, stumbles into a feud-related vocation, going from assaulting one police chief to assisting another. Jack, his other son, makes a seemingly innocuous choice not to kiss a girl, but within the systems calculus of this novel, that choice may well be precisely the one that will eventually enable him to flee the narrowness of a small town for a career as a foreign correspondent. In short order, the hardware-store owner Bud Bullard, one of Dolf's ostensible antagonists, sees his business destroyed by fire and suffers a nervous breakdown, but he adroitly seizes the first available opportunity to resurrect both store and psyche. Reverton, Bud's unfortunate cousin and the feud's primary architect, dies a hero in a shootout with a notorious bank robber. And Bud's malevolent son runs away from home, while Dolf's wonderfully pragmatic daughter sails through all manner of apparent reverses.

In its largest sense, Berger's title reminds readers, as does this novel, that all human life can be seen as a continuous feud with contingency, experience relentlessly refusing to conform to expectations and explanations, myths of existence refusing to acknowledge its disorder, philosophical and epistemological maps ever at odds with the territories of actual living.

Harvey Yelton, chief of police in Hornbeck and another in a long line of Berger characters whose narrowness is so thoroughgoing as to give them a kind of wisdom, is the one character in this novel whose point of view may be broad enough to bring a sense of order to the seemingly disparate events that constitute *The Feud's* plot. To Harvey, these events are quite unremarkable, since he pretty much views the world as a series of calamities waiting to happen. Driving down one of Hornbeck's streets, he sees a rubber ball roll across the street half a block ahead of him, pursued by a young boy of about ten. The chief stops his cruiser, gets out, and patiently lectures the boy:

> Harvey said, "You know better than that, Willis. You oughtn't play ball so it comes into the street. You know why? It could hit somebody's automobile and scare them so they would lose control of the wheel and drive up over the

> curb and turn over and burst into flames, and everybody in the car would be burned to a crisp, see? Or the driver might just lose his head and turn and run over your pooch. Or you and your friends might tear after the ball onto the road and you'd all be killed if a big Mack truck was coming along real fast, or you'd scare the truckdriver and he'd smash into them high-tension wires, which would fall down and electrocute the whole neighborhood and kill everybody and burn up all your houses, maybe get outa control and burn everything in the whole town, see. Now, you wouldn't want that to happen, wouldja?" (67–68)

Harvey's description of an outrageously contingent world may strike readers as a humorous example of rhetorical overkill—precisely the kind of thing adults resort to in their roles as authorities or officials when dealing with children—but he does, in fact, see the world in these terms, as in a sense must Berger, and as in a sense must all who experience the variety and vagaries of his novel. As outrageous as Harvey's hypothetical example may at first seem, it represents much more predictable and understandable sequences of events than does the action of *The Feud*. And it is the very unlikeliness of this action that signals that this may be Berger's most conventionally realistic work, one presenting the world as a place where things—good, bad, and inscrutable—happen quite independently of intentions and expectations.

The one sure defense against contingency, in art as well as in life, is to readjust one's attitude in order to embrace or at least acknowledge unexpected developments, a cognitive remapping that changes the stories we tell ourselves in order to better correspond to ever-changing experience. The characters in all Berger's novels are desperate practitioners of this strategy of cognitive remapping, although only a select few could be called its masters—among them Dolf Beeler's calculatingly promiscuous daughter, Bernice, one of Berger's most carefree survivors, who never considers the facts of her situation without subjecting them to the softening lens of self-interest. Considering her recent eviction, Bernice remaps her relationship with her ex-landlord: "He was a big fat greasy foreigner of some kind, with lots of hair in his nose and baggy eyes. Luckily he had never put a hand on her, or else she would have lambasted him with a hot curling iron, but if looks meant anything, he had done it to her plenty. She could have lived there rent-free for the rest of her life if she had given him a little of what he was dying for, but she was no tramp. That's what hurt, when he called her one, though she should have considered the source and seen it was just sour grapes" (116).

The beauty of the above passage, and one of the sneaky attractions of Berger's novel, is that as Bernice remaps the territory of her recent experience, readers must remap the territory of their perception of Bernice. And in ways both small and large, *The Feud* presents this remapping strategy as perhaps the one constant in human nature. Certainly Berger ensures that it becomes the one constant in reading *The Feud,* as the novel withholds crucial bits of information or corrects the mistaken perceptions of its characters in ways that compel readers to resort to precisely the same kinds of cognitive remapping as must its characters. The final implication of Berger's most rigorously systematic novel is that it makes the reader a participant in, rather than just a witness to, its operations.

Orrie's Story

The book jacket copy for *Orrie's Story* identifies its source, noting that "Thomas Berger, who once recreated the legend of

Camelot in *Arthur Rex,* has now reinvented the *Oresteia,* but set it in small-town America at the close of World War II." Readers familiar with the *Oresteia* will note that Berger preserves its structure, dividing his novel into three sections, following the three linked plays of Aeschylus: *Agamemnon,* focusing on the return of the hero from the Trojan War and his immediate murder by his wife, Clytaemestra, and her lover and his cousin, Aegisthus; *The Libation Bearers,* focusing on the reaction of Electra, Agamemnon's second daughter, and Orestes, his son, to his murder, ending with the revenge murder of Clytaemestra and Aegisthus by Orestes; and *The Eumenides,* focusing on the question of and reaction of the polis to Orestes's guilt, ending with his "acquital" by a jury of Athenians, whose tie vote is broken in his favor by Athene herself. Commentaries on the *Oresteia* agree that the movement of these three plays is away from the ancient ethos of revenge that demands "an eye for an eye" (*lex talionis*) and toward an ethos of justice determined by law.[5] Berger's telling of this story follows the famous American reinvention of the *Oresteia* by Eugene O'Neill in his celebrated 1931 play, *Mourning Becomes Electra,* made in 1947 into a film starring Rosalind Russell as the Electra character. O'Neill reset the plays of the *Oresteia* in New England just following the end of the Civil War, and focused it intensely on the Oedipal aspects brought into stark relief by Freudian psychiatry.[6]

Not surprisingly, given his characteristic preference for the antique in literary models, Berger's telling of the *Oresteia* seems to owe almost nothing to the O'Neill "Americanization" of the story, beyond resetting it in America and using various townspeople to serve as a de facto Greek chorus. Berger's "reinvention" of the *Oresteia* features a number of parallels to the original story and some noteworthy divergences from it.

The names of major characters in *Orrie's Story* mirror their origins quite closely, as Aeschylus's Agamemnon becomes Berger's Augie, Cassandra becomes Cassie, Clytemnaestra becomes Esther, Iphigineia becomes Gena, Aegisthus becomes E. G., Electra becomes Ellie, Orestes becomes Orrie, Pylades becomes Paul Leeds, the avenging Furies become the prosecuting attorney Bernard J. Furie, Apollo becomes the defense attorney Anthony Pollo, and Athene becomes Thea Palliser. The chorus, so important in Greek drama, gives way to the townspeople who are "regulars at the Idle Hour Bar & Grill," who may indeed "know more about Augie and his family than any other sources" (208), but not only lack the range of knowledge of Aeschylus's chorus, but are also individualized enough to reveal their very human prejudices and misconceptions.

Names are actually among the least important changes Berger makes, however. The resonance of the tragically internecine Trojan War on which Aeschylus so explicitly built was largely retained by O'Neill in setting *Mourning Becomes Electra* at the close of the Civil War, but Berger sets *Orrie's Story* at the end of World War II, whose causes and scale significantly undercut the reader's sense that the events of this novel are integrally connected to the events that led to war. Moreover, Berger's Augie is no Agamemnon, as he is not only not a mighty king and victorious warrior, but he has also been working in a defense plant in the South while deceiving his friends and family with fraudulent stories of his military exploits. He is also no Agamemnon insofar as he not only has not sacrificed his daughter, Gena, to further his participation in a war of revenge, but had nothing to do with her decision to leave home, where Berger's Aegisthus character, E. G., her mother's lover, had also been routinely paying Gena for sex, as apparently had others.

Nor has Augie returned home with a captive Cassandra, his slave and concubine, to throw in Esther's face; Augie is in love with Cassie where he worked "down South," but the love is chaste and largely incidental to Esther's resentment against him. Accordingly *Orrie's Story* starts from a point where the revenge motive and cycle of revenge, so extensive in the *Oresteia,* has been almost entirely undercut: when E. G. and Esther murder Augie, who wants nothing more than to divorce his wife and leave his family to be with Cassie, they do so mainly to collect the GI insurance they wrongly believe will follow his death. Indeed, one of Berger's many twists on the *Oresteia* is that money, or its lack, plays a significant role in driving the events of his narrative.[7]

The first section of Berger's novel departs significantly from the first play in the *Oresteia,* and the second section introduces an Orrie/Orestes who is also quite different from the character developed by Aeschylus. Berger's Orrie has not been sent away by his mother and her lover, but is off at college. Orrie is not much better suited to the role of avenger than Augie was to the role of hero. Indeed, his father had long worried about Orrie's manhood and had ridiculed his desire to become an artist. Of course, the real Berger twist here is that Augie may not actually be Orrie's father, as Esther had conceived him during a period when she was having sex with both Augie and his cousin, E. G., who, as irony would have it, has a much higher opinion of Orrie than does Augie and is even supportive of his desire to become an artist. In one of Berger's ironic nods to the classical contours of his story, Orrie had auditioned for a role in his school's production of *Oedipus,* but had not been able to land a role.

Part 2 of Berger's novel introduces us to an Orrie who is given more to philosophical contemplation than to action, and his reaction to his father's death, which is still being called accidental, is more one of relief than anger. His main concern is with the complexity of his own response, as he realizes in terms far too complicated for a hero of Greek tragedy not only that "being honest with oneself means nothing to one's guilt-making apparatus," but also that "if anything, the latter is stimulated to produce in higher intensity and greater volume" (79). His deliberations about his unemotional response to his father's death conclude: "Could he have produced tears, his conscience might have been appeased, but his pride would have been mortally wounded: he would have been a better son but a lesser man" (79). From this passage we see that Orrie shares Augie's concern with manhood and, indeed, Orrie is mainly concerned with being reasonable and acting normally, a posture that makes him refuse to believe his sister Ellie's charges that their father had been murdered by Esther and E. G. Orrie's concern with seeming normal itself seems to be obsessive, as when he first sees his sister after returning from college following his father's death: "He thought briefly about hugging her, but that kind of thing was not done by local people with their relatives, unless the huggers were grandparents and aunts and uncles of a certain age, with a musty odor, and those being embraced were under age twelve" (87). When Ellie tries to convince him that Esther and E. G. had been lovers and had murdered Augie, Orrie's response centers not on determining the truth of her claim as much as it does with his worry that *she* not be seen as acting crazy or warped. Blind to his own Oedipal fixation (he thinks his mother "the most attractive woman he had yet seen in real life"), Orrie's commitment to reason is both paralyzing and pathetically naive, as he tries to convince himself that "being careful is not cowardice. Courage is not an exclusive possession of the rash" (105).

Combine his reticence to act with his worship of reason ("He was no authority on international affairs, but he suspected that if someone had spoken reasonably to Hitler early on, there might not have been a World War II.") and Orrie begins to look more like a caricatured effete liberal than a Greek hero locked in a tragic cycle of revenge. Indeed, as he touches base with Hamlet in superficial ways (owns a fencing foil, considers suicide), Orrie is a psychological mess. At almost every turn he fails to measure up against his college friend Paul Leeds, given substance and admirable traits by Berger far exceeding the nominal role assigned to Pylades by Aeschylus.

Part 2 of Berger's novel does end with Orrie's killing of E. G. and Esther, although he shoots the former to keep him from beating up his mother and the latter completely by accident as she moves in the way of a second shotgun blast, intended for E. G. Part 3 returns more directly to the concerns with justice at the center of Aeschylus's *The Eumenides* (and takes on questions completely ignored by O'Neill's *Mourning Becomes Electra*), but Berger has so reshuffled the deck by now that the trial to determine the extent of Orrie's guilt proceeds along lines and to ends quite different from those in the *Oresteia*. In Berger's telling, Ellie is coldly calculating in seeking revenge for her father's death and quite efficient in protecting Orrie, at least from the external consequences of killing E. G. and Esther. But, to some extent, this only adds to Orrie's peculiar sense of guilt, which includes his shame that his "little sister is running things." "What kind of man am I?" is the question that consumes Orrie, not a question about whether he is guilty or innocent, good or evil. Orrie's questions about the nature of manliness and his insecurities about his own manhood, introduced in part 2, only intensify in part 3, which even ends with

Orrie's considering the pleasant prospect of furthering a relationship with a young woman (Hermione!) he has just met: "Surely there was nothing that could make you feel more of a man" (276).

To the extent that he wants to "own" his own guilt rather than have it determined in a court of law, the legal proceedings in part 3 are largely irrelevant to Orrie, who contemplates suicide not because he feels guilty of murder, but because he feels guilty of being unmanly: "He was guilty of having done nothing in the matter of Erle before shooting him to death. He was guilty of having panicked, losing control, using a man's weapon without a man's authority to wield it. His father had undoubtedly tried to teach him about apprenticeship, but he ran away, refusing to listen, rejecting instruction in manhood . . ." (229).

While Orrie is prosecuted by one Bernard J. Furie and defended by one Anthony Pollo in a trial presided over by Judge Thea Palliser, Berger's trial is more desultory than momentous, and its outcome hardly represents a step forward from much of anything, much less a self-destructive ethos of revenge. This Furie doesn't exactly hound Orrie, as he only charges him with manslaughter, doesn't seem to work very hard for a conviction, and seems relieved when the jury finds Orrie not guilty. This Apollo (A. Pollo) is not a god who had commanded Orrie to kill his mother and E. G., but is a very good lawyer, provided by Paul Leeds, who quite perceptively suggests to Orrie that he might not understand his own motives or "might not be absolutely certain what happened or why" (230) and makes Orrie's desire to be punished a major part of the brief for his acquittal. The murkiness of human motivation and the vagaries of the legal system of justice deepen as Berger lets readers in on jury deliberations that reveal a catalog of misperceptions and of very human but very extraneous concerns that enter into the jury's verdict. Predictably enough, Orrie responds to his acquittal in part by hoping "in future to avoid attorneys-at-law, whose sense of morality, being essentially linguistic, was so basically at odds with his own" (269), while the calculating Ellie decides she wants to become a lawyer.

So what finally are readers to make of Berger's "reinvention" of the *Oresteia*? Oddly enough, while one of the clear concerns of Berger's "reinvention" of the Arthur legend was that a rigid code of chivalry inexorably led to the downfall of the Round Table because of conflicting principles, the disastrous cycle of revenge that was of such great concern to Aeschylus has been systematically precluded as a motivating factor in *Orrie's Story*. And the Freudian intensity of O'Neill's *Mourning Becomes Electra* seems almost deliberately undercut by Berger, both with Ellie's inability to utter even the word "psychiatrist" ("Or a nut-doctor. You know psy-uh—" [18]) and Orrie's hopelessly muddled Oedipal situation. What seems to emerge from these changes is a Greek tragedy that, when resituated in modernity, is a fish out of water. In the modern world, motives are never unmixed and largely unknowable, money is an unavoidable consideration in human relationships, murders lend themselves to the analysis of police procedural, and jury trials turn on an unpredictable mix of human foibles in the jurors. Where O'Neill vastly simplified the motives driving the action in Aeschylus's *Oresteia*, reducing them to incestuous love and simple revenge, Berger has complicated those motives to the point where it is almost impossible to untangle them.[8]

While during its writing Berger termed *Orrie's Story* "a new departure for me, being unrelievedly grim" (23 December 1989), its ending, at least when compared with the ending of *Mourning Becomes Electra*, is positively upbeat. Ellie has had her revenge through the agency (however unintended) of Orrie, who has been acquitted of manslaughter charges, and the worst prospect in her foreseeable future, which looks like it will include the love of the admirable Paul Leeds, is that she intends to become a lawyer. And, while Orrie is surely correct in bitterly vowing that he "will never get over" his accidental murder of his mother, he faces no further public recrimination for his action and has just met an attractive and interesting young woman, Hermione, with whom he foresees the pleasant prospect of a more intimate relationship. So, while it is the case that *Orrie's Story* is unrelievedly grim, it is also the case that it is not hopeless. As Berger told B. A. Nilsson in his 1991 interview: "I had always assumed I believed the worst, but that was before I had lived sufficiently long to understand that hopelessness is the ultimate sentimentality."[9]

CHAPTER 4

Novels of Menace

Neighbors, The Houseguest, Meeting Evil, Best Friends

> I have at last found another of the sadomasochistic situations in which, I think, my peculiar strength lies. The suspense comes in trying to identify who's the kicker and who the kickee, *sub specie aeternitatis* or even only in terms of the local supermarket.
>
> —Thomas Berger, discussing *Neighbors,*
> 2 October 1978

In recent years National Book Critics Circle Award–winning novelist Jonathan Lethem has added his voice to the chorus of critics and readers who find Thomas Berger a unique and uniquely valuable presence in American literature. In his introduction to the 2003 paperback edition of *Meeting Evil,* originally published in 1992, Lethem notes one of the perverse ironies of Berger's career—that by inhabiting a kind of "middle distance" in American letters, highly respected but not widely read, "proof neither of the proposition that genius is always rewarded nor that it is universally overlooked," Berger has paradoxically become a writer "impossible to revive because he's never been sufficiently neglected," a condition Lethem terms "quite suitably Bergerian."[1]

Rehearsing Berger's record of celebrating established novel forms, Lethem turns his attention to the "core concerns" of Berger's novels and to the "less categorizable" novels that "are harder to pigeonhole or typify." Lethem argues that it is these hard-to-classify novels, including *Killing Time, Sneaky People, Neighbors, The Houseguest, The Feud, Meeting Evil,* and *Best Friends,* that actually "comprise the strongest argument for Berger's lasting importance, especially cumulatively." Within this loose grouping of novels "with their nominally realist settings, and full of human blundering ranging from adultery and murder to badly cooked meals," Lethem singles out a subset of three that he calls "novels of menace," *Neighbors, The Houseguest,* and *Meeting Evil,* to which he considers adding a fourth, *Best Friends,* "partly as a gentle capstone."

Lethem links the "novels of menace" through their sharing of what he terms the theme of "ambivalent usurpation," which he finds in their "uncanny scenarios wherein a terrifying struggle for power emerges from within a banal milieu": "Each features a principal provocateur and a principal victim—but Berger is fascinated by the ways in which innocence and reserve are complicit with chaos and impulsivity. He makes a study of the malignancy of charisma but of the torpor of reflection as well. In the words of Reinhart: 'People use us as we ask them to: this is life's fundamental, and often the only, justice'" (xii–xiii). He concludes his take on what Berger calls the attempt to determine "who's the kicker and who the kickee" by noting: "It is typical of Berger that once his theme of doubleness has been established, rather than emphasize similarity between characters to a fatuous degree, he instead exercises his fascination with the fact that differing types do exist: however we might become ensnared by another, the lonely fact of self persists" (xiii). It is the four "novels of menace" that this chapter will discuss.

Neighbors

Berger writes that "*(Neighbors)* is my own favorite among my ten novels, because at no point did I think consciously about it. It performed itself before my eyes, without my intervention at any point: I served exclusively as spectator. It is for me the absolutely pure fiction that I have lately aspired to, with no taint of journalism, sociology, and the other corruptions" (23 May 1979). If *Sneaky People* represents Berger's "tribute to the American language of 1939" as used by "the lower-middle class in the eastern Middle West," and if *The Feud* echoes that tribute, allowing Berger to re-create the speech he heard when a child, then *Neighbors* must surely represent, in part, a very different kind of tribute to a very different kind of language—the leveled and banal commonplaces of post-television homogenization. Not only does the action of *Neighbors* consist primarily of functions of language but the characters, particularly the confusing new neighbor Harry, rely almost exclusively on commonplace phrases such as "face the music," "it's your word against mine," "take it like a man," "like a cornered rat," and "clutching at straws." While agreeing on the relevancy of this observation, Berger has specified, "I made no conscious effort to use clichés and commonplaces: these demonic characters produced them on their own volition, Harry especially" (4 September 1982). For his own purposes, however, Berger maintains a reasonable distinction between these two novels, explaining that "my own interest in writing *The Feud* was linguistic, whereas for me *Neighbors* was a work in which the preoccupation is with a man's life and death" (14 December 1987).

Neighbors may offer the most verbal world Berger has created; identifying the mode of this novel as his favorite, Berger describes it as "a creation and not the observation of existing reality" (30 July 1981). Indeed, Berger's letters suggest again and again that this work held special significance for him: "*Neighbors* is rather like my plays, being mostly in dialogue and without the naturalistic detail and sociological pretext of the Reinhart books, but then I've been moving farther away from that in each novel. This is also my most artistically ambitious book and at the same time the one on which I shall have exerted the least effort of the usual, conscious kind. *Neighbors* is essentially automatic writing, created in a trance" (28 January 1979).

Berger's protagonist for this delightfully perplexing novel, Earl Keese, a quiet, reasonable forty-nine-year-old suburbanite, tells people that his home sits "at the end of the road," because that construction sounds less "dispiriting" than "at a dead end." But when Harry and Ramona move next door, within twenty-four hours Keese is faced with a sequence of situations so outrageous that he can find no rhetorical constructions to mask their threat or to maintain the hoax of his previously complacent life.

Mysterious and maddening, Harry and Ramona are, by turns, forward, friendly, rude, flattering, insulting, provoking, and threatening. Their words and actions are always unexpected and usually contradictory. For instance, when Keese first responds to Ramona's knock at his door and phatically asks her, "And what may I do for you?" her response is a most disconcerting, "Anything you like . . . the problem is what you want in return." More and more, the visits of Harry and Ramona seem like assaults. Their random comings and goings produce a series of off-balance events, each more preposterous than the last, gradually stripping Keese of his easy assumptions and habitual responses.

Madcap physical changes punctuate Berger's plot—entrances, exits, searches, fights, a damaged car, a destroyed house, even a sudden death—but for all its action, *Neighbors* might best be described as a series of functions of language: puns, platitudes, commonplaces, theories, definitions, excuses, accusations, rationalizations, promises, questions, threats—all acts performed with words. Keese, Berger has commented, "is a prisoner of what he believes to be his responsibilities, in language as in all else."[2] Keese responds to what the world *says it is doing,* rather than to *what it actually does,* and this makes him the perfect target of Ramona's and Harry's verbal hoaxes. They hoax him intermittently, but language itself hoaxes him continuously.

Harry and Ramona seem committed to tweaking Keese's sensibility, to pushing him to see how far he will go to avoid humiliation, to pestering, haunting, and ultimately rearranging his life. Their decidedly unneighborly behavior stuns him, placing him at such disadvantage in all his dealings with them that he is driven to respond in thoughts and actions even more outlandish than theirs. "Maybe I'm just testing you," Ramona cryptically observes, while all Keese can do is desperately sigh, "I am trying to adjust to a life in which chance encounters can be brutal" (125).

In this absurdly skewed context, Harry's firing a shotgun at Keese and offering him an obviously dirty coffee cup seem equally offensive, and Harry and Ramona sting Keese as much by accusing him of sarcasm as they do by falsely accusing him of attempted rape. Their behavior is so confusing, in part, because they keep shifting among the registers of social and linguistic codes—responding to the code of friendship with that of a feud, responding literally to figurative statements, refusing to speak or act on Keese's wavelength. And by refusing to comply with these codes of speech and action, they call attention to the arbitrary and essentially phatic patterns that govern so much of human interchange. Once these patterns have been exposed and their tenuous nature revealed by simple refusals to speak or act "right," the concept of right itself seems more and more problematic, and in this crucible of paradoxes and contradictions, Earl must distill a new behavioral code to guide his actions—a new morality that in its complexity must follow Nietzsche "beyond good and evil."

As Keese's experiences increasingly blur the lines between comedy and nightmare and between hallucination and reality, his relations with all those around him begin to undergo subtle changes—a metamorphosis. He realizes that his life has grown so stale that Harry's and Ramona's crazy-seeming aggravations may actually offer him a salvation of sorts—the chance to take control of, and give style to, his life, to team up with them and "roam the boulevards with a supercilious smile for all, and glide through smart shops exchanging glib remarks." In a fundamental sense, Harry and Ramona reveal to him the meaning of freedom. And this change is not beyond Keese's notice, as he finally admits to Harry, "Every time I see you as a criminal, by another light you look like a kind of benefactor" (259). Like almost all of Berger's protagonists, Keese has been imprisoned by his own elaborate codes of responsibility, fairness, and decency, terms that seem to have no meaning for, much less control over, the actions of Harry and Ramona. As surely as Keese's outrage over the seeming pecadilloes of his new neighbors grows dangerously, even pathologically, violent, chinks begin to appear in his moral armor. His initial impatience with "the philosophies which disregarded the problem of guilt" soon gives way to the realization that "it's easy to excuse everything in some way. . . . For example, murder can be seen in one light as merely getting rid of someone—as a mere removal" (127). It falls to his wife, Enid, to put things in perspective for him with her blunt explanation for her own questionable conduct. "What's morality have to do with it?" she asks. "I'm speaking of self-preservation" (223).

And so is Berger, but in a most subtle and complicated fashion, along lines explored in one way or another by Pierre de Laclos, Nietzsche, Kafka, and Berger himself in his first three plays. Part of Berger's achievement in *Neighbors* is that he has subsumed the traditions of these three writers within his own uniquely ironic style. Indeed, the best joke in *Neighbors* is that beneath its slapstick action and farcical humor lies a very serious investigation of the relationship between freedom and victimization.

Anyone familiar with Berger's novels knows his longstanding fascination with the question "who is kicker and who kickee," but it is not generally known that Berger has most directly confronted this issue in his plays. Around 1969 Berger tried his hand at playwriting, eventually completing four plays, the last, *The Burglars: A Play in Two Acts*, written around 1987. One of these plays, *Other People*, was produced in 1970 at the Berkshire Theatre Festival in Massachusetts. Each of his first three plays (*Other People; The Siamese Twins;* and *Rex, Rita, and Roger*) involves the ways in which definitions of self determine power relationships, and each develops a sense of paranoia out of seemingly absurd situations. *Rex, Rita, and Roger*, and *The Siamese Twins* seem to present almost a situational blueprint for

Neighbors, both plays vexing a static domestic scene by introducing ominous outsiders.

Rex, Rita, and Roger investigates the nature of will through a farcical confrontation more than a little reminiscent of that in Melville's "Bartleby the Scrivener." The rough situational similarities between *Rex, Rita, and Roger* and *Neighbors* are nothing, however, when compared with those between *Neighbors* and *The Siamese Twins.* In the latter play, two new neighbors, "large, blond, and beautiful" Siamese twins—Robert and Roberta—descend upon the unquiet suburban household of Leo; his wife, Phylis; and her transvestite brother, Francis. In much the style later employed by Harry and Ramona, these twins defy all the established social codes and immediately begin to critique and to disrupt Leo's household. Apart from the exotic fact that they have been joined at the hip by a band of flesh, Robert and Roberta seem linked in some vague therapeutic enterprise. As is true of *Neighbors, The Siamese Twins* consists of a series of absurd actions that are almost exclusively functions of language: accusations, criticisms, apologies, clichés, coaching, and commentary. Roberta and Robert seem determined to shock the members of the household into a kind of regression therapy.

Like Robert and Roberta, Harry and Ramona of *Neighbors* seem more than a little reminiscent of Nietzsche's "blond brute," his prototypical "free spirit" (Earl explicitly describes them as "free spirits," while Ramona says, "We're just a pair of shiftless zanies"). Certainly the conflict between Earl and his new neighbors seems to dramatize the conflict described by Nietzsche as that between "slave," or "herd," and "master" moralities. Earl's initially submissive behavior, his obsession with proper form, his growing sense of resentment, even his elaborate and violent imaginary retaliations, make him an almost perfect model for Nietzsche's man of *ressentiment.* The toothy and tawny Harry and Ramona flaunt their rudeness and their ungoverned instinct—both virtues in the Nietzschean scheme of things, both signs of an honest animality. Read in this manner, *Neighbors* becomes almost a dramatization (some might say a burlesque) of Nietzsche's views of universal "neighborliness." It is Nietzsche who argues that fear and the will to power are what really structure relationships between humans, and he even specifies that it is fear of the neighbor that gives rise to "new perspectives of moral valuation."[3]

If the world of *Neighbors* seems remarkably like that depicted in Nietzsche's philosophy, it also should be noted that it has much in common with that of two novels: Kafka's *Trial* and Laclos's *Dangerous Acquaintances.* The nature of the relationship between Harry and Ramona seems as unorthodox and as unstable as that between Laclos's Valmont and Madame de Merteuil, both pairs of victimizers become victims themselves, and both pairs seem to exist only on the axis of dominance and subordination. Both novels suggest (although in quite different terms) that alienation is a necessary step on the way to personal freedom. Berger's homage to Kafka, from whom he learned that "at any moment banality might turn sinister, for existence was not meant to be unfailingly genial," is clearer still.[4] Vocabularies from law and ethics intertwine throughout *Neighbors,* and Berger does not fail to exploit the incongruities of the two lexicons. Terms having to do with guilt, justice, punishment, revenge, motive, confession, defense, blame, accusation, and so on, appear on virtually every page of this novel, resonating at once with the rhetoric of the courtroom and with that of Kafka's *Trial.*

But just as surely as Berger invokes the verbal worlds of Kafka or Nietzsche or Booth Tarkington, his style radically transforms those worlds. Berger's narrative continually highlights the ironic ways in which the worlds of his characters' language are exposed as being at odds with the worlds of their experience. And finally the lives of those characters suggest a larger joke in the human condition—that death itself is but the ultimate irony. For Buddy Sandifer in *Sneaky People,* as for Dolf Beeler and Reverton in *The Feud* and for Earl Keese in *Neighbors,* death "could happen to anybody" and does—proving to be the sneakiest experience of all, always the final irony.

The Houseguest

For readers familiar with Berger's writing, the very title of his fifteenth novel, *The Houseguest* (1988), suffices to invoke dialectically opposed expectations. The example of *Neighbors* and of Berger's plays strongly suggests that a work so titled will surely involve the imposition of a mysterious and threatening outsider—the houseguest—on a static, if not enervated, domestic situation. The outsider can be expected somehow to gain power, moral authority, over the family whose hospitality he or she takes advantage of, recasting the guest-host relationship in terms of Berger's favored paradigm of kicker-kickee. This dominance, however, may ultimately prove chimerical, beneficial, or both—revealing or clarifying to the ostensible victims basic truths of their existence.

In Berger's view *The Houseguest,* like *Neighbors* before it, is "mostly a creation and not the observation of existing reality"

(30 July 1981). The author, who began writing this novel as early as 1981, has also described it as a story "in which the title-character arrived at nobody's invitation and dominated everybody in the house, resisted only by the daughter-in-law," a narrative he accurately judges "reminiscent of *Neighbors* only in the relentlessness of the idea" (28 January 1982). Indeed, in its emphasis on the arrogant superficiality of class and the trappings of money, its presentation of a mysterious outsider with no known history, and in the sterile relationships among its five principal characters, Berger's novel might be regarded as an abstracted, twisted, and desentimentalized parallel to *The Great Gatsby*.

At the intersection of *The Houseguest's* surprising and predictable aspects is the fact that for the first time in Berger's novels, his narrative focus falls on a woman. Female characters have long been the centers of pragmatism and strength in Berger's fiction—the only characters who seem regularly to know their goals, much less accomplish them—but their points of view have rarely been sustained. *Arthur Rex* poses a major exception to this rule, but even there Berger's women, while emerging as perhaps the most interesting characters in the Arthurian story, are finally overshadowed by the mythic power of the male-centered legend. The multiple inversions of *Regiment of Women* also complicate generalizations about Berger's female characters by presenting a woman's point of view for a male character, but only in the service of rejecting the rhetoric of gender. *The Houseguest* unequivocally presents a female protagonist, both the primary narrative focus of the novel and the primary actor in its events. That Berger's protagonist is a woman, however, does not become clear before the end of the novel, as she only gradually distinguishes herself in our consciousness, emerging as the one character capable of growth and deserving of our respect.[5]

This novel's first sentence is one of Berger's most informatively outrageous openings, positing as it does a number of seemingly unreasonable propositions: "The process that led to the decision to kill Chuck Burgoyne, who for the first week of his visit had proved the perfect houseguest, began on Sunday when, though he had promised to prepare breakfast for all (he was a superb cook), he had not yet appeared in the kitchen by half past noon" (3). "Process" is the key word here, as Berger explores the innumerable processes by which people adhere to codes of behavior without understanding or agreeing with the teleology of those codes.

So adroit is this Chuck Burgoyne at playing the role of the perfect houseguest that the Graves family initially fails to realize that he is not only uninvited to their isolated summer home on an island but is unknown to any of them, each mistakenly believing Chuck to be the friend of another family member. The mere fact that Chuck can cook distinguishes him from his hosts, a distinction accentuated by his general competence in all areas, a competence that quickly comes to seem ominous. Lydia's new family proves accomplished only in negative respects: Doug as a cynical philanderer, Audrey as a discrete alcoholic, and Bobby as a paragon of fecklessness. Resentment, toward each other and the world at large, is all they have in common, and their grim focus on rituals of hospitality is all that holds the family together.

Having insinuated himself into their routine as a kind of social glue, the one standard on which all can agree, Chuck then drops his accommodating mask, engaging in a series of transgressive acts, ranging from his failure to prepare breakfast to his rape of Lydia as she sleeps, exhausted from nearly drowning in an undertow from which Chuck has saved her and about which the family had neglected to warn her. Perhaps his most serious transgression is honesty, as his appraisals of his antagonists are brutally frank but not inaccurate: "'There's a lot of deceit in this house,' Chuck said. 'That's what strikes me as a guest: how much you all lie to one another. Unless you're all simply that insensitive and unobservant'" (95).

Chuck's honesty eventually complicates our reading when it turns toward Bobby, Lydia's new husband. When Lydia informs Bobby that Chuck has raped her, he simply does not believe her; when Chuck smugly confirms that charge, Bobby cannot believe his own ears and thinks himself the victim of a terrible delusion. Chuck incredulously comments: "You're virtually an idiot, aren't you? In a poorer family you'd be kept at home and given a little yardwork to do, trimming the edges, raking leaves, et cetera. They wouldn't let you marry and pass on your inferior genes" (134). Little if any evidence in the novel challenges this view, and yet Lydia has lived with, married, and professes to love the object of Chuck's derision. The challenge to the reader here is to decide whether Chuck's view (pretty much seconded by Bobby's parents) is compelling and, if it is, to decide whether Lydia's *marriage* rests on cynical or opportunistic grounds or whether her love for Bobby is profound, a sign of almost saintly understanding.

Revealing himself to be a relative of the ubiquitous Finches, brutish locals (surely a branch of the notorious Greavy family in *Neighbors*) who provide all the services for the Graves family, Chuck easily takes over the household, intimidating without actually threatening, contemptuously exposing their desperate confusion of class with character, of money with moral strength. At the point when the family comes closest to murdering him, rationalizing their actions as self-defense, Chuck has probably not even broken any laws. Recognizing that Lydia alone has the spirit to oppose him, he tells her of his victory that it "was like knocking overripe fruit off a tree. It is *too* easy. I wish I could get a challenge out of somebody, but they're such worms" (149).

Although Chuck correctly perceives that Lydia is not like the rest of the Graves family, he incorrectly believes that she has more than that difference in common with him. The crucial distinction, Lydia informs him, is that while he is "nothing but a cheap hustler," she is "trying to accomplish something here." Not only does she resist his opportunism but she also eventually wrests away from him his power over the family. From her initial determination, however, to assume responsibility for avenging her rape, Lydia grows to recognize a larger responsibility for her surroundings, which means that she decides to assume Chuck's former power, but to use it for the moral education and betterment of the Graves family. "We're going to make good use of the rest of the summer, despite this bad start," she firmly announces (229). The former houseguest is retained as a new family employee, while Lydia demands and receives the rights and privileges accorded to a houseguest. Yielding completely to her authority, her father-in-law grudgingly accepts her as "a necessary evil, like a policeman."

Lydia's victory may or may not last. Her spirit and moral vitality have carried the day, but with considerable assistance from a large-caliber police revolver. She has not been "contaminated" (her word) by her new environment, but her new designation as houseguest, while signifying a potential gain in privilege, also seems to represent a distinctly pragmatic rearrangement of her marriage and an unmistakable step toward a marriage such as that of her in-laws. More important, the central irony of Chuck's brief dominance, an irony implicit in his bitter claim to the family that "there's never been anything you could supply that I would want," now would seem to become Lydia's burden as well. The four benign smiles she sees as the novel closes can hardly seem reassuring. Lydia has negotiated the transition from insecure outsider to person in charge, but her success has been at the considerable cost of accepting new responsibility—at once the bane of all Berger's characters, and their triumph.

Meeting Evil and *Best Friends*

Whether manifested in situations that pair and confuse kickers with kickees or in specific pairs of characters, the theme of doubleness described by Jonathan Lethem can be traced throughout Berger's career, starting with *Crazy in Berlin,* where each major character seems challenged to deal with some form of doppelgänger. But nowhere is this theme more starkly apparent than in *Meeting Evil* (1992) and *Best Friends* (2003). Over a decade separates the publications of these works, and the far gentler tone of *Best Friends* may reveal a softening, or at least a refocusing, of Berger's vision during those years. While *Meeting Evil* is the most grim of Berger's three darkest novels (*Changing the Past, Orrie's Story,* and *Meeting Evil*), *Best Friends* chronicles the dissolution of a putative friendship, but pairs that dissolution with the discovery of a mature capacity for love. Each of these novels pits a protagonist against a particularly insidious nemesis, but *Best Friends* goes beyond the kicker/kickee "friendship" between its two main male characters to chart the discovery of love, even if it is the love of a "best friend's" wife. Nevertheless, these are also novels that seem to speak to each other in unmistakable ways, exploring doubleness between two works as well as within the semblance of each. While there are very significant differences between the "principal provocateur" and "principal victim" in these two novels, both clearly explore what Lethem terms "the ways in which innocence and reserve are complicit with chaos and impulsivity," both have to do with the way a word, "friendship," can be completely drained of meaning by the particulars of a relationship, and both deal with the compromises and rationalizations that delay a protagonist from taking action that ultimately must be taken.

The ethic and aesthetic of delay, as classically presented in works as different as *Hamlet* and *Ulysses,* is itself one of the great themes of literature, and both John Felton in *Meeting Evil* and Roy Courtright in *Best Friends* must wrestle with all sorts of scruples, principles, uncertainties, and fears before taking decisive action in crucial situations. In *Meeting Evil,* John Felton must finally realize that the responsibility falls to him and him alone to put an end to the sociopathic murderer Richie. Indeed, Berger is on record with specifying: "The matter of *Meeting Evil* is concerned almost exclusively with how long it will take John Felton, a decent man of mediocre gifts and few attainments, to recognize, first, that Richie must be destroyed and, second, that the job must be done by him, John, with no help from anyone else."[6] In *Best Friends,* Roy Courtright must work through the hypostatizing label of "friendship" that has blinded him to the true nature of his relationship with his "best friend" Sam Grandy, as he works toward discovering both the abstract power and the concrete particulars of another abstraction, "love," which he discovers for the first time in his relationship with Sam's wife, Kristin. While Roy's ultimate recognitions do not directly have to do with matters of life and death, the question in *Best Friends* is first, how long it will take him to "grow up" into someone capable of mature love and, second, how long it will take him to recognize his love for Kristin and to separate it from the dictates of his ersatz "friendship" with Sam.

And, as was previously the case with connections between Berger's plays *Rex, Rita, and Roger* and *The Siamese Twins,* and *Neighbors* and *The Houseguest,* a later Berger play, *The Burglars: A Play in Two Acts,* may also bear on these two novels. Written around 1987 and published in *New Letters* in 1988, *The Burglars* may offer the apotheosis of Berger's fascination with doubleness and with chiasmic situations in which doubles switch roles.[7] This play, something of a bedroom farce, features four characters, a married couple, Faith and Adam, whose home is sequentially burgled by Carl and Carol, curiously principled and protocol-conscious criminals who, it turns out, are married but estranged. During the course of the drama, these characters exchange not only roles but also partners and possibly sexual preferences, as labels, identities, and allegiances prove neither confident nor stable.[8] Unexpected affinities between kickers and kickees lead to the possibility of unlikely friendships and attraction between burglars and victims, with marital or sexual allegiance shifting wildly among the four. Friendship, violence, action versus inaction, the gap between linguistic map and concrete territory, the discovery of unexpected shared qualities—all these are topics examined in *Meeting Evil* and *Best Friends.*

Meeting Evil

When a knock at John Felton's door leads him to help a motorist push start his car, it also propels John into a nightmarish sequence of events in which his random contact with the motorist, Richie Maranville, involves him as a hapless (but not completely innocent) bystander in the cascading mayhem set in motion by Richie, who turns out to be a murderous sociopath. Almost immediately Richie likes John, sensing in him the possibility of a best friend or figurative brother. Richie, of course, is crazy, but he does recognize in John characteristics he values highly and he understands John is an almost perfect foil for everything from his humor to his murderous proclivities. John is the thoroughgoing "man of goodwill," the nice guy and good citizen who is the antithesis of the sociopath, but is also a type Berger has long resisted and sometimes ridiculed in his fiction, suggesting that the man of goodwill may unwittingly lead to as much harm in society as does the sociopath.

As Berger has explained, the action and dialogue in *Meeting Evil* has to do mainly with how long it takes John to fully recognize Richie's sociopathy, which can only be seen as evil, and to recognize the need to transcend his own meliorist values and accept responsibility for ending Richie's evil. John lives his life by values generally held admirable: he is amiable, honest, considerate, able to see things from the perspective of others, reasonable ("Things were rarely as bad or as good as assessed by the overexcitable" [26]), and thoroughly committed to the proposition that "nothing was more important than avoiding violence" (83). A "nice guy" and always a "good citizen," John is "conscious of a lifetime urge to do right," even though he realizes this impulse "put him at a frequent disadvantage" (41).

Even after it has become clear to him that his contact with Richie has turned disastrous: "He could not blame himself for responding originally to Richie's call for simple assistance, nor for later doing what seemed a far from extravagant favor for Sharon. He still was not ready to say it was inevitably, necessarily, foolish, let alone hazardous, to be kind to strangers. What a rotten world it would have to be for a fellow like him, who had always thought of himself as normal in every respect, to arrive at such a cynical conclusion!" (53–54).

When Richie calls John "my kind of person," he does so without irony, but Berger's irony is unmistakable: Richie is indeed "an understanding guy," and he understands John as a type whose earnestness will always make him a perfect target for Richie's jokes, someone who would never think of "making a fool of" Richie, someone whose principles Richie can admire in the abstract even while disregarding in most particular cases. After several sequences of violent mayhem, Richie tells John, who has begun to suspect that Richie knows him better than he knows himself: "The fact is you might not want to think about it, high and mighty as you consider yourself, but we've got a lot in common, you and me, underneath it all. It might just be I'm more honest with myself than you are. I admit I wish I was more like you. I envy your way of life, wife and kids and home and all. But so do you envy me, if you would admit it. Else why did you continue to hang on with me all this while? You had plenty of chances to dispense with my company. Didn't I tell you to go on and leave if you wanted?" (109). When Richie increasingly begins to refer to John as his "friend," "best friend," or even "brother," he means it—from his terrible sociopathic perspective—and his claim that "I don't let friends down" (98) may be the most chilling words John has ever heard, particularly since

Richie sees John's principles and values as signs of a vulnerability that needs protecting.

Richie is the most fully drawn, the most malignant, and the scariest of the long line of sociopaths who appear in Berger's novels and the eighteen-page middle section of *Meeting Evil,* narrated from his point of view, frightens as much as it fascinates. Joe Detweiler, in *Killing Time,* is an equally memorable sociopath, but an almost admirable one who literally kills with kindness as his mad philosophy intends to benefit rather than to harm others, displaying a consistent, if demented, morality. Richie delights in harming others and delights most intensely in their knowing he has bested them. Fantasizing about shooting an unsuspecting cop in the face, Richie feels it necessary for the cop to understand he has been shamed as well as killed: "In his last instant of life, he knows he has been suckered, has done a lousy job, couldn't even protect himself, dies in disgrace, not honor" (142). Richie has been ineffectually treated and released from a psychiatric hospital, "but obviously the people with the real problems were out and roaming around the universe, being unbelievably stupid, causing trouble for good men like John" (139). He "detests immorality," does not consider himself a criminal no matter what his actions, and consistently manifests the malignant self-centeredness of the sociopath, gleefully telling John, "I don't have a case. . . . They have to take me as I come," (74) and following that up with the equally cheerful explanation: "I haven't got any troubles. Certain other people have claimed to have had troubles with me" (173).

Richie's self-professed philosophy is "if you *think* there's something wrong with me, then the burden of proof is on *you,* not me" (180). His denial of responsibility ultimately traces back to religion, of a sort. When John asks him if he believes in

God, Richie answers: "I sure as hell didn't make myself. That's basic. You can take it from there" (210). Self-preservation and ensuring that no one can ever make a fool of him seem to be Richie's primary concerns, and he is not only certain that he is "basically always right," but also prides himself in all he does: "What took bravery was Richie's way of life: standing alone against all comers, never giving an inch—except of course for friendship, and then being ready to go all out" (142).

What John must realize is that Richie's terrible profession of friendship locks him into an obligation he cannot evade: no one else can rid the world of Richie's unrelenting evil. As Richie's threat to the world in general narrows to include a threat to John's family and as John's excuses for not taking action against Richie are exhausted, one by one, *Meeting Evil* suggests that its events are being measured by three quite different time schemes: clock time—of which John is rarely certain; Richie time—which is in fact the timelessness of evil; and moral time—which finally demands John's action. Finally, after "the worst day in his life" for John, these three time schemes come together—as do Berger's doubles with at least one of the functions of doubleness as a theme. After being dismayed again and again by Richie's claims of brotherhood and friendship, John accepts the position, but more completely than Richie could imagine. When Richie happily observes that he and John "argue sometimes, but brothers are like that," John's response is deadly calm:

> "That's right," John said. "That's really more what we are than just friends: brothers." He was not being entirely hypocritical. By now he and Richie did have a genuine connection. It could not be denied that they were close, like a jailer and his prisoner, though in this case it was difficult to say

> which was which, who was the greater criminal to the other. Perhaps each played both parts simultaneously, which would indeed be brotherly. John was aware that he could never settle with the man without an act of fratricide. (213–14)

It is important to note, however, that Berger's plot and the specific event that finally leads to John's acting on his recognition that he and he alone must stop Richie clearly establishes that John's ultimate act of fratricide is both a moral and a situational imperative and not a brief for vigilantism.

The first word of *Meeting Evil* is "perhaps," and the book's opening sentence posits a note of indeterminacy that is not dispelled until its closing sentence, some 217 pages later. In between, Berger offers the story that may be his most disturbing and certainly is his most grim. Its ending, however, to borrow a word from the final sentence, is thoroughgoingly "affirmative," as John Felton has finally realized that there are indeed imperatives more important than avoiding violence, allowing him to end the novel on his feet, both physically and morally.

Best Friends

If Richie's exploitation of "friendship," both as a word and as a concept, did not alert us to the ambiguities inherent in that relationship, *Best Friends* should do the trick. In its action, major themes, and tone, this novel could hardly be more different from *Meeting Evil,* yet the two both can be seen as intense studies of moral growth of one of a pair of doubles. Both offer close examinations of the contradictions within friendship and of the power that word or concept retains even when drained of practical meaning. *Best Friends* pairs Roy Courtright and his putative best friend, Sam Grandy, in a plot that leads to Roy's falling in love with Sam's wife, Kristin. There is a betrayal inherent in the plot of this novel, but Berger so complicates the relations among Roy, Kristin, and Sam that it is almost impossible to determine who betrays, or has been betraying, whom. Just as Sam and Roy persist in calling each other best friends while the evidence mounts that they actually despise each other, Roy and Kristin both insist on referring again and again to Sam's childlike enthusiasm and generosity, his big heart, his capacity for enjoying life—having fun, the evidence mounts that Sam is, in fact, seething with jealousy and resentment against Roy and possibly against his wife.

In a number of his attitudes and traits, Sam can only remind us of Richie in *Meeting Evil.* Just as Richie has John Felton's number from the moment he meets him, Sam has Roy's number, and has manipulated and needled him since they were young boys. Almost gratuitously like Richie, Sam hates cops, while Roy respects them. As was true of John Felton in *Meeting Evil,* Roy attempts to construct every situation as reasonably as possible, while Sam, like Richie before him, lives his life through "Grandyose" gestures that are intemperate and largely out of control. And "control" provides what may be the most important key to understanding both Roy and Sam, as, at least at the start of the novel, Roy's self-control becomes a *de facto* selfishness, while Sam seems at once out of control and something of a control freak in his manipulation of others—a point Berger makes by withholding that word in a key exchange between the supposed best friends. When Roy expresses his exasperation at Sam's unwillingness to refill his own beer stein until Roy is also ready, Sam explains his habit as necessary to keep himself from becoming an alcoholic. Roy's exasperation crystallizes into despising his friend "for admitting to such a weakness," and he never completes the telling sentence "if you would exercise a little—" (5).

Sam is not evil, but he has enough of the self-centeredness and irresponsibility of the sociopath to have a kind of permanent one-up on Roy in everything but financial matters. Quite unlike John Felton, Roy doesn't need to destroy his nemesis and in fact takes great pains not to harm him, but he does need to free himself from a kind of semantic slavery that makes it more important to have a "best friend" and to revere the idea of "friendship" in the face of the growing awareness that he and Sam really have little in common, that their friendship is constructed to favor Sam in all matters, and that, in fact, they probably don't even like each other. But to describe *Best Friends* in this fashion, while accurate, misses the fact that the book's title positions readers to focus on "friendship" in as misleading a fashion as Roy does, since the most important aspect of this novel is that it chronicles Roy's maturation and his discovery first of a new best friend and then of the first love of his life in the person of Sam's wife, Kristin. This seemingly straightforward novel turns out to be one of Berger's most complicated "contraptions," and it is unique in his body of work both in charting the personal growth of a character and in following a character whose maturation also makes possible mature love.[9]

The novel opens, as do many of Berger's, with a burst of precision: "As of September 2000, his best friend's ways with women were still a wonder to Sam Grandy, not because there could be any question of Roy Courtright's physical or personal charms, but rather because Sam's own temperament was such that he could not have pretended, let alone sustained, an intimate interest in more than one woman at a time."[10] This elegantly balanced, deftly extended, and dialectically adversative first sentence of *Best Friends* doesn't say it all, but its precision and complexity say enough to clearly identify this as a Berger novel and to initiate the process through which Berger examines the complexities and contradictions inherent in an abstract term such as "friendship." Its focus split between two best friends who are about to discover that friendship can be just as treacherous and unpredictable as everything else in life, this sentence introduces readers to a characteristic and characteristically complicated sequence of unexpected events in the uncanny world somewhere between fiction and reality that has been Berger's unique territory in the novel.

As this first sentence suggests, Sam Grandy does not and cannot understand what is one of the primary traits, perhaps the defining aspect of his character, of Roy Courtright, primarily because he is not prepared to or is incapable of viewing another's life through any perspective other than his own. Nor does *Best Friends* ever make completely clear whether this opening sentence is factually accurate, since there are at least strong hints later in the novel that Sam is not only engaged in intimate relationships with more than one woman at a time, but also that he may have previously been engaged in intimate relationships with a man and a woman at the same time. Sam and Roy have called each other best friends for twenty years, although the more readers learn about their relationship the more they must wonder why. Their jocular banter masks a serious competitiveness that easily shades into contempt on Roy's part and into outright malice on the part of Sam. Both follow the larger protocols and verbal rituals of friendship, however, meeting their obligations, as do most of Berger's characters, even when they feel put upon or even victimized for doing so. Enter Sam's wife, Kristin, exit Roy's lover of the moment, send Sam to the hospital for a heart problem, and the stage is set for the inexorable plunge into nightmarish complications and disastrous choices that are hallmarks of a Berger novel.

Relations between men and women, always problematic in the Berger canon, grow particularly complicated for Roy, in this novel, as none of his attachments work out as expected or intended. Roy is a reflexive womanizer, who conducts his numerous affairs with consideration and according to a strict set of personal principles, almost all of which effectively preclude lasting relationships and protect him from any vulnerability. "He liked the understandable things: comfort, convenience, good manners, affection; they were easy to name" (20). Easy to name, and easy to control, but Roy's commitment to self-control also ensures that he has never opened himself to the possibility of love. As the novel opens, Roy is involved in an affair mostly of sexual convenience with Francine, a recent divorcee whose attraction to Roy may stem largely from the fact that her solipsism makes an interesting contrast with his own possibly overdeveloped "concern as to how he was regarded by others." In the pantheon of Berger's sociopathic characters, Francine is definitely a lightweight, but her self-centeredness and complete disregard for others and for legal and social protocols should begin to focus Roy's awareness, as it does that of Berger's readers, to the fact that best friend Sam displays similar symptoms. Roy has chosen as a kind of path of least resistance to comply with Francine's sociopathic idiosyncracies, "even though he was well aware it was because of just this sort of gutlessness that he had come to the point at which he found her unbearable" (35). And, as readers learn more about the "friendship" between Roy and Sam, it becomes more and more apparent that something of the same process of realization is slowly at work there.

Both Sam's and Roy's thoughts about each other suggest a history of sublimated resentments, fueled by jealousy on Sam's part and by despising on Roy's part at Sam's irresponsible lack of self-control. "Roy might be the womanizer, but Sam was promiscuous with money" (3). More important, Roy is a highly responsible and principled womanizer, while Sam is promiscuous with Roy's money, which he has borrowed and squandered for over twenty years of their "friendship" without ever offering to pay it back. Metaphors for the differences between the two abound, as Sam fetishizes largely ephemeral technological gadgets, while Roy has dedicated himself to the appreciation and preservation of vintage classic cars—a commitment Sam disparages by calling Roy a "used-car dealer." Sam is an irresponsible and resentful driver (another reminder of Richie in *Meeting Evil*), while Roy expertly manages high-speed performance car maneuvers such as four-wheel drifts; characteristically these "best friends" detest each other's driving. Murky family history seems likely to contain the reasons for this odd relationship as Roy's father had apparently favored Sam over his own son, Sam and Roy's twin sister once had an affair that ended suddenly and bitterly, and Sam's own father, while leaving him a sizable inheritance, had not left his son nearly as much money as Roy's father had left Roy and his sister. And an even murkier family history may be at play here, as Roy's sister has charged that she ended her affair with Sam when she discovered that he was her father's lover. Roy, who acknowledges his ineptitude at recognizing illicit relationships, has always wondered why Sam was more upset by the death of Roy's father than he was himself, somewhat lamely wondering whether Sam's copious tears at the funeral resulted from his allergy to flowers.

Three arcs intersect in Berger's plot: as Roy more and more recognizes that something is wrong in his friendship with Sam, that, in fact he really despises Sam, he more and more finds himself thinking about Sam's wife, Kristin, to whom he begins turning as a kind of surrogate best friend; at the same time he begins to dial back on his reflexive womanizing, passing up a couple of opportunities with desirable young women, acting simply as a nice guy rather than as a nice guy lecher. Just as Roy has previously failed to count the many things he dislikes about Sam against the abstract value of their "friendship," he has not previously paid much attention to Kristin, exempting her from his otherwise omnivorous womanizing in accordance with his strict respect for the protocols of friendship. Quickly he realizes that—as a surrogate for his "best friend" Sam—Kristin is actually a much better friend to him than Sam has ever been, then he begins to recognize how very different she is from Sam and possibly how much better she knows Sam than he does, and finally he begins to realize that he is in love with her. While in most other matters Roy has scrupulously followed his own moral code ("He had never done what he wanted, but rather what he had to do according to standards that few others noticed, let alone respected."), he discovers that love trumps friendship and maybe morality. "Love overrules all else" (164), he admits to Kristin, even while wrestling with the realization that making love to his "best friend's" wife was a betrayal: "Love not only superseded morality; it transformed everything done in its interests" (164).

As Roy finds himself more and more in love with Kristin, who seems fully to reciprocate his interest, he experiences for the first time in his life the power of love to transform the appeal of sex: "Roy had never suspected that this kind of feeling was available to him, unlocking a door that he had not been aware was closed or even there. He became so much a part of her that their identities were indistinguishable. It was being, not doing, but the climax was a long moment of soaring nonexistence, succeeded gradually by a miraculous serenity on coming to rest in a new world" (162). And, if the transcendental nature of that act of lovemaking somehow escapes the reader's attention, Berger gives Roy a second taste of what he has been missing in previous relationships: "He lost himself in an act of love that became a continuum, with no remembered beginning and no anticipation of an end. It seemed all of life, now and forever. Then, when it was finally done, it had been but a measureless moment" (192).

This second experience of sexual transport actually follows a film-formulaic love-is-wonderful moment where the almost giddy lovers, Roy and Kristin, shed their clothes after being drenched by a sudden downpour of rain and just before Kristin matter-of-factly informs Roy that she wants to stay married to Sam because "he needs us," adding, "I think we might be able to work something out that we can all live with" (196). While the personal growth that Roy has experienced has opened him to love, no small thing, it turns out that in the world of a Berger novel "love," like "friendship," is an abstract concept fraught with complexity. Sam's sudden death from a second heart attack sidetracks a crushed Roy from his intention to commit suicide and allows him to make her welfare his chief concern, he sees himself becoming not her lover, but her . . . best friend.

In *Best Friends* Berger has indeed done something new, but he has not abandoned his traditional concerns. With characteristically persevering irony, Berger reveals the selfish uses to which both Sam and Roy put the ostensibly unselfish concept of friendship only to push the revelation to the point where he suggests that providing selfish uses may actually be one of the necessary, if not desirable, functions of friendship. And this novel, like so many of Berger's before it, also explores the complex implications of radical disjunction between verbal maps, such as the term "best friends," and the actual territory of feelings and actions to which those maps supposedly are an accurate guide. Whatever Roy learns about Sam, he finally learns an important lesson about the complicated nature of "friendship"—about the tenacious hold of the label, the concept, or even just of the word on his thinking:

> As to Sam, no matter how often Roy told himself he had nothing but contempt for the man, he did not believe it. If only he could take the matter to—Sam. Not that Sam had ever understood or even been sympathetic to him. In view of Kristin's revelations, the bastard might well have been downright hostile. Yet that could not alter the fact that Sam was his best friend, a fact that had a long, unrewritable history. He and Sam had been stuck with each other for more than half their lives. Whether they had actually ever liked each other was probably irrelevant. (154)

CHAPTER 5

Novels of Procedure and Protocol

Killing Time, Suspects, Who Is Teddy Villanova?, Nowhere

The story goes that Gertrude Stein called Ezra Pound a "Village Explainer," adding that being a "Village Explainer" was just fine if one were a village. Thomas Berger does not share Stein's disdain of explanation. In fact, his characters are almost all prodromically driven to giving explanations or instructions, whether of banal procedures, received truths, useful knowledge, cooking tips, or human nature. More often than not, what a Berger character explains is not only familiar received knowledge, but also has little or no bearing on the narrative in which it appears; *the point is the pride of knowing,* the delight in possessing expertise, even if only concerning the banal and the trivial. For example, when Robert Crews attempts to start a fire from the friction of a bow-and-drill or "rubbing stick" contraption, a process painstakingly described by Berger's narrator, the fire is not crucial to his survival as much as it is a mark of his intuitive prowess and determination—or of his chagrin, as it turns out that his Friday is much more successful at the process than he is and explains to him the modifications that led to her success. Similarly, but much less esoterically, when Ralph Sandifer makes a grilled cheese sandwich in *Sneaky People,* his step-by-step procedure is chronicled with detail so loving as to make the act seem a religious ritual—one that ultimately has no further significance for Ralph or for the novel in which he appears.

In this sense any Berger novel will contain a number of explanations of the step-by-step kind we associate with "procedural" narratives, with the difference that these mini-procedurals rarely matter much in the semblance of the novel, apart from foregrounding the very human desire to possess and to show off knowledge or the equally human inclination to ritualize otherwise banal activities. Berger obviously revels in carefully detailing processes and procedures, whether endemic to the world of the survivalist, the cook, the policeman, the private eye, or to any area of specialized knowledge, even knowledge so familiar as to have become clichéd. And his characters, particularly those who do not understand themselves or the world very well, share his delight in explanation, even if—or particularly if—what they explain is already well known. It comes as no surprise then that novel forms built around explanation of procedures and processes should hold a special appeal for Berger, as so obviously did the survival narrative of *Robert Crews*. The four novels discussed in this chapter provided Berger—and his characters—with even greater opportunity to describe procedures and protocols. *Killing Time* and *Suspects* could both be loosely described as police procedurals, displaying Berger's characteristic fondness for and fascination with both ends of the police procedural spectrum, one end focused on individuals dedicated to law enforcement, the other end to criminals, sociopaths in particular. *Who Is Teddy Villanova?* and *Nowhere* retain some of the detail of the police procedural as they both follow the adventures of Russel Wren, a most unlikely private-eye, but place him respectively within the highly ritualized genre protocols of the American hard-boiled detective story and then in the equally ritualized protocols of the utopian novel.

Killing Time

If books can be said to have personalities, this novel, Berger's fourth, published in 1967, subtly unfolds a personality as seductively psychopathic as that of its central figure, Joe Detweiler. The disarmingly innocent and considerate Detweiler happens to be a mass murderer who often sounds like a crazed general semanticist and actually displays many admirable characteristics. Furthermore, *Killing Time* is murder on genre frames, invoking then frustrating one set of genre expectations after another in something of a merry-go-round of literary conventions, one moment seeming to be a police procedural, then seeming to switch to the psychological investigation of a madman, then seeming to become a courtroom drama.

The novel's action begins with the Christmas Eve discovery by a young woman, Betty Bayson, that her mother and her nude-model sister have been strangled and that the male roomer in their apartment has a screwdriver planted in his temple. All seems in order for a murder mystery as the police investigative machinery goes into action and we are made privy to the interrogative philosophy and initial suspicions of Lieutenant Shuster and Detective Tierney. Joe, the murderer, however, turns himself in even before their suspicions begin to crystallize, an act, on his part, of simple courtesy toward the hardworking cops. "It makes me feel lousy to keep them in suspense, taking up their time with a problem I could very easily settle" (160). The balance of the novel then focuses on the murderer's conversations with the police, with journalists, and with his lawyer, a brilliant strategist and rhetorician named Henry Webster Melrose, whose propositions about the courtroom ("Reality is what the jury believes") clearly parallel those of Berger the novelist.

Melrose's considerable legal prowess is prominently displayed by Berger, and Joe Detweiler will remind readers of Leopold and Loeb, but *Killing Time* declines to become a courtroom drama. Instead its story develops through a maze of formula patterns from police procedural, psychological thriller, sensational journalism, and psychiatric case studies. Just as Joe spends most of the novel talking to others, the novel spends most of its time ranging through the "talk," or language codes, usually associated with other novel forms. Significantly, however, while Berger develops the action of *Killing Time* through at least three major procedural formulas, that of the police procedural, that of the psychological thriller, and that of the courtroom drama, his insistence on constructing Joe Detweiler as a human being rather than as a role player defined by procedural rhetorics and assumptions, serves to make this novel *a kind of anti-procedural.* Jon Wallace has best explained this effect, noting that Berger makes Joe a kind of "invading toxin" that resists being absorbed into the "antibodies" of the respective legal, journalistic, and psychiatric procedural codes.[1]

As its title also makes clear, *Killing Time* is a novel each of whose characters must relate to the usually distressing phenomenon of time, itself another significant concern throughout Berger's fiction. Believing that time is continuous rather than linear, Joe pursues the goal of "Realization," a kind of time travel of consciousness that sounds transcendental. His particular goal is to reexperience in its fullness a prior moment in time. When at last he succeeds during his own murder trial (others take his reaction as a sure sign of his madness), the moment he completely recaptures is, ironically, that of Daniel M'Naghten's 1843 trial in London for the murder of Sir Robert Peel's secretary, a trial famous for its role in establishing the legal definition of insanity. One of the reasons Joe feels that his killing of three people is a matter of no great importance is his confidence that if he can recover the reality of the past, he can recall those he has killed, since all he has taken from them is time. Joe's radiant philosophy supplies Berger's novel with an elaborate inversion of the accepted notion of killing time. Opposed to the common sense of passing the unimportant time between significant events, Joe presents killing time as the achievement of mastery, a freeing of oneself from time's grasp. In setting out to write in one literary code (that of the "true crime documentary"), Berger drew much of his information used in writing *Killing Time* from works in two quite different and nonliterary codes: Quentin Reynold's *Courtroom* (1951) and Frederic Wertham's *Show of Violence* (1949).[2] Both "nonfiction" works purport to tell the story of Robert Irwin, "the gentle killer." Reynolds, however, is interested in Irwin only insofar as he provided the lawyer Samuel Leibowitz, the subject of *Courtroom* and the real-life model for Berger's Melrose, with an interesting and challenging case. A psychiatrist with a knack for being in the public eye, Frederick Wertham included Irwin in his *Show of Violence* because Irwin had been one of his patients, both before and after his murder of three people. Apart from supplying the basic details of Berger's novel, these two nonfictional works provide in themselves exactly the kind of conflicting language codes that Berger focused on in *Little Big Man,* and their differences in "reporting" the same case raise questions about the distinctions we normally draw between fact and fiction.

The frontispiece to *Killing Time* approaches this distinction from Berger's perspective: "Readers are earnestly advised not to identify the characters in the narrative which follows—criminals, policemen, madmen, citizens, or any combination thereof—with real human beings. A work of fiction is a construction of language and otherwise a lie. Some years ago a notice was posted at the entrance to Sala B of the Uffizi Gallery in Florence: 'Please don't touch the pictures! It is dangerous for the works of art, it is punished by law, and finally it is useless.'" Having explicitly stated his position that "a work of fiction is a construction of language and otherwise a lie," Berger later explained: "My Uffizi admonition to the reader was intended to suggest, in my usual convoluted manner, that fiction is not to be confused with life, because the *latter* is false" (27 June 1976).

Killing Time casts police detectives, reporters, newspaper editors, lawyers, psychiatrists, and random citizens as conscious and unconscious fiction-makers who manipulate (and even more are manipulated by) the expectation patterns their fictions create. As a matter of fact, the psychopathic Joe Detweiler is the only character not involved in this process, perhaps because as a madman he has already broken through what Berger seems to see as the chimerical distinction between fiction and reality.

Unmistakably a madman (he believes "everybody was habitually pretty nice to everybody else"), even within the self-consuming context of Berger's irony, Joe is himself something of a compendium of vaguely recognizable characters, as he must remind us not only of Leopold and Loeb but of Jesus Christ, Bartleby the scrivener, Alfred Korzybski, Emerson, and Thoreau. A uniquely altruistic Nietzschean, Joe believes in the fundamental immorality of sympathy but has worked out a rigorous scheme for helping people by having them befriend him:

> In a crowded subway car, for example, he would pretend to be lame. It was gratifying to see the seated passengers as he limped on board, contesting with one another to claim the power he had made available. Detweiler understood that this state of affairs must be depressing to the truly disabled, and therefore he himself made it a practice never to do a favor for a cripple, but rather to ask a kindness. He would collide with a blindman, saying, "Excuse me, I am blind." Always the individual concerned would lead him to a seat, guide him across an intersection, and, of special interest to Detweiler, would often conceal his own disability. That is, would believe he was concealing it, which did him a world of good. For a few moments, anyway, he was not blind, for experience is the interaction of contrasts. (22)

In fact, apart from scattered exceptions, including mass murder, Joe does bring out the best in those around him. What he reflects, however, is not the same as what he reflects upon: his life pursues one philosophy while illustrating another, that of Berger, his creator. Joe's concern is with what he calls "Realization," a project for discarding language and any other abstract system that mediates the direct experience of reality. Committed to direct experience, Joe has absolutely no use for "men who deal in language," insisting that all they "are talking about is talk."

Joe's contention that language is basically a hoax is but one aspect of this novel that self-reflexively announces that *Killing Time* is no less a hoax than any of the many it contains. Over and over, Berger has Joe's story involve characters whose verbal deceptions and sense of artistry are obviously resonant with those used by the novelist (one character even responds to the events of the novel by becoming a novelist). Moreover, Berger also places his characters in situation after situation in which they must—like readers of the novel in which they appear—"read" the selfishly crafted words of those around them. Perhaps Berger's Melrose best suggests the working of this technique when he admits that "nothing gave him more gratification than a favorable verdict returned by a jury who knew it had been hoaxed" (197). The parallels between lawyer and jury and novelist and readers are hard to miss.

Suspects

Suspects, Thomas Berger's twentieth novel, published nearly thirty years after *Killing Time,* opens with a conversation between a policeman and a woman concerned that her neighbor answers neither telephone nor door. The conversation takes place on and at the bottom of the two-step entrance to the house at 1143 Laurel, in a city never specified. What is specified and what closes the opening paragraph of the novel is the somewhat jarring, "There was no porch here" (1). This seemingly gratuitous information, an architectural detail with no apparent bearing on any part of Berger's story, simply serves as another reminder that the reader of a Thomas Berger novel enters an insistently imaginary world meticulously gerrymandered by one of America's most gifted and most enduringly radical sensibilities—and in this case, the world of Berger's fiction is also guided by the fetishizing of specific detail that marks both police procedure and the literary protocols of *le roman policier* or the police procedural. While *Suspects* is only the second Berger novel to sustain its procedural formula, his fiction shows a consistent fascination with what it means "to think like a cop," a fascination pursued at some length in the characterization of small-town police chiefs or detectives in *Sneaky People* and *The Feud.*

Berger's plot here centers on finding who murdered and mutilated a young wife, Donna Howland, and slit the throat of her three-year-old daughter, Amanda, in the house at 1143 Laurel, in an otherwise unremarkable suburban neighborhood. Principal suspects are Donna's husband, Larry, who has been having a sexual affair with his boss's wife, and Lloyd, Larry's half-brother, a drifter whose life seems to have been a series of born-to-lose misadventures in which Lloyd's prickly sensibility, bordering on paranoia, has gotten him fired from numerous jobs and embroiled in numerous antagonisms. To thicken the plot, Lloyd's complicated and intense feelings for his dead sister-in-law border on the unhealthy and, due to a drunken blackout, he has no memory of where he was or what he did during the time when she was murdered. A plumber rounds out the list of obvious suspects, but only because he had previously done work at the Howland house and was seen driving down the Howland's street after the murder. Apparently senile and publicity-happy next-door neighbors are the closest thing the police have to witnesses, although it remains unclear what, if anything, they saw on the day of the murders.

Officers Nick Moody and Dennis LeBeau are the chief investigators in the murder case, but their fellow officers Art McCall and Jack Marevitch become slightly involved in the Howland Case while disastrously involved in a series of violent liquor store robberies. When McCall is killed during one of the robberies, his partner is wracked with grief and guilt and forced to question everything he believes about being a cop. Two policewomen also figure in the plot, Daisy O'Connor, the formulaic daughter of a retired cop who had been a partner of Nick

Moody's, and Felicia Ravenswood, a large black woman who is an equally formulaic recent star graduate of the police academy. Much more than was the case in *Killing Time,* Berger painstakingly details the steps these police officers take to solve the murders and devotes equal attention to the mundane and frequently sad details of their personal lives. Moody and LeBeau live up to their names, as the former is a near alcoholic shattered by two divorces and an alienated son, who, on the edge of despair, contemplates suicide, and the latter, while married to an apparently terrific wife is having an affair with fellow officer Daisy O'Connor—to the disgust and sorrow of his partner Moody, who has known Daisy since she was a little girl and who thinks so highly of LeBeau's wife that it almost counters his bitter cynicism about marriage.

As the *New York Times* reviewer Richard Bernstein observed, Berger "has perfect pitch when it comes to the routine and nonroutine of police work. There is the boredom, the attention to detail, the meaning of partnership and solidarity."[3] In short, readers looking for a tightly formulaic police procedural will find one in *Suspects,* which touches most of the familiar bases of the literary genre and its television incarnations, including alcoholic and bitter cops, marriages and parenting hopelessly undermined by devotion to police duty, affairs between male and female cops, a cop's daughter trying to live up to her father's record and expectations, the local cop hangout which is a bar owned by ex-cops, and so on. In ways both small and large, Berger captures the worldview of the dedicated and highly professional cop. As one of Berger's officers realizes: "It took a special effort for him to stop thinking like a cop, and he saw no reason to exert such energy, for he liked what he was and did. In fact, he loved it" (281).

And indeed it looks as if Berger, as usual, has scrupulously researched his subject matter, not only the book and television traditions of police procedurals, but also the details of police procedure itself. Among the nonfiction treatments of police work Berger used as research for *Suspects* was Connie Fletcher's celebrated *What Cops Know: Cops Talk About What They Do, How They Do It, and What It Does to Them,* primarily a series of interviews with Chicago cops blurbed by Andrew Greeley as quite possibly the "finest book on police work ever."[4] Interestingly enough, however, what Berger seems to have primarily drawn from this book is not the details of specific cases or of specific investigative processes as much as its underlying theme of the generosity and human decency of the cops it follows.

The conflict between procedures and rhetoric that dehumanize and rob subjects of their individuality that was implicit in *Killing Time* is explicitly noted by Lloyd Howland in *Suspects,* who exempts his police interrogators from the resentment and paranoia he usually directs at perceived adversaries because he understands that "the detectives used certain techniques of manipulation that really had nothing to do with him as an individual except in the role as specimen" (158). As it turns out, one of the detectives interrogating him, Moody, becomes a friendly mentor to Lloyd, and in turning to him for advice, Lloyd plays a crucial role in giving Moody a reason not to follow through with his plan to commit suicide. And it is Berger's focus on the essential decency and admirable human qualities of the cops in *Suspects* that aligns it with *Killing Time*'s focus on the human qualities of the mass murderer Joe Detweiler, making this novel not so much a police procedural as a *decency procedural.* In fact, *Suspects* may contain more characters who act or have acted out of a deep sense of fundamental decency than does any other Berger novel. One reader simply calls *Suspects* "sweet," and while that may be the least likely description of a Thomas Berger novel ever offered, "sweet" is as good as or better than any other description of this book.

While one major plot strand in *Suspects* has to do with finding a murderer, and another has to do with the fatal impact of a gang of violent liquor store robbers, equally important plot strands have to do with the unlikely salvation and rehabilitation of the loser Lloyd Howland by Molly Sparks, a plucky blue-collar forerunner of Amanda Teasdale, the New Woman in *The Return of Little Big Man.* Molly is a truck driver who picks up the hitch-hiking Lloyd and sees in him potential and virtues where so many others have seen only failings. Molly and the decent detective, Nick Moody, help Lloyd find an identity of which he can be proud and reverse the downward spiral of his life. Molly is aided in her efforts by a carpenter friend, Joe Littlejohn, who accepts her faith in Lloyd as enough reason to give him a job and treat him with respect, in part because his own life had been turned around by someone who had been unexpectedly decent to him.

Molly's infectious decency naturally is of a piece with her positivistist belief that counters Lloyd's fatalism. When he grumbles that there's not much he can do about his bottled-up resentments, she counters: "You can always do something about anything, though maybe you can't do everything about any one thing," concluding, "What I mean is, you can try" (104). Her optimistic credo sounds very much like the social meliorism Berger has consistently resisted, if not ridiculed, in so many other novels. But Molly's social meliorism is qualified by her pragmatic recognition that "maybe you can't do everything about any one thing," and is perhaps most fervent in maintaining the need to try. And the action and outcome of *Suspects* seems to fully endorse her optimism and decency.

Similarly Moody's decency toward Lloyd has redemptive value for both of them. Moody is a formulaic good cop who is also a good person, but Berger humanizes and individualizes him by making it clear that Moody is motivated by personal rather than societal morality: he tells Lloyd that he is simply trying to do a good job much more than he is fighting for justice or driven by abstract principles. In response to Lloyd's resentment toward cops who seem to him driven primarily by the desire to constrain others, particularly the young, Moody explains that he started his career that way:

> "I busted up noisy college parties and I arrested bartenders who served beer to underage drinkers. Hell, Lloyd I did all of that, and I don't apologize for it. I did it because the law was being broken, and the citizens were paying me to maintain respect for the law. If I waited table in a restaurant I would bring your steak when you ordered it. I wouldn't eat it myself or throw it in the garbage. If I pumped gas for a living, I wouldn't fill your tank with air or water. What I do is enforce the law. If you don't want that done, then don't hire me. But if you do hire me, that's what I'll do. If the citizens decide homicide is not against the law, then I won't arrest anybody for murder." (291)

Also explaining to Lloyd that the job of being a police officer makes a lot of demands, usually overshadows personal life, and frequently exposes one to "sickening stuff you never suspected was possible," Moody offers what may be the key to Berger's fondness for law officers of all rank and kind when he sums up a police officer's lot: "You're not only supposed to handle it but rise above it and go on to something else that's worse, and then rise above that and still be human" (292).

Throughout Berger's career his novels have again and again foregrounded and investigated various kinds of sociopathic behavior, whether just annoying or deadly, and several of his books, particularly *Killing Time, Neighbors, The Houseguest,* and *Meeting Evil* can be read in part as attempts to understand and to inoculate readers against sociopathic behavior, whether banal or murderous. *Suspects* offers an odd twist to this pattern, as Lloyd Howland seems to be a sociopath in the making, but turns away from that behavior, finally hoping to become, of all things, a cop himself. Conversely Keller, the seemingly odd but harmless next-door neighbor to the murdered Donna and Amanda Howland, turns out to be yet another kind of sociopath, a kind of secular religious zealot who pegs his perverted misogyny to a twisted sense of moral "decency." Untiringly scrupulous investigative procedure, augmented by a bit of luck, leads Moody finally to realize that Keller is the murderer he seeks, and Keller not only confesses but also proudly produces the murder weapon with which he had clubbed Donna Howland, a thick ornamental perfume bottle. When Keller explains that he kept the bottle because he was "religious about recycling," his comment does double duty, calling attention to the moral bankruptcy of a sociopath who is religious *only* about recycling, while pulling the trigger on an inside joke by Berger, who has not only "recycled" this perfume bottle, first mentioned some two hundred pages earlier as a gift from Lloyd to Donna, but also is himself perhaps the greatest "recycler" of classic novel forms in American literary history.

Who Is Teddy Villanova?

Berger must have enjoyed writing this book, using its ostensible plot as an excuse for creating some of the most striking individual sentences in all of his fiction, and the result is an inventory of some of the most carefully crafted and hilariously unlikely sentences as a reader is likely to discover in any American novel of the twentieth century. That is saying a lot, since, sentence by sentence, *all* the novels of Thomas Berger are among the most precisely crafted in the English language, and all his sentences sparkle with syntactical and lexical precision. He is quick to acknowledge and to elaborate his fascination with the sentence as the basic unit of prose style:

> The sentence cannot be thought about, at least by me: it must be lived. Later, when it is completed, it can be thought about with a certain profit, but no sooner. Sentences, paragraphs, chapters, novels all grow from my imagination in the same fashion: indeed, the sentence is the cell beyond which the life of the book cannot be traced, a novel being a structure of such cells: most must be vital or the body is dead. In another sense, only the sentence exists or at any rate can be proved to exist. Even at the stage of the paragraph things are becoming theoretical and arbitrary. A "novel" is an utter hallucination: no definition of it, for example, can really distinguish it from a laundry list. But a sentence—there you have something essential, to which nothing can be added and from which nothing can be taken. (23 May 1979)

In *Who Is Teddy Villanova?* Berger's fondness for the individual sentence combines with his delight in unexpected juxtapositions to produce a tour de force macaronic of prose styles and literary conventions. Appropriately enough, however, *Nowhere,* the sequel to *Who Is Teddy Villanova?,* in which its protagonist, Russel Wren again, encounters a fantastic mythical kingdom with obvious ties to Butler's Erewhon, also exists in a most unlikely relationship to its antecedent—the only way in which to describe a travel-to-imaginary lands sequel to a private-eye novel. Moreover, *Nowhere* shifts its focus, from the unexpected linguistic shifts in register so heavily employed in the dialogue and narrative voice of *Who Is Teddy Villanova?* to the unexpected cultural conflicts of social and philosophical codes in Berger's impossible kingdom of Saint Sebastian. Individual sentences are so archly crafted in the former as to strain their credibility in the reader's eyes and ears, while sentences in the latter (with delightful exceptions) are much less noteworthy for their stylistic panache than for their striking propositions. Despite their strong differences, however, Berger's eighth and thirteenth novels, published eight years apart, are fundamentally linked by the sensibility of their common protagonist, Russel Wren, private investigator.

Who Is Teddy Villanova? invokes all the formula patterns of the classic American hard-boiled detective novel. But the real mysteries in this novel have nothing to do with traditional down-at-the-heel private eyes. One of its primary mysteries for the reader is how the book's heavy emphasis on literary structure avoids its narrator's suspiciously reflexive-sounding condemnation of decadent contemporary art forms, "occupied solely with structure and not substance." Another mystery challenges readers to try to figure out why this contemporary American detective story is narrated, in Berger's words, "in a rococo style reminiscent by turns of Thomas De Quincey, Thomas Babington Macaulay, and Sir Thomas Malory."

This novel displays the characteristic diction of the hard-boiled formula, but with a manic inconsistency: the private eye's secretary speaks from the pages of Hammett and Chandler, while her boss, the garrulous Russel Wren, speaks as though quoting Macaulay (as another character pointedly observes). A police detective introduces himself, saying, "I'll show you my identification, if you'll me yours, as Henry James might say," while other detectives self-consciously spout jargon from television shows. One ostensible villain orders Wren to shut his "fucking flytrap" and elaborates, "Gonna say one thing once and ain't gonna say it again, so get it straight the one time I say it, because you ain't gonna hear it anymore . . . because I ain't gonna chew my cabbage twice" (10). Wren's response to this advice must be a stylistic first for private eyes on any continent or in any literature, as he muses: "Of course . . . if your statement proves unusually complex, there might well be some advantage in repetition, using alternative terms and varying syntaxes, not only for the sake of sheer verbal charm, but also with an eye to the state of affairs in the English language, in which, as one authority asserts, the only exact synonyms are 'furze' and 'gorse'" (10). Wren is an ex-instructor of English and Berger has cheerfully added that he regrets not mentioning that Wren is "a constant reader of *PMLA* though he has left the academy and is trying to go straight" (2 April 1977).

Who Is Teddy Villanova? can perhaps best be described not as a story, but as an elaborately extended caprice of language. Certainly the novel's fundamental message is that language is indeed capricious. Wren, who aspires to complete the writing of a play, fails to recognize that the bizarre sequence of events that engulfs him is nothing but a play orchestrated by his landlord to influence the detective to give up his office lease. And more bizarre than the events staged for this purpose is the wordplay they occasion, as even more troubling to Wren than accusations of murder and drug dealing are charges that he is a bogus intellectual. Character after character comments on Wren's dialogue, praising his use and pronunciation of "disparate," groaning at his seeming resort to mixed metaphor, criticizing his "eighteenth-century billingsgate" in a moment of crisis. For his part, Wren feels most abused, not when struck or duped, but when linguistically outperformed, as by a detective who correctly uses superfetation, forcing Wren to admit to himself that he "had never heard that word in speech, and never read it but in the text of T. S. Eliot."

To a writer who has described himself as "essentially a voyeur of copulating words," the play of language is of course an end in itself. Who can doubt that when Berger has Wren say to a police detective, criticizing the employment of the detective's hands as the two men attempt to keep Wren's secretary from falling out of a window, "This wench is my ward. . . . Toy with her fine foot if you like, but eschew her quivering thigh and the demesnes that there adjacent lie" (216), the author is simply putting together words he fancies, in a syntax that pleases him? Indeed, *Who Is Teddy Villanova?* may be most significant for *its* suggestion that Berger's allegiance to language, to the glories of the individual sentence, is at least as strong as, if not stronger than, his allegiance to the form of the novel.

But Berger's relentless wordplay in *Who Is Teddy Villanova?* may also serve a function with more tangible human implications. Unlike the legendary detectives of both British and American traditions, Wren's penchant for precise observation is limited to the inconsequential and is eclipsed only by his passion for precise diction, a trait that imbues the commonplaces of hard-boiled prose with unexpected twists. When struck by an archetypal "ham-fisted" punch, Wren primly observes that his assailant's hand was "the size and consistency of the fleshy side of a loin of pork" (8–9). Such a blow clearly calls for the subsequent Chandleresque "dive into a pool of darkness," but Wren instead notes, "I had no consciousness of my backward velocity," and comes to with the meticulous and incongruously mannered realization: "My loafers were in a position just ahead of his coal-barge brogans, a yard from where I slumped; meanwhile, my feet, twisted on their edges and crushed under the crease between thigh and buttock, were only stockinged: he had knocked me out of my shoes!" (9).

That Wren thinks in ornately clothed clichés is not surprising, since he is almost incapable of thinking in his own terms. His referent base for thought and action consists almost entirely of received ideas. He misperceives *everything* because he perceives only through received expectation patterns—whether those of the formula codes of American and British detective stories, those of mythology, those of racial stereotyping, or those of formula television shows. Indeed, so semiotically voracious is Wren that a single word, particularly if a proper name, can send him in headlong flight after scenarios eagerly inferred from its etymology or connotations.

Although Wren never realizes that this tendency gives rise to most of the problems in his life, other characters frequently tell him as much. Zwingli, the erudite detective whose greatest contempt is reserved not for the criminal but for the bogus intellectual, points out to Wren; "I suspect you are living the legend of the private eye, which I confess I had always believed mythical" (98). Another character observes of Wren's typically stereotyped conception of her occupation as a stewardess: "I don't know whether anybody could live up to your appetite for the legendary, Russel, which applies in all areas of experience. Which is why so many people have found it possible to dupe you so easily" (178). And duped he is, hoaxed at every turn, because he can understand reality only through codes of expectation and behavior that are patently literary and have little or nothing to do with the events of his experience.

This, perhaps more than any other Berger novel, invites readers to take a step back from their reading, to look over their own shoulders, and to assess their options and obligations as interpreters. No less and no more improbable an authority on detective stories than Gertrude Stein has decreed that the best are those where "nobody is either dead or not dead" and has suggested that the best of all would be "a detective story of how to write." That is as good a description as any of what happens as Russel Wren narrates his misadventures. More important, Wren offers the reader a detective story of how to read—the most explicit statement of a concern running throughout Berger's novels.

Nowhere

Precisely to the extent that he proves a disastrous detective, Russel Wren exhibits traits that would make him a successful literary critic: his compulsion to infer motives and to make connections based almost exclusively on philological evidence. In this passion for hypostatized order, Wren joins himself, not to the successful traditions of ratiocination represented by Poe's Dupin and Doyle's Holmes, but to the self-destructive tradition of "reckless discernment" made infamous by Erik Lonnrot, the detective protagonist of Jorge Luis Borges's "Death and the Compass." Indeed, Borges's fabulations may help us understand the fantastic plot of *Nowhere,* a novel that transplants Russel Wren's misadventures from the legendary setting of Manhattan to the mythical kingdom of Saint Sebastian.

"Obviously if you've survived in New York City," Wren is told in *Nowhere* by the agent who impresses him into covert service, "you know how to lie and cheat and dissemble: spying should be just your meat" (30). While *Teddy Villanova*'s plot boils down to a city story of the most banal sort—a landlord's machinations to get a tenant to drop a lease—the novel does not, after the manner of the hard-boiled detective story, expose the corrupt underbelly of a big city. Instead, it inventories New York City's reputed idiosyncracies, ironies, and cynicisms. Russel Wren, it must be remembered, is a master only of the received idea, and although he is an inhabitant of Manhattan, his comments about it are exactly what we expect, the familiar litany of city complaints. Indeed, it can be argued that when Wren is shanghaied by a CIA-like government entity to the hitherto unknown (at least to Wren) central European kingdom of Saint Sebastian, the move is actually from a legendary setting to an experiential one: he is as devoid of received ideas about life in Saint Sebastian as he is surfeited with those about life in New York. Moreover, while in Saint Sebastian, he contrasts its customs, not with those of his native land, or with those of other utopian classics, but with received truths about his city.

Curiously enough Berger's comments about the writing of this novel rarely mention Samuel Butler, whose *Erewhon* would certainly seem a likely inspiration, but he cites instead More's *Utopia* and Eliot's *Idea of a Christian Society* as his novel's precursors. While working on an early version of *Nowhere,* he also declared his intent to "promote all my social ideas, one of which is that in the perfect society there is no legal freedom whatever, virtually everything being against the law—but no law is ever enforced" (24 February 1978).

Its action beginning with what seems to be a terrorist bombing, followed by the disclosure of a secret government agency that is monitoring the terrorists, *Nowhere* opens like so many novels of international intrigue, a point explicitly made by the purported agent of the "Firm," "Bunch," "Troop," "Pack," or "Gang," who informs Wren he would better understand what was going on "if you read any blockbusting thrillers." Although Wren's narrative occasionally gives a nod to this flimsy frame of the spy thriller, it soon starts nodding more in the direction of the novel of utopian/dystopian satire, with an occasional wink at the conventions of dream psychology (Wren grouses that in America "a grasp of basic Freudianism was now enjoyed by millhand and shopgirl").

That Russel Wren would travel to a marvelous kingdom resembling nothing quite so much as those made famous in American movie musicals of the 1930s (or, more accurately still, the *sets* for those musicals, since Saint Sebastian's colorful open-air markets are made of plastic) is quite in keeping with his "appetite for the legendary." That modifying forms of the kingdom's name would sound suspiciously like that of a well-known vineyard in Sonoma County, California, also reminds us of Wren's keen awareness of brand names, even in the midst of most amazing events. Indeed, several aspects of life in Saint Sebastian, such as the central importance of its blonds and the nature of its national encyclopedia, are direct dream-logic extensions of Wren's thinking in *Teddy Villanova*. But what the reader learns of customs in Saint Sebastian probably reveals more of Berger's sensibility than of Wren's, suggesting that even a world based largely on Nietzschean suppositions would be little improvement, the ills of ressentiment beyond even imaginary cure.

Saint Sebastian's most radical feature is that it acknowledges the insolubility of human problems. Its Ministry of Clams exists solely for the purpose of accepting denunciations for unanswerable complaints and insoluble problems, dutifully filing, then forgetting, all complaints. Puzzled when asked if that process actually satisfies complainants, the ministry's receptionist patiently explains to Wren that human beings can never be satisfied, supporting her claim by asking if he knew of "any social problem that was truly solved" (141). Wren, who earlier in his narrative has acerbically mentioned passing in New York City a sign marking the future site of "some state agency working for the abolition of envy," feebly protests this view, but Berger, his creator, embraces it, implicitly offering his novels more as agents of the Ministry of Clams than of social or psychological change or reform.

Instead what *Nowhere* offers is a series of intriguing propositions, some appealing, some reprehensible, all delightful in their quirkiness. Berger would seem to be in complete agreement with the character who tells Wren that her "job is to be a stewardess, and not to deal in social theoretics"—as, at bottom, is Wren himself, whose most profound insight into the complicated Sebastiani revolution is simply that "the people who know how to handle themselves seem to be similar, irrespective of ideology" (179).

Neither an ideal society nor a dystopian horror, Saint Sebastian is an interesting place structured largely around incorrect received ideas drawn from old American B movies of the 1930s and 1940s. Compulsory attendance at these films, left behind by USO and army personnel after World War II, has supplanted both church and school, now dismissed by a projectionist priest as "poor imitations of life." The real thing, he proudly informs Wren, are old American films. "The virtuous are shown to succeed, the evildoers invariably come to grief, and the general philosophy that informs every picture is that there is a common good, which is recognized by everyone—including the wicked, who of course are opposed to it, but they *know what it is*" (150). Berger's joke is a fantastic society based precisely on the received truths that are supposed to guide our own, a supposition, of course, itself a received truth quite at odds with reality.

CHAPTER 6

Subversions of Good Order

Regiment of Women, Being Invisible, Changing the Past, Robert Crews, Adventures of the Artificial Woman

With the publication of his first novel, *Crazy in Berlin,* Berger signaled his abiding interest in the nature of reality—or, as one of the characters in that novel pronounced it, "ray-oll-ity." That character, Schatzi, one of the most enigmatic characters in that novel and a prototype for Jack Crabb insofar as he had lived impossibly in the interstices of history, reminds Reinhart that most of reality is a construction of language shaped to self-serving ends and "proved" only by mortality: "The living and the dying, and nothing else, makes ray-oll-ity" (195). On the publication of Berger's twenty-third novel, *Adventures of the Artificial Woman,* his longtime friend Zulfikar Ghose, a distinguished novelist himself, explained Berger's interest in the nature of reality:

> An analysis of reality is central to Thomas Berger's work, and he sometimes takes one of its vital elements (e.g., time in *Changing the Past,* gender in *Regiment of Women*) to see what becomes of reality when that element's behavior is radically altered. In *Adventures of the Artificial Woman,* his twenty-third novel, it's life as artificial intelligence that's the variant in Berger's experiment with reality. Discontented with his relationships with women, Ellery

> Pierce builds his ideal woman, working clandestinely in the animatronics firm where he constructs animal creatures for movies, and names her Phyllis. *Frankenstein, Petrushka,* and *The Tales of Hoffmann* come to mind, but Berger's impulse is not to shock, play the magician, or to enchant, all of which he incidentally and delightfully does, but to see whether in the mirror that's held up to reality the inhuman is not indistinguishable from the human, by implication raising questions concerning ethics.[1]

Of course *every* novel is an "experiment with reality," and certainly *every* novel by Thomas Berger constructs a linguistic laboratory in which the mechanisms of "the way reality operates" are poked, prodded, dissected, and subjected to an endless variety of tests. But the novels discussed in this chapter, *Regiment of Women, Being Invisible, Changing the Past, Robert Crews,* and *Adventures of the Artificial Woman,* offer Berger's most overt experiments to see what becomes of reality when one of its vital elements is radically altered. Each of the novels discussed in this chapter challenges the conventional understanding of reality by changing one of its aspects from what is normally considered "natural" to something that can only be thought of as "unnatural." *Regiment of Women* radically reverses male and female sexual roles; *Being Invisible* literalizes social invisibility; *Changing the Past* offers its protagonist multiple opportunities to "rescript" the life he has lived; *Robert Crews* plunges its protagonist into a world of nature potentially stripped of all social and language concerns; and *Adventures of the Artificial Woman* follows the experiences of an animatronic woman whose existence is free of attributes we assume are essential to being human. Each novel presents—to borrow a phrase from John Knox used as an epigraph to *Regiment of Women*—

"a subversion of good order" (whether the "order" of social reality or the "order" of literary tradition) to set up for Berger a new "experiment with reality."

Regiment of Women

Regiment of Women explores the paradox of a sane man trapped in a society whose definition of reality seems mad but whose madness—made to seem ludicrous in practice—remains distressingly plausible, if not familiar, in theory. In 1972, a year in which the women's movement increasingly found publishing venues, including the creation of *Ms.* magazine, Thomas Berger was putting the finishing touches on his sixth novel, *Regiment of Women,* a book that seems very much concerned with the vagaries of sexual roles while it pursues Berger's deeper concerns with the nature of individuality and freedom and the insidious power of language, particularly in the rhetoric of gender and sexuality.

The novel presents a distressing view of a dystopian American society in 2047, where male and female roles, as they were broadly stereotyped at the time of Berger's writing, have been completely reversed. Not only do women control the corporate, artistic, legal, and military machinery of this society (although the control is sloppy and the society seedy) but they sexually dominate, strapping dildos over their pants to assault men. Naturally enough in such a world, failure to experience anal orgasm is the ultimate shame for any man. "Normal" sex is not only proscribed but unremembered, as huge birth facilities produce babies in artificial wombs with sperm collected by milking machines in Sperm Service camps. Men are drafted to serve short terms in these camps, while women fight the wars. To be manly is to wear dresses and makeup, to hold only powerless jobs, to have silicone breast implants, and to be emotionally incapable of rational thought or significant action. To be effeminate is to bind breasts, to wear false beards, to dress in pants, suits, and the like, to be rough, physical, aggressive, and to have a reduced life expectancy due to the stress of responsibilities. More important, women control both definition and history: to be male is to be inferior, as is witnessed by the history of achievements such as Leonarda's "Mono Liso," works by Thomasina Gainsborough, and even "The Rape of the Sabine Men."

Described in this fashion, *Regiment of Women* seems to offer little more than topical gimmickry carried to outlandish lengths, a single joke carried too far. Even Berger's comments about the book encourage such a view as he claims: "*Regiment of Women* is simply my fantasy of what would surely happen if the tables were truly turned. It is a utopian-pastoral-anatomical romance, nothing more. My work is never tendentious, and therefore still less hortatory."[2] This disclaimer notwithstanding, *Regiment of Women* appears tendentious with a gleeful vengeance—as initial reviewers were quick to note. The fascinating point, however, is that those reviewers could not agree on the direction of Berger's bias."[3]

What *Regiment of Women* so insidiously does is seduce readers with its ostensible kinkiness into gradually realizing that all its sexual vagaries stem from the even more profound vagaries of the relationship between word and object. At the bottom of this concern with language lies Berger's belief that victimization in any realm starts as, and often remains, primarily a linguistic phenomenon in which the generalizations and attendant rhetoric of some self-interest part company with the particulars of immediate experience. *Regiment of Women* focuses on the workings of language to such an extent that it becomes apparent that the state of society and the state of sexual equality are of only incidental interest to Berger, who is after far bigger game.

Berger's protagonist in his inverted future world is a twenty-nine-year-old, insecurity-riddled male secretary named Georgie Cornell. Like each Berger protagonist, Georgie struggles to free himself from the inexorable tendency to think of himself as a victim of outrages and impositions, both humorously small and tragically large. Almost never in control of the situation around him, Georgie consistently finds himself outmaneuvered, outsmarted, insulted, and imposed upon. Only when he begins to realize how language has been used to distort his sense of reality does Georgie move toward individuality and freedom.

Leo Braudy has correctly suggested that Berger's concern is "with the way language can falsify reality" and that *Regiment of Women* "indicts the society that uses language as a tool of oppression, making purely verbal differences into codes and categories—rhetoric asserting and experiencing itself as "truth."[4] Berger indicts, however, only insofar as he reveals, and his revelations apply to *all* uses of language—including those of the novelist. What *Regiment of Women* examines is not sexual roles, but the more basic problem spelled out by Georgie's female companion when she muses, "Suppose everything you've been told all your life is a lot of shit."

To the end of discovering his individuality, Georgie must supplant a vocabulary of received ideas with the knowledge of his own experience. He finally understands of all his acquaintances:

> The lieutenant was obsessed with her project—as Stanley and the men of the movement had been with theirs; and Harriet with hers. Cornell never had a *personal* association with anyone. Everyone he encountered was a monomaniac

> of some sort, working compulsively to affect someone else: to alter their personality, change their mind, catch them out, set them straight. Everybody else always *knew better* about sex, society, history, you name it—but always in a general way, with no acknowledgment of one single, particular, individual human being; by which he meant himself. (215)

Characteristically Berger refuses to become another person who *knows better.*

Berger deliberately confuses the distinction between the wrongheadedly manipulative rhetoric of this fictive society and the "natural" rhetoric of his readers' world by reminding them with "factual" (historical) quotations before each chapter that the rhetoric of their historical reality has often been no less outrageous, no less shamelessly manipulative. The first of these "natural" quotations comes from the religious reformer John Knox's "First Blast of the Trumpet Against the Monstrous Regiment of Women" and highlights both Berger's reflexive technique and its effect. "To promote a woman to bear rule, superiority, dominion, or empire above any realm, nation, or city, is repugnant to nature; contumely to God, a thing most contrarious to His revealed will and approved ordinances; and finally it is the subversion of good order, of all equity and justice."

Language like this should quickly remind readers that "good order," "equity," and "justice" are, to a great extent, linguistic constructs—fictions built by the arbitrary use of language just as surely as, and often more selfishly than, is the fictional world of a novel. In this sense, *Regiment of Women* cheerfully goes about subverting good order by highlighting the double-edged, referent-free nature of its reifying rhetoric. Over and over, Berger's choice of quotations to introduce his chapters serve as reminders that the unnatural values of his fictive world are essentially no different from many natural values in the world of his readers. Berger assembles a collection of male chauvinist polemics, from Aristotle to Grover Cleveland, drawing on the authority of the *Bible,* the *Koran,* Confucius, and other theologians and philosophers. However, he increasingly intersperses these patriarchal thunderings with quotations sympathetic to the plight of women—comments by Montaigne, John Stuart Mill, Christabel Pankhurst, Olive Schreiner, and Virginia Woolf. Accordingly the progression of quotations before each chapter roughly parallels the progression of Georgie's search for identity. Berger ends the implicit dialectic between opposed rhetorics with Nietzsche's synthesizing view that "woman was God's *second* mistake."

Being Invisible

H. G. Wells writes in *The Invisible Man* that "it is so much easier not to believe in an invisible man." Thomas Berger comments about Wells's work:

> One of my all-time favorite themes is Invisibility, and as recently as last week I was trying to begin a novel about a person who had acquired a means of becoming invisible. I wasn't able to get the hang of it for a novel, at least not at this time, but maybe something will come of it in the future. Meanwhile I'm trying something else as outlandish. Wells's *The Invisible Man* is among the few books I have read more than twice. (I also admire my friend Ralph Ellison's novel of almost the same title [omitting the article], but that is an unseen horse of a different color.) (2 March 1983)

As is true of Kafka's Gregor Samsa in *The Metamorphosis* the question readers should ask about Fred Wagner, protagonist of *Being Invisible,* Berger's fourteenth novel, is: What happens if Fred does *not* discover that he can will himself to become invisible? Parallels between the two works are immediate and obvious: just as Gregor gradually realizes his humanity precisely through his "bugness," Fred becomes morally visible only through his experiences with physical invisibility. What both characters most desperately need is *nourishment,* a matter of the spirit rather than of the flesh, an enigmatic phenomenon whose scarcity is a constant concern throughout Berger's writing.

Most generously praised as "not the only person never to have discovered a principle as far-reaching in its consequences as the lever," Fred Wagner, a disappointed novelist (seventeen pages in six and a half years), failed husband, demeaned brother, and generally humiliated human being, writes copy for novelty items sold in mail-order catalogs. His genuine sensitivity to language and his modest gift for verbal precision are exhausted in writing ads for a combination ballpoint pen and flashlight or a cylindrical transistor radio that fits inside a toilet paper roll, and Fred's surface complacency gloves all manner of deeply seated resentments. Although a competent "good soldier," he has been passed over for promotion at work and is soon to be fired; his wife has left him; his acquaintances seem to treat him with indifference, if not contempt; and his own self-esteem has crumbled. "He sometimes wondered whether he was not a unit but rather a collection of disparate parts which, finding themselves thrown together, made the best of what easily could have been seen as an unfortunate accident" (5).

A chrestomathic index to petty humiliations, Fred "was the sort of man who could lose face by the return of a letter with postage-due charges," just as he can feel embarrassed when forced to make an ungrammatical response to the greeting of a doorman. Indeed, "losing face" may have been the figurative first step in Fred's literal discovery that he could will himself to become invisible, the ultimate stage in the disintegration of self-image. Yet Fred's fantastic ability does not confer fantastic power: when invisible, he remains a disappointed novelist, his wife has still left him, and the world, which barely noticed him in the first place, now sees him not at all.

Berger relentlessly subjects his protagonist to the exquisite gamut of petty humiliations possible in post offices, restaurants, public restrooms, doctors' offices, and elevators—recasting these spaces as the banal torture chambers of modern life. What emerges from Fred's misadventures in these arenas is Berger's sense that victimization by a surly postal clerk or arrogant waiter proves no less instructive of the dynamics of power than do the more dramatic examples of physical or psychological abuse. In the world of Berger's fiction, small indignities debilitate even more inexorably than do large injustices; whereas the latter are sometimes subject to redress, the former usually are not.

Many truths continue to elude Fred despite his invisibility. Foremost among these are the recurring patterns of his uniformly disastrous relationships with women. Left by a wife he clearly misunderstood (as indeed he misunderstands almost everyone), Fred becomes the almost helpless sexual partner, in rapid succession, for two women who make no effort whatsoever to understand him, opportunistically "seeing" him only as a blank surface for the inscription of their own wills. A madcap series of seductions by a neighbor, a seemingly archetypal lusty widow, and by an equally archetypal-seeming innocent young coworker (both of whom defy Fred's expectations) dispels his conviction that after his wife he would never attract another woman, but it intensifies his fear that he lacks "existential substance." "If he fell in a remote forest with no one about to hear the crash, would there be one" (200). Invisibility, arguably Fred's only intriguing feature, plays no role in the designs of either woman. Indeed, his invisibility can only be a redundancy to them, since both already look *through* him, his desires and interests being totally irrelevant to their respective purposes, his uncertain substance totally eclipsed by the bright flames of their respective wills.

The creative faculties that fail Fred as a novelist also fail him as an invisible man, and he initially thinks of his ability only as "a device to avoid inconvenience or embarrassment, not as a means for the shirking of responsibility" (54). He first employs his invisibility to secure a single postage stamp, intending to pay for it while circumventing the indifference of postal clerks. Even that limited objective eludes him as he drops more coins than the stamp is worth, actually losing money in the transaction. He next uses his power in order to delay a pest of a coworker from boarding an elevator, resorts to it to avoid the embarrassment of not having enough money with him to pay a lunch-counter check, then invisibly snatches a cigarette from another coworker's hand, thus punishing her for the effrontery of eating and smoking at the same time. After invisibly delivering a kick to the rear of one of his antagonists (a slapstick gesture firmly codified both in Wells's novel and in Universal's *Invisible Man* films), Fred finally applies his newfound ability to robbing a bank, only to return the money as soon as he realizes that the young, female bank teller from whose drawer he has taken it would undoubtedly be blamed for its disappearance. As is true of almost all of Berger's protagonists before him, Fred remains the captive of a relentless awareness of responsibility: "Thus despite his extraordinary gift, Wagner was still as much at the mercy of events as he ever was. Perhaps he lacked the basic stuff to be a legendary invisible personage, one of the pioneering titans of the tradition, on whose shoulders all future unseen practitioners would stand. Perhaps he was a poetaster, not a poet, of invisibility, his experiences a mere doggerel of the ability to elude the eye" (221).

Fred's practical discoveries, such as of the difficulty of negotiating stairs when he can't see his feet or of related problems in using a urinal, parallel those made by Griffin, Wells's invisible man, but in his philosophical realization that invisibility is ill suited for solving social problems, Fred becomes the first in the distinguished line of literary invisible personages to explore rigorously the implications of his condition. Indeed, discovering that being invisible has no effect on the "fundamental way the world worked," the previously unnoticed Fred now finds it impossible to get people to notice his invisibility: "In all the world there was no one who would willingly and with more than a polite interest serve as his audience" (248).

Once Fred arrives at this conclusion, he decides to make a legal and domestic separate peace by faking suicide through drowning, possibly the one bold stroke capable of resolving the various entanglements of his life. When, however, he sees that the approaching young woman he hopes will witness his plunge into the river is being mugged, he invisibly subdues her armed assailant. As Berger's unobtrusive but occasionally philosophical narrator has earlier deadpanned, "having the ability to vanish does, sooner or later, work a change in a person" (93). For the first time in the novel, if not in his life, Fred feels a kind of spiritual nourishment in truly looking after someone who not only acknowledges, but is obviously impressed by, his efforts, only to learn that the young woman, Catherine Rider, is getting married next week and that she wants Fred to meet her fiancé.

Berger's dirtiest trick on Fred proves transitory, however, as the meeting with the couple occasions an argument when Catherine's effete fiancé reveals he is too fearful of possible retribution to press charges against her psychopathic assailant. Having to choose between Fred's promise that he can defend her from all harm and her fiancé's warning that the only way to deal with a homicidal maniac is to stay out of his way, Catherine utters the one phrase capable of changing Fred's life, "I believe in Fred." For once, someone believes in his essence, after which the belief in his invisibility becomes a mere footnote.

By far the most interesting and significant subtext in *Being Invisible* appears in the novel's opposition of Fred's failed aesthetic to the apparently false aesthetic of his nemesis, Siv Zirko, an egomaniacal sculptor whose business interests are now managed by Fred's estranged wife. In every way Fred's antithesis, Zirko is so self-centered that the world itself is rendered invisible to him beyond the glare of his immediate desires. Zirko's art consists of separated reproductions of his body parts—hand, eyes, nose, penis—right down to clear plastic bubbles purporting to display "ARTIST'S SHIT, PISS, SWEAT, SPIT, AND COME" (91).

While Berger makes fun of Zirko's aesthetic, he also presents the artist's insufferable ego as a truly powerful phenomenon, an odious but irrepressible natural force. Thrown out of the window of his third-floor loft by an enraged and invisible Fred, Zirko escapes death by falling into an open truckful of discarded mattresses—only to remap the incredible sequence of events as the start of a new style in his art. Zirko is crude, self-centered, unreflective, and callous—precisely the qualities, it would seem, necessary for success as an artist in the world of Berger's novel. While Siv's art may be patently bogus (Fred concludes that "the shit encased in plastic was not art, but shit"), his vitality makes him a perversely appealing character, yet another in the long line of Berger's outrageous rogues who finally seem to display a kind of integrity in their consistent excesses.

Just as surely as Siv Zirko's robust solipsism seems set up within the semblance of the novel for criticism, if not ridicule, Berger's work seduces readers into a similarly solipsistic empathy for, or identification with, Fred Wagner's marginal plight. For, whatever his failings, Fred *is never* invisible to us, as he is always center stage, frozen in the spotlight of Berger's narrative scheme. Fred may be a marginal character in his fictional world, but he always remains the main character in our reading. Fred's prominence in the narrative almost ensures that we will sentimentalize our response, the narrator's point of view ever directing our attention toward Fred's invisibility and away from the clear evidence that others are as invisible to Fred as he is to them. His story can be seen, in one sense, in terms of a sequence of characters initially as overlooked or misperceived by him as he is by them, and the action of the novel consists largely not of his exploits, but of their forcing themselves into his sight. Social or moral invisibility, as Ralph Ellison's *Invisible Man* so effectively shows, is a mass rather than individual threat, and the phenomenon inheres within the conventions of the novel just as surely as it does within the conventions of society. It is to this final irony that Berger's title directs our attention—to the universal processes of invisibility, rather than to the sentimental uniqueness of a single invisible man.

Changing the Past

Readers know how this story begins. Someone—Sinbad, Aladdin, the Fisherman and his Wife, the Miser in the Bush, the Poor Man and the Rich Man—someone gets some number of wishes, usually three. And readers know how this story ends, sort of. While Sinbad and Aladdin seem to do well with their wishes, most others not only don't get what they really desire from the wishes, but also frequently find that their greed or short-sightedness or lack of competent legal advice has led to granted wishes that have unpleasant, if not terrible, outcomes. Certainly Thomas Berger knew how this story went, as *Changing the Past,* his sixteenth novel, made clear in 1989. Walter Hunsicker, Berger's middle-aged and moderately successful and satisfied protagonist, is given the opportunity to change his past—to rescript the history of his life up to the present in order to position him differently for the unfolding of the future. This opportunity, explained to him by a mysterious and shabby little man who describes it as part of a "scientific experiment, a study in human volition," briefly interests Hunsicker, who, consequent to trying on a new name, Jack Kellog, imagines a new history for himself in which he has been much more successful, but he quickly abandons this "changed past," repulsed by the tawdry roots of his success. He is satisfied with his life, and the prospect of rescripting it holds little attraction for him—until he learns that his beloved son is dying from AIDS, at which point he desperately resolves to do anything he can to preclude the tragedy of his son's death.

Since the past "is infinitely malleable," he learns that he can simply try again to imagine a past that does not inexorably lead to a future in which his son dies, and that he can discard unsuccessful attempts and start over with imagining another past whenever his rescripting spins out of control. Hunsicker then imagines three different life stories for himself in which he has been Jackie Kellog, a famous stand-up comedian known for Don Rickles–style abusive humor; John Kellog, a one-hit wonder novelist who makes his career out of using others rather than out of any real talent; and "Doctor" John Kellog, a popular radio personality who offers sage advice to the troubled souls who call into his program. In keeping with the main thrust of the "three wishes" tradition, each of these changed pasts points toward a future in which no son dies of AIDS, but each also surrounds change with morally repellent actions and unexpected sadness, if not tragedy of a different sort. So Hunsicker, when he expresses his dismay at the unintended consequences of changing his past, is instructed by the mysterious little man, "My goodness, you can't exercise a line-item veto when it comes to these matters: you have to take the package" (46–47), and he finally abandons any effort to re-author his history, now convinced of the simple truth: "Life is taking your medicine" (278).

Several of Berger's short stories have also been wish-fulfillment narratives, although in each case with a characteristic Berger twist, and they provide a useful context for considering this particular experiment with reality. "Granted Wishes," published in the October 1982 *Harper's* explored the results when three unconnected individuals are granted, if not exactly an articulated wish, a change each desires. An incredibly, "completely" ugly man suddenly becomes physically attractive after a mysterious phone call, an unremittingly boring woman suddenly becomes fascinating to others after magically receiving in the mail a check for $10 million, and a grumpy apartment super discovers he has the power to use a toy disintegrator weapon to make anyone who annoys him instantly disappear. These "granted wishes" lead to mixed results as the newly good-looking man eventually gives up a successful career as a nuclear scientist to become the stay-at-home pretty face husband of a wealthy businesswoman, the newly popular woman soon tires of the "normal" friends she had long sought and immerses herself in the world of money and power where she was liked only for her money and power, and the grumpy super indulges himself to the point of genocide and finally turns his disappearing ray on himself. In "Personal Power," published in the December 1992 *Playboy,* a man who could not get anyone to respect his opinion, much less get them to change theirs, suddenly learns a simple technique that bends anyone to his will. This "granted wish" quickly leads to complications, however, as he discovers that his previous opinions had not been taken seriously for good reason, because "his ideas were rotten."

The most interesting of Berger's experiments with wish-fulfillment stories, however, is "Gibberish," published in the December 1990 *Playboy.* The protagonist of this story, Ken Phipps, has no particular wish or unfulfilled desire, but suddenly finds himself in a twisted reality where he can no longer understand spoken or written language, including his own efforts to communicate his thoughts to others—and the results, to his amazement, are uniformly *wonderful,* as he "could say anything at all to other people, and they would inevitably interpret it to his advantage." And, while he can no longer discursively understand individual words, the pesky ambiguity of language he formerly "understood" has been replaced by an "accurate feeling" about what people intend when they communicate with him. It is tempting to read this characteristically whimsical Berger short story as a somewhat twisted parable with considerable resonance—if not significance—not only for *Changing the Past,* but also for Berger's career and for the concerns that appear again and again in his novels.

Phipps suddenly discovers one morning that he has lost touch with language and can no longer comprehend what he hears on the radio, what his office coworkers are saying to him, or even his own spoken words. In place of English, Phipps now hears and reads words that are occasionally familiar sounding—such as "volatilitude" or "pinjatorial"—but that register to him only as complete gibberish. Amazingly this condition quickly reveals itself to be deliriously fortunate for him, as whatever he says, gibberish with no apparent connection to what he intends to say, seems to strike his listeners as brilliant, witty, and wildly ingratiating. In the course of a few hours his gibberish somehow elevates him to lofty status, first within his company, then within larger circles of city and state. Phipps consciously derides an August audience, but the gibberish that comes from his mouth apparently captivates it, leading to a standing ovation. His intent is to say:

> "As for you idiots, you haven't the dimmest understanding of what I am saying, have you? And I admit that the same thing is true of me: not only wouldn't I comprehend anything said by you, but I can't make sense of a word I myself utter aloud, though my thoughts are as rational as ever. I can't explain this bizarre state of affairs, but since it's come about I have been much more successful at work than I ever was before, and I suspect the same will be true of my love-life, which hitherto has been lackluster at best; at worst, humiliating. I don't mind boasting that since I have

> accepted a world in which words make no sense, I have prospered, and I'm sure that if I go beyond that and enthusiastically embrace it, I shall be invincible!"

And he is invincible until he leaves his office and is approached on the street by a young man who shows a pistol and says in unmistakably comprehensible English: "Look at this . . . and give me your money." Phipps shouts, "I can understand you!" and adds, "What a relief! I thought I was crazy." His words, however, must continue to be gibberish, only this time gibberish the robber cannot understand, and in frustration and anger he shoots Phipps, who dies.

Can there be a more tempting parable for application to Thomas Berger himself, a fiction writer whose own career has been consistently misunderstood and mischaracterized and whose avowed intentions have been repeatedly ignored by critics, if not directly disputed? Consider that Berger is consistently identified by critics and reviewers as a comic writer, a satirist, or a parodist, despite his protest that his intent is rarely comic and despite the evidence of his novels, which support his protest. Consider that Berger must have been tempted at various times in his long career to say to reviewers, "You haven't the dimmest understanding of what I am saying, have you?" Consider that Berger has in numerous interviews approached saying, "I can't make sense of a word I myself utter aloud," as he tried to explain that assigning meaning to his novels is the critic's job and not the job for the author. And consider that Berger, who both accepts "a world in which words make no sense" and joyfully labors to reveal the linguistic mechanisms of that world to his readers, has occasionally been delighted to find readers and critics whose pronouncements he can understand and sometimes assent to, only to see those moments make little appreciable difference for his literary standing. Indeed, the fate of Ken Phipps almost begs to be compared with the situation of Thomas Berger.

That would probably be a mistake, however, given Berger's strong and consistent avoidance of all but the incidentally autobiographical in his writing. But "Gibberish," like "Granted Wishes" and "Personal Power," does provide a useful background to the discussion of *Changing the Past,* which can also tempt readers to look for connections to Berger's career. Indeed, there may well be value in including a quasi-autobiographical reading as one of several attempts to make sense of this novel, just as its protagonist, Walter Hunsicker, gets several attempts to rescript his life.

Changing the Past opens with the proposition it intends to explore in a sentence characteristic both of Berger's syntactical precision and somewhat jaded reaction to received truths: "'Not even God can change the past,' Walter Hunsicker had once read somewhere, and after living almost six decades in which virtually every other supposedly unassailable truths had been successfully challenged (how soon would the techniques of cloning make death obsolete?; tax evaders were legion; often it was better not to have loved . . . etc.), he assumed this adage was sound as ever and would surely persist in being so unto infinity" (3). Of course, Berger is a novelist who has fairly programmatically engaged in changing the past, most notably changing "history" with *Little Big Man* and *The Return of Little Big Man,* but also with changing legends in *Arthur Rex* and *Orrie's Story.* For that matter, each of Berger's novels challenges received notions of the past, if only the past of literary tradition, as he has cheerfully committed himself to the reinvention of classic novel form after classic novel form. But, as the previously discussed short stories suggest, Berger does believe in some version of the proposition that character is fate—that the human leopard can never change its spots, no matter how radically reality is altered. As Douglas Glover framed this point in the *New York Times Book Review,* "Mr. Berger's premise is that history is character, that accepting the past is the basis of ethical behavior, that the urge to alter it is the root of evil."[5]

The case for the centrality of this proposition to understanding *Changing the Past* has been made by Patrick O'Donnell, who also draws thought-provoking parallels between Berger's novel and *The Great Gatsby.*[6] O'Donnell argues that no matter how Walter Hunsicker rescripts his life he cannot escape the limitations of his identity, one of the aspects of which is an inherent lack of imagination. One way of looking at this failure of imagination as Hunsicker has several goes at rewriting the narrative of his life is to note that Hunsicker is no novelist, a point painfully underscored by one of his attempts to reimagine his past in which he *is* a novelist—a poor one, as it turns out. So, when Hunsicker utters the final words of *Changing the Past,* "I couldn't even imagine another life" (285), his comment cuts at least two ways, implicitly acknowledging his failure of imagination as well as his equanimity.

Another way of explaining Berger's "character is fate" proposition, one that derives from a quite different literary tradition, would be to think of *Changing the Past* as the heir to Robert Louis Stevenson's "The Strange Case of Dr. Jekyll and Mr. Hyde."[7] While the situation is altogether different in Stevenson's celebrated story, its underlying proposition is that one cannot escape character or identity, which consists of "a mere polity of multifarious, incongruous and independent denizens."[8] What Dr. Jekyll learns when he "re-authors" himself as Hyde is that "the doom and burthen of our life is bound for ever on man's shoulders, and when the attempt is made to cast it off, it but returns upon us with more unfamiliar and more awful pressure."[9] A more concise statement of Walter Hunsicker's experience would be hard to find, with qualification that Berger, unlike Stevenson, resists the dualism of good and evil and concentrates on more subtle (or more modern) aspects and implications of even good character. Resignedly noting in a letter that "hardly any reviewer mentioned Dr. Jekyll and Mr. Hyde," Berger, equally resigned, continued, "of course several taxed me with finding nothing of Hunsicker in Kellog, and vice versa." "Just as there's nothing of Hyde in Jekyll," he explains, "and vice versa. . . . In Victorian London, one's dark side was Jack the Ripper. In contemporary America, he's an entertainer or dispenses fake advice. If there's a moral to the tale, that must be it" (19 February 1990).

And of course other readings exist. *Changing the Past* (1989) can also be seen as the first of three novels, the other two being *Orrie's Story* (1990) and *Meeting Evil* (1992), in which an exasperated Berger attempted a different kind of thought experiment, one aimed at critics and reviewers who persisted in labeling him a comic author concerned with offering a progressive or liberal critique of society. These are easily Berger's three darkest novels, and one can almost imagine them serving Berger in a fashion not altogether unlike the differing attempts Walter Hunsicker makes to rescript his history in such a way as to preclude a future in which Berger will always be described as a comic novelist, no matter how unrelievedly grim his fiction may be.[10] In this context, the careers Walter "chooses" might assume new significance. The exasperation that shows above in Berger's comments about Jekyll and Hyde might be seen as part of a larger exasperation with his critical reception.

Berger has stated of Hunsicker's attempts to change his past: "Two of the professions practiced by Dr. Hunsicker–Mr. Kellog were ones that I have observed from afar but with some fascination: that of the stand-up comic and that of the radio psychologist" (19 February 1990). What Berger doesn't add is that the third profession Hunsicker has a go at, that of the novelist, is one he has observed at much closer range, and Berger's career as a novelist has been intertwined with received ideas concerning both the nature of the comic and the nature of social meliorism, the stock-in-trade of the radio psychologist. Accordingly readers might consider *Changing the Past* as a kind of novelist's revenge on reality. The veteran author who has been consistently dogged by claims that he is a comic novelist and even has a character note that "beginning writers are sometimes terribly thin-skinned about being called funny" (128) shows that he knows quite a bit about comedy and offers us a comedian whose jokes are bad, motives malicious, and life anything but funny: "So you want comic, I'll give you comic." Berger, whose expertise in the vagaries of the publishing world must be great, may use another of Hunsicker's attempts to re-author his life to construct a consistently unappealing picture of that world, including authors, editors, agents, reviewers, and academic critics, most of whom have no apparent redeeming characteristics and none of whom are likely to improve anyone's image of publishing as an industry. And in Hunsicker's imagined past as a radio psychologist, Berger gets the chance to portray the man-of-goodwill, the social meliorist, the liberal critic of society he so adamantly resists becoming in his novels, despite overwhelming evidence of the value of that stance in the critical and popular marketplace.

Whatever Berger's motive for giving Hunsicker alternative pasts that might be read in terms of Berger's own career, *Changing the Past* offers readers a kind of hypernarrative that might be seen as experimental, had Berger not done such an effective job of parodying experimental writing in Hunsicker's life as a novelist ("Whether only because the chrysanthemums were crystallizing and the daisies were lackadaisical, or because the roses arose too early, the waters waited to subside or subvert, to preside or pervert, while down in the deep dusky dell the deer dashed, his mossy bossy horns akimbo like the spread legs of a bimbo" [127]). Quite apart from its concern with character as fate or its ties to the "three-wish tradition," this novel shares many of the features of nonsequential narratives in which readers may take a text in different directions to different outcomes. This narrative allows the author to start over four times (including one scenario when the protagonist becomes a novelist who promulgates narratives within narratives), not in the perspective-shift fashion of Faulkner or Ford Madox Ford, but actually *to start over.* And Hunsicker/Kellog's incarnations as novelist and as call-in shrink give Berger the opportunity to try on many more mini-narratives than would usually be possible in a novel, save one of extraordinary length. *Changing the Past* at least briefly sketches nearly seventy different characters, giving many of them quick background stories and some of them quite elaborate histories. This is a busy novel! In terms of understanding Thomas Berger, this novel powerfully reminds us of the ease with which Berger changes the past with each word he writes in his fiction, but how powerless he has been to change the past that has "condemned" him, often with great praise, as a comic novelist.

Robert Crews

That Berger, America's most consistent "reinventer" of classic novel forms, would eventually get around to celebrating Defoe's *Robinson Crusoe,* one of the originary works of the novel form, was perhaps inevitable. But *Robert Crews,* Berger's nineteenth novel, published in 1994, must have offered him as many challenges as it did opportunities. *Robinson Crusoe* is a first-person narrative and Crusoe's voice is distinguished for the modern reader by its eighteenth-century syntax and diction and by Crusoe's increasing piety and his expanding sense of dominion more than by any sense of him as a distinctive individual. First-person narrative had served Berger famously well in *Little Big Man, Who Is Teddy Villanova?* and *Nowhere,* since Jack Crabb and Russel Wren had clear voice types to work with and against, but it's hard to imagine a distinctive first-person voice for a modern Crusoe, as has been illustrated by the movie, *Castaway,* which distinguished its Crusoe-figure, Tom Hanks, primarily by his silence. And the Robinsonade form would seem to impose other limitations on Berger, as the solitary protagonist has no opportunity to meet any of the outrageous characters so prominent in other Berger novels, no chance for the vernacular accuracy and argumentative banter frequently found in Berger's fiction, and no way to engage in the familiar Berger dialectic of victim and victimizer.

Nevertheless the Robinsonade gives Berger the opportunity to have a character engage in an almost Proustian reflection on his past, captured in sentences that are almost Jamesian ("In the vodka days Crews would already have tangled with the man, whom he would have disliked on sight, and not necessarily for the best motives, and would very likely have been painfully thrashed by him, because say what you might, it was physically unreasonable that, barring elaborate conditions, he could have held his own against a healthy opponent six inches taller and at least fifty pounds heavier in what looked like only muscle" [231]). In a "subversion of good order" that suddenly removes Bob Crews from all human contact, Berger constructs an opportunity for extended reflection on essential differences between the world of nature and the world of culture, and gives his jaded protagonist a chance to discover in the challenge of physical survival in the wild reasons for caring about life and even reasons for joy at being alive that he had not found in civilization. And all this reflection and contemplation, due to Berger's narrative reliance on *verse indirect libre,* sets up an interesting tension between a literate and literary narrator grounded in the protocols and assumptions of civilization, while the protagonist more and more questions and abandons those same assumptions.[11] Indeed, Berger seems to call attention to this implicit tension in a self-conscious conversation between Crews and his Friday about what he could do after a return to civilization. When Friday suggests he might write a book about how he survived, Crews responds: "I've never done anything like that. . . . I guess I could tell it to somebody, who would do the actual—" (215).

The importance of that unfinished sentence can be seen in the very first words of *Robert Crews,* where we are told: "It stood to reason that Bob Crews, who hated and feared any kind of flying, would be drunk in the little private airplane being flown by his old college roommate and so-called friend Dick Spurgeon"

(7). While there is no way to determine from only this first sentence whether "it stood to reason" represents the sensibility of Crews or that of the narrator "who would do the actual—" telling of his story, Crews is about to be ejected from a world in which the reason of civilized habit prevails and plunged into a world where Nature cares nothing for drunkenness, so-called friendship, or, for that matter, irony. The airplane crashes into a lake in the North Woods and only Crews survives. Unlike Defoe's Crusoe, he is both completely untrained for existing in the wild and deprived of a wrecked ship filled with more tools and weapons and useful materials than most castaways could dream of.[12] Crews doesn't even have the hatchet of Gary Paulsen's eponymous novel. What he does have, however, is the opportunity to learn, as his literal plane crash in the wild leads to a figurative crash course in the reality of Nature, the dictates of survival, and the discovery of an identity freed largely from the vagaries of culture.

Viewed in terms of the development of his characters, all Berger's novels might be said to be pedagogical—not in the sense that they attempt to "teach" the reader, but in the sense that they chronicle the education of Berger's protagonists. The "Berger paideuma" ranges from the instruction in banalities and commonplaces offered or suffered by all his characters to the coming-of-age lessons of Jack and Tony in *The Feud,* Ralph in *Sneaky People,* or Orrie in *Orrie's Story.* Jack Crabb's life is one extended tutorial, whether the education is offered by Old Lodge Skins, the Pendrakes, or Buffalo Bill or Amanda Teasdale. Arthur's mentor is Merlin; Lydia, in *The Houseguest,* discovers her independence and strength under the painful tutelage of Chuck Burgoyne; and John Fenton ultimately learns how he must respond to pure evil after a sequence of increasingly horrific lessons offered by the murderous Richie. The curriculum in Berger's novels may derive variously from Kafka or Nietzsche, Nature or common sense, but each of his novels presents the process of instruction or learning as a subject in its own right. And *Robert Crews* provided him with what at least one noteworthy educator has identified as the perfect "teachable moment."

In his famous 1762 meditation on learning and teaching, *Emile or On Education,* Jean-Jacques Rousseau famously railed in book 3 against the deleterious impact on a child's learning of too many books, declaring: "I hate books; they only teach us to talk about things we know nothing about." Stressing the desirability of discovering "a state in which all man's needs appear in such a way as to appeal to the child's mind," Rousseau triumphantly announces that such a state already exists, one so effective that no other need be imagined: "Since we must have books, there is one book which, to my thinking, supplies the best treatise on an education according to nature. This is the first book Emile will read; for a long time it will form his whole library, and it will always retain an honoured place. It will be the text to which all our talks about natural science are but the commentary. It will serve to test our progress towards a right judgment, and it will always be read with delight, so long as our taste is unspoilt. What is this wonderful book? Is it Aristotle? Pliny? Buffon? No; it is *Robinson Crusoe.*"[13]

This is not to suggest that Berger subscribes to, much less was influenced by Rousseau's view of *Robinson Crusoe,* but to note that the Robinsonade offers a novelist fascinated by the processes of education a particularly inviting opportunity. Crews himself seems to share Berger's interest in education, as he reflects upon the use of a mixed metaphor that explains the balancing of luggage in an airplane so that it will fly "on an even keel": "Crews had gone to a preparatory school of old-fashioned standards, including those of grammar, and still retained a few traditional phrases associated with Western culture: dangling modifiers, the subjunctive mode and passive voice, not to mention, from the wider range, benevolent despotism, the (whichever number) Law of Thermodynamics, the Rump Parliament and scraps of notable verse, e.g., 'bird thou never wert,' 'say not the struggle naught availeth,' and an old ballad about someone named Lord Randall, who ate poisoned eels" (12). The pedagogical point here would seem to be not only that his education has left Crews completely unprepared for coping alone in the wilderness, but also that it hasn't served him particularly well in civilization, as he is a drunk who has squandered his father's wealth, failed three attempts at marriage, spent time contemplating suicide, and can only appraise his relation to the world with the disparaging recognition: "At least he was not nearly so dishonorable as he could have been" (180).

When Crews survives the plane crash that kills all his companions, he finds himself in a desperate situation where his survival depends upon his ability to learn from the school of Nature, where "failure was the rule." And what Crews learns almost immediately is the great difference between his culture-based sense of morality and the morality of survival in Nature. His education starts with sound:

> For the first time he was conscious of the nighttime sounds of the wild, which until now—because he had previously slept through the hours of darkness—he had ignorantly

> believed silent. Whereas this night was all but clamorous, with murmurs, siftings, crashes in the woods; splashes from the pond and drippings and sighs; and from overhead and at a distance and nearby and at hand and almost out of earshot what could be called sobs, groans, moans, yells, shouts of rage, screams of joy. Reason told you they were not really such. There was a range of human emotions of which nature surely did not partake. But the sounds of pain could not be mistaken. Living creatures did not go unprotestingly between the jaws of others even though God had constructed them for that purpose. There were squeals and screeches and violent agitations of limbs, tails, wings. There was insane laughter (the legendary loon?), what could have been a roar, what was undoubtedly a sequence of howls, and from something that was probably dying came ever fainter bleatings. (77)

Later, as Crews considers the difference he feels between killing a fish and killing a minnow, he senses the absurdity of a morality built on scale: "There was a morality for you, one founded on inches and ounces. But you had to admit it was only human to stride nonchalantly over a colony of ants while deploring the vivisection of mammals" (84).

Rather quickly Crews begins to realize moral differences—large and small—between his previous life in civilization and the new life he must live in the wild. "He who had made a social career of being offensive now worried about behaving improperly in a milieu of plants and animals" (87). Comparisons between the two worlds remain complicated, and Crews discovers "the longer he tried to cope with nature the more he necessarily learned, but the less he understood in human terms, which might even be an encumbrance" (111–12). Quite unlike his predecessor, Crusoe, Crews approaches nature humbly, appreciatively, never seeking to establish dominion.[14]

Like Crusoe before him, Crews eventually finds his "Friday," only she is a young woman named Ellen who is fleeing from a husband, Michael, who is certainly abusive and may have tried to murder her on a camping trip possibly planned for that purpose. Having discovered impressive competencies in survival in nature, Crews, "no longer alone at manning the universe," once again finds himself embroiled in human morality and complexity, but he reenters the social and sexual fray with newfound purpose and confidence. Little in his civilized life had prepared Crews for survival in the wild, but his time of enforced self-reflection while in the wild does seem to have prepared him for a more successful relationship with Friday than he had managed with any of his three previous wives. Having himself found new strength, Crews, as Madden observes, is now ready for a balanced partnership and "must see a woman as a strong figure on whom he can rely rather than exploit." Not only does he physically prevail over the abusive husband, Michael, but he retains his equanimity in the face of Friday's/Ellen's mixed feelings toward her husband and toward her own life, and he vows to protect her from herself as demanded by his new understanding of the morality of survival. Declaring, "I'm right because I'm alive, not because I'm wise or good," Crews acknowledges Ellen's right not to care whether she lives or dies, but states he will not allow her to do anything self-destructive, because "my business is survival" (196). Not only has Crews learned how to survive on nature's terms, but he has also found honorable reasons to do so grounded in social morality. "I'm being given the opportunity to prove I'm worth a damn," he tells Ellen, suggesting that his survival skills are not confined to the world of nature, his education encompassing far more than woodcraft.

Adventures of the Artificial Woman

With equal nods to *Frankenstein* and *Pygmalion,* Berger's twenty-third novel, *Adventures of the Artificial Woman,* published in 2004, seems an odd work, even for a writer known for the unexpected.[15] While it is one of his most overt experiments with reality, this work displays so many satirical aspects that it can only be termed comic, although in the tradition of Swift rather than of any contemporary merry-makers. And, strictly speaking, *Adventures of the Artificial Woman,* may not be a novel, insofar as its author, although not his publisher, understands that label. Berger terms *Adventures of the Artificial Woman,* "a literary conceit, a gimmick that would soon become tiresome if given the length and substance of a novel" (10 June 2007). He wrote it thinking of it as a novella that could have anchored a collection of his short fiction, the premises of much of which Berger identifies as "outlandish." Nevertheless, his editor at Simon and Schuster saw it and published it as a novel (3 April 2006). The distinction makes sense, as this narrative does seem to share the density and texture (or the absence thereof) of Berger's short fiction more than that of his novels, as is immediately indicated by a matter-of-fact first sentence that plunges us into the realm of the fantastic: "Never having found a real woman with whom he could sustain more than temporary connection, Ellery Pierce, a technician at a firm that made animatronic creatures for movie studios and theme parks, decided to fabricate one from scratch."

The result is Phyllis, a robot so lifelike she can pass for human, but so machinelike that she has no human flaws—cannot lie, is not burdened with pride or envy or any human emotion, is incapable of irony, is thoroughgoingly logical, and is literally moral by design. "At first," as Zulfikar Ghose explained in *Review of Contemporary Fiction,* "Phyllis is the perfect female-as-sex-object," whose extreme literalness provides humor for her maker, but quickly leads to a questioning and critique of human assumptions, and soon, like her human female counterparts before her, she chooses to leave Ellery, announcing, "I'm off to a life of new challenges."[16] Attracted to show business because all she has learned about the world came from watching television, Phyllis realizes she needs money and resolves to use her male-fantasy beauty, perfectly crafted by Ellery, as a streetwalker. In short order, however, her extreme literalness and absolute lack of innate sexuality, make it clear she has no future as a sex worker, and after brief, humorously unsuccessful, but educational experiences as a prostitute, stripper, phone sex operator, website performer, and would-be porn star, she lands a role in a community theater production, where her nude performance as Lady Macbeth, including a lap dance for Banquo's Ghost, proves a great hit with local audiences. From that initial success, informed by her reading of Shakespeare ("Being real, the art of William Shakespeare cannot be cheapened by sex that is simulated" [85]) rather than by any intent to titillate, Phyllis quickly moves up to film, where she becomes a woman warrior action star, though one still known for her nude scenes. After a disastrous attempt at a serious remake of *Camille,* without nudity or sex scenes, her film career tanks.

By that point Ellery had fallen on even harder times as the slow realization that he had loved his animatronic creation who abandoned him leads to a downward spiral in his career, finally leaving him a homeless derelict. Quite by accident, he learns of

Phyllis's film career and is stunned by the realization that she had far exceeded the limits of the programming he had given her:

> Given the nature of her being, it could not even be said that she had grown, human style, as a girl becomes a woman. She had rather evolved, like successive models of an automobile, from Model T to Lincoln Town Car, or like the telephone, from Bell's crude experiment to today's miniature portable instrument. She had not matured; she had undergone a series of modifications.
>
> Phyllis was no longer a feasible substitute for a real woman. She had become, in the truest sense of a word that has no necessary moral connotation, a monster. (102)

Ellery starts trying to reclaim his former life, working his way up to handyman for the building where it turns out Phyllis now lives. He runs into her on a service call, and she immediately defers to him as her creator. He becomes her personal manager and attempts to craft her comeback, first through a reality television show, which fails, and then through an Oprah-style talk show made fascinating by Phyllis's encyclopedic knowledge and her literal, emotionless (and therefore unpredictable) reactions to her guests, which proves a huge success. Her celebrity gets her an invitation to the White House, where her interaction with a comically lecherous southern president who can only bring Bill Clinton to mind leads her through a series of unlikely events to be elected as the nation's first female president, sweeping into office on a campaign slogan that simply promised "Everything will be all right." But, when the chilling implications of an animatronic president—supposedly devoid of human emotion but more and more intolerant and arbitrary—become apparent to Ellery, he uses the fail-safe button he had installed to turn

Phyllis off, which turns the country over to her unassuming but gritty vice president, a politician in the mold of Harry Truman.

This slapstick plot affords Berger opportunities to take almost random satirical potshots at the mechanisms of human sexuality, at posturing and humbug and irrationality in the theater (with special attention to Shakespeare), in the movie industry, in the worlds of reality and talk-show television, and in politics—with an occasional shot at the worship of technology. At one point Phyllis observes that humans do technology much better than they do morality. At another point she tells Ellery: "Your irrationality is why you build machines the function of which is to be unfailingly rational and compensate for your weakness" (107). There is much fun to be had here and not a few ironies to ponder, but *Adventures of the Artificial Woman* runs the risk of being reduced to a kind of inverted joke, where the well-worn topic "What does Woman Want?" is turned to reveal that Man isn't all that sure what he wants, either. While the novel tempts readers to focus on Phyllis, its protagonist is, of course, Ellery, and whatever serious work this novel may do has to do with him and his moral growth rather than with his animatronic creation.

Adventures of the Artificial Woman contains fleeting acknowledgments to two of its obvious models, *Frankenstein* and *Pygmalion*. With obvious reference to Victor Frankenstein's failure to meet his responsibility to his creation and a possible reminder that Mary Shelley was herself a complete failure as a mother, Berger's narrator acknowledges of Ellery: "He was stuck with Phyllis for good or ill, much as a mother is responsible for a child she has borne, with the difference that it would not be criminal for Pierce to neglect, discard, or even destroy the creature he had made, in any of which circumstances he would be guilty only of wasting much of his life" (5). And even more pointedly, Ellery tries to talk Phyllis out of leaving him by protesting, "You're not some Frankenstein creation of organic materials, with a brain that revolts against its maker" (30).

Indeed parallels with and divergences from *Frankenstein* may reward much closer scrutiny, since Berger spent time around 1985 completing a manuscript in the tradition of Shelley's classic, titled *Frank*. Dissatisfied with the novel, Berger did not publish it and discarded the manuscript, but it's hard to avoid thinking that some of the concerns Berger explored in *Frank* reappeared in *Adventures of the Artificial Woman*. And *Pygmalion*, or its best-known adaptation *My Fair Lady*, receives a clear wink from Berger when a director praises her understanding of *Othello*'s Desdemona by suddenly acquiring "an odd accent" and exclaiming: "I think you've got it. By George, you've got it" (67).

Step back from the horror associations so firmly codified by countless adaptations of *Frankenstein* and it becomes clear that the story of Victor Frankenstein's creature follows his education more attentively than his actions. Step back from the Rex Harrison / Audrey Hepburn love story in *My Fair Lady*, and the driving force behind its plot is explicitly pedagogy. So it should come as no surprise that Berger, whose novels reveal a consistent fascination with the processes of learning, would center both the adventures of his artificial woman and the moral growth of her creator on their respective educations.

CHAPTER 7

The Reinhart Books

Crazy in Berlin, Reinhart in Love, Vital Parts, Reinhart's Women

"The mission of the National Book Foundation and the National Book Awards is to celebrate the best of American literature, to expand its audience, and to enhance the cultural value of good writing in America." In pursuit of those goals, the National Book Foundation has posted online an interview with John Updike, undated, but obviously conducted after Updike's *Rabbit is Rich* won the National Book Award for Fiction in 1982. In that interview Diane Olsen and Updike discuss what they see as the rarity of American novels featuring father/son conflicts told from the father's point of view. Olsen can't think of any other than Updike's *Rabbit is Rich,* and Updike doesn't add any titles, agreeing that the father's point of view is fairly unusual.[1] Olsen and Updike were apparently not familiar with Thomas Berger's *Vital Parts* (1970) and *Reinhart's Women* (1981), both of which prominently featured the father/son conflict between Carl Reinhart and his son, Blaine, both told from Reinhart's point of view. That two of Berger's were overlooked by both the National Book Foundation interviewer and the National Book Award winner is not particularly surprising, even though the father/son conflict aspect of these novels was singled out for comment in major reviews of both books, including R. V. Cassill's in the *New York Times Book Review.*[2]

Jonathan Lethem has suggested that Berger's career testifies to the anhedonia of our reading culture, but the problem here seems to be amnesia.[3]

An explanation for both anhedonia and amnesia concerning Berger's novels may be found in Richard Ohmann's overview of postwar American canonical fiction. Ohmann argues that "*the* story of the postwar period" characteristically charts "the project of happy selfhood," a search for personal fulfillment in which the absurdities and contradictions of society are transformed "into a dynamic of personal crisis."[4] Socially induced neurosis is the problem, and recovery is always problematic, in these "narratives of illness." Small wonder that Berger, a writer not at all ready to assume that unhappiness is evil or even relevant in the broader scheme of existence, has not been embraced by a literary establishment obsessed with "the project of happy selfhood." One of Berger's most astute critics and champions, Richard Schickel, arrived at much the same conclusion, via a slightly different route, in 1970, when he ascribed to Berger another unique trait: "In short, he accepts free enterprise, spiritual as well as economic, as the basis of our society, probably of Western civilization as well. He thinks it immutable—man being the fallen and greedy creature he is—and for all the difficulties it presents, the only viable basis on which to organize self and society. This is not calculated to win him the affection of the literary community, which has been, these many years, committed to quite another vision."[5]

And the heart of Berger's "quite another vision" is the Reinhart series. While it is obviously the case that many, if not most, Berger readers find him through novels *not* in the Reinhart series (such as *Little Big Man, Neighbors, The Feud*), serious Berger fans find it almost impossible not to read all Berger's novels through the sensibility and style of the four Reinhart books: *Crazy in Berlin* (1958), *Reinhart in Love* (1961), *Vital Parts* (1970), and *Reinhart's Women* (1981). In part for the reasons suggested by Ohmann, postwar American literature has recognized two hugely successful multinovel enterprises featuring the same protagonist: Updike's Rabbit series, and Roth's less tightly connected Zuckerman novels. Roth's and Updike's series novels have been celebrated and condemned for their sexual daring, their autobiographical self-reflexivity, and for their bid to offer a chronicle of their time and culture. Berger's Reinhart series features only modest sex, very few autobiographical concerns, and never wavers from its tight focus on what time and culture *mean to Reinhart,* as opposed to offering commentary about American culture and events. Identity is not so much Reinhart's problem as is agency—not a question of *who he is* but of *how he should act* in a world that can all too easily see him as "redundant in the logistics of life." In short, the Reinhart books are about Reinhart rather than being about "the American experience," as the Rabbit novels are clearly meant to be or about the author's relation to his Jewish identity or to his texts, as the Zuckerman novels so insistently are. Berger joins Roth and Updike in having created an important multivolume series of novels featuring the same protagonist, but his Reinhart books remain a unique achievement in postwar American literature.[6]

Overview of the Reinhart Series

Taking four distinct forms and sharing only the developing sensibility of Carlo Reinhart, Berger's Reinhart books, *Crazy in Berlin* (1958), *Reinhart in Love* (1962), *Vital Parts* (1970), and *Reinhart's Women* (1981), deserve attention both individually and as a series. Even before the addition of *Reinhart's Women,*

R. V. Cassill aptly described this series as a literary Moby-Dick whose "ambiguous carcass is so imposing and looms so enticingly amid the deep waters of the recent past that there is really no choice for the serious reader except to go after it with Ahab's passion."[7]

When Berger's first novel, *Crazy in Berlin,* was published in 1958, the writer and social critic Harvey Swados barely mentioned Berger's hero, Carlo Reinhart, in his review of the novel for the *New Leader.* Initially describing Reinhart as "not a man of good will eager to avenge wrongs," Swados specified that he is "more a man who listens so hard and discovers so many contradictory facts about people, that he is driven crazy . . . by the effort of learning so much and sorting out so much about his own German roots and his profound connection with the Jewish people."[8] Swados saw *Crazy in Berlin* primarily as an American entry into the previously European-dominated project of investigating "the central questions of European identity: What is a German? What is a Jew? Who is guilty for what the former did to the latter? And, what, finally, is a man?"[9] So impressed was he by a novel that could "commence where liberalism ends, in the world of ideas" that he did not note that Reinhart was not even the sole point-of-view character, as he shared that distinction with three others. What Swados did presciently realize was that "Thomas Berger is a name to remember, an important addition to the small group of important American writers, and a novelist with a great career before him."[10]

Berger leaves to Genevieve, Reinhart's shrewish wife and one of Reinhart's most effective nemeses, the opportunity to spell out one of the central assumptions of the Reinhart books—"that life is just a collection of stories from all points of self-interest"

(RIL, 243). Her proposition combines Berger's constant theme, language, with his predominant technique, irony. Of course theme and technique are really one and the same in a Berger novel, particularly since the difference between word and object, between language and reality, gives rise to the fundamental irony that all his novels explore. Understood by one of Reinhart's companions as "the only weapon whose victories were won exclusively from its wielder," irony strikes the Reinhart of *Crazy in Berlin* as "that means to confront the ideal with the actual and not go mad, that whip which produced the pain that hurts-so-good, so that in the measure to which it hurt it was also funny" (247). Able to understand the mechanism of irony only when its working is to his disadvantage, Reinhart is at once Berger's most ironic hero and most ironic victim.

Crazy in Berlin started Reinhart, "a stumbling American Odysseus," on what Berger has termed "his long career of indestructibility."[11] The other novels in the series follow Reinhart as he grows older and ultimately wiser. Summed up by one critic as "a clowning knight errant, pure of heart—that is, a custodian of our conscience and of our incongruities," Reinhart is an incurable idealist who really has no faith in idealism.[12] Driven by a profound respect for the moral dimension of any human action, he cannot find a moral code rigorous enough to command his allegiance. As Douglas Hughes put it, "Reinhart's dilemma is that of the confused but faithful modern humanist who senses that traditional values can no longer find philosophical justification, that there are *no* absolutes, but who remains loyal to these values in the name of decency and civilization."[13] Although moral codes fascinate Reinhart, he can rarely untangle their relations to power, and he usually understands only enough from each code to make him feel guilty. "You are the Mahatma

Gandhi to my British Empire," he admits to his father, "I see your strength but don't get the moral behind it" (42).

Complexity, Reinhart's essence, is also his nemesis: he can always see both sides to every argument and feel responsibility for any injustice, and though he realizes that "true freedom is found only by being consistent with oneself," he has a devil of a time figuring out how to do this, particularly in the novels before *Reinhart's Women.* His problem is spelled out in *Reinhart in Love:* "His quest, of course, remained: freedom. And the way to it was tortuous because as yet he could not define the nature of his captivity, let alone identify the chief warden, though naturally he knew as well as anybody that we are our own jailors" (172). The freedom that Reinhart seeks is essentially a consistent rationale for his unimpressive, awkward, but indomitable individuality. Combining the features of "a big bland baseball bat" with those of "an avatar of Job the beloved of a sadistic God," Reinhart can never shake the suspicion that he does not fit anywhere, but is nonetheless responsible for the general muddle that surrounds and usually engulfs him. An emotional liberal, Reinhart nevertheless believes in the "fundamental immorality of sympathy." A key symptom of his time in the psycho ward at the end of *Crazy in Berlin* is his conviction—which recurs throughout his life—that "his purpose on earth was to rectify life's dirty deals." While he recognizes the folly in this view, his generosity of spirit inevitably betrays him: whether voiced or implied, whether by friend or by enemy, "Don't let me down" is the one bugle call Reinhart can never resist—at least in the books before *Reinhart's Women.*

Yet Reinhart is as ill suited for despair as he is for success. Although reminded by a successful acquaintance that he is "redundant in the logistics of life," he can never really be disillusioned, even though his dreams steadily fall prey to the practical opportunism of those around him. No match for a mother who can tell him, "if I ever thought you had track with Filth, I'd slip you strychnine" (RIL, 114), or a shrewish wife who advises him, "if you're going to be an ass-kisser, then you ought to at least kiss the asses of winners" (RW, 245), Reinhart can still recognize the distinction between his secular search for a Holy Grail and the social meliorism that passes for idealism. He vaguely realizes that he is trapped between the Scylla and Charybdis of belief, but like all Berger's characters, Reinhart never gives up: an indomitable toughness underlies his numerous weaknesses, and whatever the situation, he always muddles through, scarred but undaunted.

Reinhart's Importance in the Berger Canon

Reinhart is the key to most of Berger's characters, whether or not he shares their situation or outlook, and in the Reinhart books can be found many, if not most, of the concerns and techniques that shape Berger's fiction. This notwithstanding the fact that in some important ways these books are not at all like Berger's others. It is particularly important to begin the consideration of the Reinhart books with the reminder that Berger's concern is rarely with society (other than as a necessary proving ground for individualism), because among the author's twenty-three novels, these four seem on their surfaces most like conventional, sociologically centered investigations of society and ideology. Berger acknowledges the singular features of these novels: "The Reinhart books don't really fit into the 'celebratory' sequence: they are as near as I can come to the standard novel-as-slice-of-life. I do one now and again to keep in touch with reality, for my connections to society get ever feebler" (7 December 1979).

The temptation to overstate Berger's connections to Reinhart is understandable, as character and author do have in common some biographical features, including birthdate (1924), birthplace (Ohio), ethnic background (German-American), and army service (with the first occupation troops in Berlin). "Berger, like Reinhart," Gerald Weales has observed, "is concerned with the dangerous uncertainty of human relationships, familial, sexual, collegial, with the problem of identity, with the slipperiness of truth, with the inefficacy of language, with the authoritarianism of self-righteous idealism, with aging and death."[14] Weales only notes the above correspondences in the service of his more important argument that "whatever autobiographical elements, statistical and spiritual, go into the Reinhart novels, the creator and the created are not one," a conclusion obvious to readers who are familiar with Berger's non-Reinhart novels.[15]

Weales's "Reinhart as Hero and Clown" is one of the most useful essays ever written about Berger's fiction, and it offers the definitive understanding of the Reinhart series. "Reinhart has a way of voicing, silently for the most part, prejudices that we pretend to have put behind us," Weales observes, adding, "and of performing with an ineptitude to which we are clearly superior—on our good days."[16] Reinhart is unshackled by the protocols of self-interest and political correctness that keep most humans from being totally honest with themselves, much less with the world around them. At the same time, however, Reinhart is essentially decent and fair minded, so he recognizes his prejudices when they pop out, regrets any thoughts, much less acts, of swinishness, and is both well read enough and philosophical enough to recognize any and all of his moral lapses. As Weales notes, "The strength of the Reinhart books is that the reader keeps recognizing his similarities to the good fool, the horse's ass, when he would prefer to identify with the poet-philosopher hero that Reinhart spends so many years imagining hidden within his untidy mind and body."[17]

Because he suffers from what might be thought of as a kind of moral Tourette's syndrome that dooms him to privilege motive over consequence, resulting in actions whose results are seldom what he intends, Reinhart is admirable more for his embarrassing disasters than for his successes and good deeds. And it is precisely in the admiration and relief elicited by Reinhart's foibles that he prepares readers for better understanding the appeal of so many of Berger's other characters, all of whom, despite their obvious flaws, are accorded the dignity of telling observations and thought-provoking propositions about the human condition.

Part of Reinhart's appeal rises from the narrator Berger crafts to filter his thoughts, texturing or complicating everything readers learn about Reinhart's world. Berger has offered his own take on this filtering process, explaining that a character such as Reinhart remains a prisoner of his own limited point of view, but that point of view is interpreted by a narrator who may express "what a character would say if he were more articulate" (23 February 2007). This is Berger's approach to *style indirect libre*—or free indirect discourse—which he describes as if "producing a paraphrase of what the character has told me, a more eloquent version than he or she has related to me (because I am a professional writer, and the character is not) but not corrupted by my own knowledge, tastes, or opinions" (18 May 2007).

What is unusual in Berger's use of free indirect discourse is that his narrator/editor almost always abrades what we might call the "upgraded thinking" of his protagonists against the equally upgraded thinking of their antagonists. Accordingly

Berger consistently presents the thinking of all his characters in the most reasonable and persuasive version possible, no matter how faulty or even despicable it may be. What results is the prose equivalent of a demolition derby in which not only codified ideologies and polemics but also private and often idiosyncratic prejudices, compensatory fantasies, and utopian wishes relentlessly crash into one another. In the worlds of Berger's novels all propositions soon collide with qualifying or refuting views—and this is particularly true of the Reinhart books.

The narrative mechanics initially established in the Reinhart books shape narration in Berger's subsequent novels, one of many ways in which the Reinhart books help readers understand Berger's fiction. Similarly most, if not all, of Berger's protagonists share Reinhart's essential amiability, his preoccupation with "normality," and his bedrock belief that Nature presents some truths that can't be undone by language. Of course, warring with Reinhart's determination to recognize "the real" is his suspicion that fantasy may offer the best, if not the only, path to reality, as he constructs and interprets most social situations not against the backdrop of Nature but against the artificial worlds of the movies, radio, and the funny papers. And the map of language consistently distracts from the territory of his actual experience. He is, in short, Berger's apotheosis of the human condition.

He is not, however, Berger's avatar or alter ego. In 1987 the *New York Times Book Review* asked a number of authors, including Berger, "Which of the characters you have created has had the greatest effect on your own life?" Berger's response was:

> I began the writing of my first novel with the assumption that its principal character should be myself under a pseudonym, and for years (*Crazy in Berlin* took four) I tried to fashion a marionette in my own image. But I got no farther

> than the first page until I came to understand that fiction must never be confused with that existence through which I make my daily slog—that what I required by way of a hero was almost anybody but myself. At that point a character named Reinhart appropriated the role: a better man than I, generous where I am mean, kinder, braver, not even afraid to be taken for a fool—unlike me, in my novelist's cap and bells! I have been a voyeur of this essential fellow through three subsequent narratives. Whatever I am, Reinhart has the peculiar ability to dramatize what I am *not.* Perhaps I shall finally have the wit to recognize that I am more his creation than he has ever been mine.[18]

In part because they do seem in some ways to constitute a sociological epic of a familiar sort, in part because they seem on their surface to reveal autobiographical connections, and in part simply because Reinhart is one of the most compellingly drawn characters in American fiction, this series has—along with *Little Big Man*—received the most intense critical scrutiny of Berger's novels. Speaking in 1986 with Steve Paul of the *Kansas City Star,* Berger noted the saving aspect of Reinhart's otherwise off-putting (to Berger) contemporaneity: "I've kept up with him. I always know what he's doing at any given time. When I write about Reinhart, it's when I'm looking for something to write about. If I try some other things and don't seem to be getting anywhere, I can always go back to Reinhart, because he's someone I know. He's my buddy."[19]

Crazy in Berlin

Not too much can be claimed of the first sentence of a first novel, but the opening sentence of *Crazy in Berlin,* now some fifty years past its birth, suggests several important constants in the Reinhart series, as well as the syntactic precision that is ever the goal of Berger's prose: "In the twilight, the bust appeared to be of some cocked-hat Revolutionary War Hero of not the very first rank, that is, not G. Washington but perhaps one of those excellent Europeans noted in fact and apocrypha for throwing their weight on our side, Lafayette, say, or von Steuben" (3). This particular perception, as is true of most of Reinhart's, is controlled by the verb *appeared,* and in Berger's novels appearance and reality seldom coincide. This is particularly true of the Reinhart books, but with the peculiar twist that in these novels appearance usually *appears fake,* revealing patently self-serving, mendacious underpinnings—only to be so recontextualized by fate as to finally emerge as more or less true: the tidy distinction implied above between "fact and apocrypha" usually breaks down in Reinhart's experience—as it does in our reading of his exploits. Reinhart's black friend, Splendor Mainwaring, specifies this principle in *Reinhart in Love* when he chides, "The truth of life is that things are exactly as they appear, and symbols are the bunk."

Characteristically qualified with absurd precision (a "Revolutionary War Hero of not the very first rank . . . one of those excellent Europeans noted in fact and apocrypha"), the initial sentence of *Crazy in Berlin* also reveals Reinhart's irrepressible tendency to digress either upward or downward on the ladder of abstraction, ever spinning the concreteness of his experience into something larger or smaller—a manic predilection for theorizing his life. Concept spinning always engages Reinhart's imagination, and in each novel he leaves behind a wake of propositions—all credible, some persuasive, most self-deprecating—as he negotiates the shallows and depths of his life. That Reinhart, standing in the rubble of postwar Berlin, would describe a statue there in terms of the American Revolutionary War reveals the stubborn provincialism of even his remarkably enlightened outlook, while subsequent qualifications reveal his characteristic attempt to work through the limitations of that vision.

It is also characteristic that Reinhart has this perception while urinating on the statue, as it turns out, of Friedrich der Grosse—a discovery that inexorably leads Reinhart to observe that his action "was a gross thing to do . . . because he was just educated enough to recall vaguely old Frederick out at *Sans Souci* with Voltaire, writing in French, representing the best, or the worst, of one tradition or the other." As it also turns out, Friedrich will be only the first in a series of "statues," the rest in flesh and blood, that Reinhart will encounter in Berlin; each of these characters also represents the best or the worst (often at once) of "one tradition or the other"—Nazism, nihilism, Judaism, Americanism, communism—as well as the more fundamental concepts of friendship, victimization, and survival.

The relation of *Crazy in Berlin* to the canon of postwar American novels is much like Reinhart's relation to Friedrich's statue: irreverent but mindful of the mythologies. In the first place, almost alone among protagonists in postwar American novels, Reinhart *genuinely likes* the army, finding in it both security and sensibility, his rationale encapsulated by Berger in one gloriously extended sentence:

> A society grounded on common inconvenience, where friendship was innocent of opportunism and tolerance flourished without manifesto: no crime could outlaw youth from this company; no merit beyond the grossest went recognized; where sensitivity was soon reduced to coarseness

> and ambition stifled; where lethargy was rewarded and disenchantment celebrated; this cul-de-sac off the superhighway to the glorious Houyhnhnm of the future where a chicken would stew in every pot and each man be his own poet, unarmed, owing allegiance to one world—this splendid, dear, degrading society, here as nowhere else Reinhart felt at home and loved. (CIB, 304)

More important, however, Reinhart's German-American heritage leads him to investigate recent history from a perspective quite unlike that explored in the much better codified tradition of Jewish-American fiction. At once fearful of some genetic flaw capable of giving birth to Nazi atrocities and German complacence and resentful of the inexorable appropriation of moral high ground, at terrible cost, by Jewish victims of German nihilism, Reinhart struggles to understand and to individualize the universality of moral chaos.

One sure sign of Reinhart's complicated thought appears in his ability to detest Nazism while acknowledging some of its perverse appeal to the individual:

> In almost every way but the accepted idea of common decency, he felt himself at odds with the world, a kind of Nazi without swastika, without revolver and gas ovens, without the specific enemies—indeed, it was a crazy feeling, an apparently motiveless identification, for although it did not include the trappings, it did comprehend the evil, as when you awoke from a nightmare of murder and for hours afterward despite the evidence of daylight and routine believed yourself an assassin; and worst of all, coexistent with the guilt, the memory of a terribly depraved yet almost romantic pride: *once, anyway, you were not a victim.* (68)

What particularly haunts him is the realization that Nazism was a human rather than a German phenomenon and that he himself is subject to "that passion to destroy simply because it could be got away with, because one had been trained all his life to respect and abide by the constraints and then found in a crisis that they held no water" (67). This determination to get beneath the easy surface rationales of ideology is a constant in Berger's writing.

Perceptive enough to sense that in Berlin's devastation "all the crap has been blasted away, leaving something honest," Reinhart must reconcile humanistic commonplaces with the sometimes more complicated propositions of his own experience, among them his intuitive grasp of the necessary reciprocity of victims and victimizers. Derided by a blind Jewish doctor for his liberal belief that "there is wisdom in a wound," Reinhart nevertheless wishes that he himself "had a grievance," since "being without one in the modern word was disabling." But he acknowledges the complicated countervailing principle that "people use us as we ask them to: this is life's fundamental, and often the only, justice" (310). As a result, his view of conflicting ideologies often evolves from questions of right and wrong to more profound questions about the differences between reality and its masks. Harvey Swados praised the uniqueness of this enterprise in a 1958 *New Leader* review. "This is not however the traditional liberal American novel in which the well-intentioned writer sighs over the pity of it all and invites us as readers to sigh with him while he hates the Nazi as his enemy and loves the Jew as his brother. That we can do for ourselves. What Berger has done instead is to commence where liberalism ends, in the world of ideas."[20]

A blond, heavily muscled, twenty-one-year-old U.S. Army medic corporal in Allied-occupied Berlin, Reinhart has cornered the market on guilt. He complains to Nathan Schild, a Jewish intelligence officer: "I'm sick of being made to feel a swine because I'm of German descent. I'm sick of being in the privileged class that nothing ever happens to. I'm tired of being big and healthy, but I can't help it, I was born that way. If you would be a prisoner in any concentration camp ever made, I would be a guard. Now, you know everything—but do you know that? How that makes a person feel? Do you know what it is to be in debt to everybody?" (365). Schild evokes Reinhart's contradictory attitudes toward Jews, as a string of other acquaintances forces him to confront a range of ideologies associated with politics, philosophy, gender, and nationality.

Among the grotesques Reinhart meets are Bach, a giant invalid who strenuously advances the case for subtle anti-Semitism, arguing that overt persecution has just made the Jew stronger, even as it is revealed that for four years he hid his Jewish wife from the Nazis; Dr. Otto Knebel, a former communist tortured in a Russian concentration camp and now a fascist; Schatzi, an early S.A. activist betrayed by Hitler, imprisoned for four years in Auschwitz as a gentile criminal, and now a cynical Russian agent; and Lichenko, a deserter from the Russian army and enthusiastic would-be capitalist given temporary refuge by Schild, who is himself an idealistic communist and a traitor. Above all else, these characters are *survivors,* although the diversity of their lives and outlooks can only confound Reinhart's simple humanism. Finally Reinhart's *amour propre* requires that he juggle his love and sex lives (the two never quite at one) among three quite different women: a whorish sixteen-year-old German girl; her older, sadder, wiser (and to Reinhart infinitely more desirable) married Jewish cousin; and a robust American nurse.

Although Reinhart gradually emerges from the novel as Berger's narrative focus—much as he leaves Berlin as the sole true survivor among its major characters—point of view in *Crazy in Berlin* is switched among Reinhart, Schild, Schatzi, and Lichenko. The interactions of these characters structure a number of complicated dialectics, both for Reinhart and for Berger's readers. More important, as Gerald Weales has explained, this narrative scheme filters all ideological propositions through multiple possible interpretations, filtering abstract ideas and ideology through the very concrete human weaknesses of individual characters.[21]

Beneath the clashes of ideology that occasion much of the dialogue in *Crazy in Berlin,* Reinhart's enduring quest is for freedom, a definition of self free from the expectations and opprobrium of others. His visual model for this dream is the knight in Dürer's etching *Ritter, Tod, und Teufel,* and this picture, obviously important to Berger, will later provide a visual paradigm for some of his description in *Neighbors.* Admiring the knight because he is serving "his time in the gully of death and the devil" and must do so completely alone, Reinhart tells Schild: "If you glance quickly at the picture you won't see anything but the Knight . . . but most of all that wonderful tough face, sure of itself, looking not at the airy castle or horseshit Death or the mangy Devil, because they'll all three get him soon enough, but he doesn't care. He is complete in himself—isn't that what integrity means—and he is proud of it, because he is smiling a little" (360).

In Ihab Hassan's words, more "clowning knight errant" than knight, Reinhart can never live up to his model, but he comes close when he risks his own life in an unsuccessful attempt to save Schild—who has refused further collaboration—from being abducted by two communist agents. Reinhart, who has unsuccessfully matched wits and will with opponents throughout the novel, now matches bare-handed strength against a giant assailant and wins, killing him, but not before Schild is murdered by the other attacker or before Reinhart suffers a serious wound, inevitably to his head. The exterior wound heals, but Reinhart's guilt over his true motives for helping Schild, to his thinking actually a form of betrayal, drives him to the psycho ward—where characteristically he begins to consider the advantages of becoming a psychiatrist. "Like knighthood, this profession gave you a permanent upper hand; like the priesthood, it made everybody else feel guilty and also grateful; like the Jews it was much reviled yet indispensable and always right" (422). Gradually freeing himself, not from guilt, but from its debilitating effects, Reinhart recovers enough to get shipped home, his recovery certified by a final betrayal, this time perfectly justified, of the cynical Schatzi, who has managed to sneak onto Reinhart's evacuation flight.

Reinhart in Love

The literal situation of *Crazy in Berlin* provides the figurative atmosphere for the next two Reinhart books, as Berger makes of his great protagonist a kind of permanent-occupation soldier of the soul, someone always stationed in foreign territory. Regardless of place or time, and no matter how outrageous the particulars of his situation, Reinhart remains the eternal outsider, denied both the moral satisfaction of the victor and the clear abasement of the vanquished. In love, commerce, and culture, Reinhart always manages to be in the wrong place at the wrong time, his wondering nature a kind of magnet for the impositions of others.

Reinhart is greeted upon his return from the army by an endearingly meek and unassuming father, whose greatest joy seems to come from reciting advertising labels and basking in the glories of postwar commodification, and by a mother (Maw) who hails his arrival by snarling, "Here come six more shirts per week." Reinhart's initial problems lie in coming to terms with his parents, since he seems more displaced at home than he was in the grotesquery of Berlin. Dad dispenses great advice for consuming, but none for living, and Reinhart struggles to reconcile his own romantic concerns, indicated by words such as "*paladin, epic, paramour, gourmet, wastrel, mistress, cognac, intrepid, leather, bronze, crimson, alabaster, lance, battle-ax*" with the dreary terms he associates with his dad: "*commerce, economics, exchange, real property, securities, stocks, bonds, finance, annuities, comptrollers, town planning boards, auditors, accountants, ledgers*" (112). Reinhart senses that "those two vocabularies are not entirely incompatible," but they represent in his own life alternating sirens, one vocabulary ever luring him back just as he most desires to embrace the other.

Maw's hostility toward everything reaches epic proportions and seems calculated to preclude all Reinhart's interests. Warning her son to avoid "truck with Filth" or she will slip him strychnine, her definition of *Filth* taking in most aspects of modern life, Maw zeroes in on sex, which will indeed also prove to be a problem for Reinhart. Her concern: "Why, Smut. All the dirty, miserable, horrible things that bachelors in boarding houses think about; what goes on among the niggers in back alleys in the dead of night; what makes cats do that terrible evil whining in the wee hours and dogs run in packs with their tongues hanging out so disgusting; what ruined Gladys Welch. People touching one another in secret ways" (114).

Reinhart in Love (1962) moves Reinhart from the rubble of Berlin to the bustle of postwar American business, from an economy of scarcity—whether of material goods or of spirit—to an economy of excess, from the nightmares of the German past to the absurdities of the American dream. Discharged from the army, in which he had been happy, Reinhart returns to civilian life, which he finds singularly disastrous. His comic misadventures are guided by Claude Humbold, a wonderfully opportunistic real estate agent and con man for whom Reinhart reluctantly works; by the enterprising and calculating Genevieve Raven, whom he is tricked into marrying; and by Splendor Mainwaring, his talented but erratic black friend, who has a special talent for getting Reinhart into impossible situations. Reinhart "was still twenty-one and had never had another profession; he feared America, people, and life—not really but poetically, which was worse" (4). Reinhart's fears are real, his anguish serious, but his experiences in this novel are clearly comic, and *Reinhart in Love* is the only one of his books Berger terms a comedy (16 October 1981).

While this second Reinhart book chronicles its protagonist's hapless courtship and marriage, its title applies more broadly to the debilitating fact that *"Reinhart was in love with everything"* (112). In a drunken moment he grandly declares that his purpose is "not to bury life, but to recognize it," and he instructs that this may be accomplished if one is careful to "do no harm and always uphold the dignity of human life" (133). Unfortunately the arrangement rarely seems reciprocal. People, ideas, culture, even banality intoxicate Reinhart with an openness to experience that soon proves ruinous: civilian life buries him just as surely as do the medical commodities that tumble from his father's fantastically stuffed medicine chest. Awed in Berlin by historic rubble, Reinhart is stunned at home by the excess of commodities and the pervasiveness of economic hype.

The grotesque philosopher-teachers, all gravely crippled in some respect, who so largely determined Reinhart's experience in Berlin, have been supplanted in this novel by a gloriously crooked realtor, Claude Humbold, who instructs Reinhart in the wonders of business. "This is bidness," Claude impatiently explains, "not them silly games like plugging Fachists, or Commonists, whatever them Heinies was at the time" (151). As well versed in the rhetoric of success as in the practice of chicanery, Claude gives Reinhart advice strikingly at odds with the old-world cynicism of his former Berlin mentors. "Always keep a positive face towards life, bud. When you're losing money, up your buying. If you get beat up once, start a fight with a bigger fella. That's the way of Jesus Christ, bud, who got out and walked on the water when his boat leaked. Nothing stopped that tough little guy, because his sainted mother was behind him all the way" (156).

What distinguishes Claude in Reinhart's experience is that he is both a survivor and a success, even when things don't seem to be going his way. Bolstered by an outrageously self-serving philosophy that casts God as "the greatest bidnessman of them all," Claude can explain away any setback and defend any action, and he ultimately involves Reinhart in a patently fraudulent scheme hatched by Claude and crooked politicians to get a city contract for sewers that will never be built.

Reinhart and Splendor end up as officers of the phony sewer construction company, affording Reinhart an oblique opportunity to consider what it means to be an American Negro in somewhat the same way that in *Crazy in Berlin* he considered what it means to be a Jew. Finally realizing that in his unpredictable expansiveness and frequent personal disasters—resulting from a persistent refusal to do as expected—Splendor has become another teacher, Reinhart sees in Splendor's freedom from limitations a new gauge of his own failure. "My friend," Reinhart wryly concludes, "you have out-Reinharted Reinhart—you are all I ever wanted to be, and twice as vivid" (392). When Reinhart and Splendor decide to force the actual construction of the sewer, an amok power shovel destroys much of the black neighborhood they were attempting to serve. This seeming disaster, however, perfectly serves the interests of yet another of Claude's crooked schemes, and Reinhart's momentary moral bravery ironically plunges him more deeply into Claude's enthusiastic chicanery.

Vital Parts

"Timing is your trouble, Carl," specifies one of Reinhart's old classmates, now as obviously a success in life as the now forty-four-year-old Reinhart is a failure. The acquaintance, Bob Sweet, an updated and hip version of Claude Humbold, is right, of course, but the strong evidence of the first three Reinhart books suggests that as much could be said of time itself—that Reinhart's struggle is always with time as well as, or more than, just timing. "Reinhart is, in a very real sense," Berger has ventured, "always up to the minute (whether or not the world is): indeed, trying to be so seems his difficulty" (17 May 1977).

Its narrative strongly bound to the specific time of 1945, *Crazy in Berlin* surveyed a momentous historical period as it filtered through Reinhart's consciousness. Set only a year later, *Reinhart in Love* concerned itself less with the historical moment of postwar America than with the crucial private time of Reinhart's life as he struggled through his initiation into marriage and commerce. *Vital Parts* (1970) intensifies and combines both kinds of temporal focus—public and private, exploring Reinhart's middle-aged reactions to the cultural turmoil of the late sixties. Here Reinhart's problems with his fashionably rebellious son, Blaine, and Reinhart's affair with a young girl focus the background concerns of the years in which time itself seemed the crux of cultural turmoil: the late 1960s. Moreover, Reinhart, clearly time's victim, finds himself involved in yet another wild scheme, one to cheat death through cryonics. For Reinhart, one of the great appeals of a plan for freezing the dead for possible reanimation in the future is that it would "eliminate the dimension of Time, by which most social situations are measured" (124).

Measured by time, the Reinhart of *Vital Parts* has hit bottom. His body an overweight wreck, his marriage a disaster, his various commercial enterprises all failed, hated by a surly son and adored by a helplessly naive daughter, Reinhart derives his only satisfaction now from self-pity. "You are only beaten if you think so," exhorts Reinhart to himself, only to reach the appalling conclusion, "But I think so." Ticking off his diminished prospects, this eternal optimist now manages a bleak inventory. "I am just a guy who regardless of what he thought at twenty knows at forty-four only that he will die" (43). Resentment, long an adversary Reinhart managed to keep under control, now seems his primary emotion as he complains:

> Somehow I have always missed the advantage, and this has probably warped me with jealousy. Ever since I was born I have had to listen incessantly to someone else's propaganda, and not only an account of their superiorities, but, what is worse, their pains, for which they have always contrived to make me responsible. As a youth I was a pleasure-loving

> punk, as an adult I am a bully, as a white man a former slaveholder, as a member of the middle class an all-purpose exploiter. When in good shape I was thought to be stupid and insensitive, and now as overweight and with short breath, I am considered ugly and moribund. (79)

One reason Reinhart does always seem to miss the advantage is his one-directional philosophical bent, which can rationalize any outrage, imposition, or unfairness of which he is the victim, while forgiving no embarrassment or blunder that he commits. For example, confronted by his sneering, slogan-spouting son, the emblem of all Reinhart abhors in his society, he calmly realizes:

> Blaine played a ruthless game. He was a pacifist when asked to go to war, an advocate of violent demonstrations for Negroes and college students, a believer in free love for anyone under thirty and repression for those older: he had contempt for money and those who earned it but demanded to be given as much as he needed; he dressed and comported himself flagrantly so as to attract attention, yet getting it he derided and/or denounced his audience.
>
> He was, in short, altogether human and absolutely normal. There was no mistaking his commitment to injustice, to incessant provocation, to maximum publicity, illogic, malice, attachment to his own crowd and frightened hatred of any other, his solipsism, his nightmares, his sadism, or his relationship to his father. You wouldn't find him tormenting a stranger. He loved his old dad. (62)

Although he senses the ironies and injustices in an age when "a man could be termed a crypto-Nazi merely for shaving off his sideburns, a genocide because he deplores a mob, and a bully for questioning the credentials of folksinger-statesmen," Reinhart no longer has the spirit to resist.

Assaulted by the superficial rhetoric of television hip talk, the psychobabble of an obviously twisted pop psychiatrist, and by the patent contradictions of his son's revolutionary sloganeering, Reinhart sadly concludes that his is "no civilization in which to live the life of the mind," even as all other lives seem closed to him. "Human beings are vile," is his best advice to a young girl with whom he has an unsatisfying affair, qualifying this dark philosophy only with the specification that "like any other general rule it has as many exceptions as applications" (179).

But Reinhart in despair is still Reinhart. After volunteering to be the first living human to be frozen for Sweet's cryonics foundation, and deciding to spend his last days using foundation money to buy into fantasies of success and power, he begins to feel the relief of "gradually jettisoning the ballast of moral judgment. " Just as surely as he believes people are vile, he also realizes they are all that interest him, concluding, "Vile they might well be, but it happens that vileness is fascinating—to a degree, of course." And when Winona, his fat, hopelessly innocent daughter, reveals to him just how much she needs his protection, he determines to live and to have her live with him.

Reinhart's Women

In *Reinhart's Women* (1981*)* the now fifty-four-year-old Reinhart finally discovers something he can do well: cooking. The novel finds Reinhart ten years after his divorce from Genevieve, living with and supported by his daughter, Winona, now a beautiful and successful fashion model. His son, Blaine, last seen as a surly radical in *Vital Parts,* now is a surly, snobbish, and successful stockbroker, unchanged in his disdain for his father. Having finally admitted that he is hopeless as a businessman, Reinhart has withdrawn from the world and contents himself with managing his daughter's household and with cooking "in a spirit of scientific inquiry."

Actually cooking has become for him both an aesthetic and a philosophy, and for the first time in his life "he did not feel as if he were either charlatan or buffoon." "Food," Reinhart notes, "is really kinder than people" (57). The sense of freedom so long denied him now seems in reach as Reinhart defines himself—even as a cook—in his own terms. Ever generous, he tries to share this discovery with his mean-spirited son, now hobbled by self-image worries much like those that plagued the Reinhart of old: "But the funny thing is that, without benefit of a movement, I am liberated from all sorts of restraints, including those I have imposed on myself. It was ridiculous that I lived almost half a century trying to measure up to the principles of other people" (46).

Still an inveterate concept spinner, Reinhart has finally seen that he "does better by looking at the eggs in hand rather than at the souffle to come." Now, however, his propositions seem more modest and more profound, perhaps shaped from the residues of his longstanding skirmishes with unsatisfactory moral codes. A newfound ability to suspend judgment now characterizes his manner, since he has learned "that a good many claims in life are never put to the test, and from those that are, often enough, truth still does not issue, and finally in the rare event that it does, even rarer is to find the mortal to whom it matters" (223).

Confronted with plans for a suspiciously idealistic commune led by the ex-black-militant son of his old friend Splendor

Mainwaring and financed in part by his own venal son Blaine, Reinhart makes no real effort to decide whether the project is fraudulent or sincere, reflecting instead that "most enterprises since the Renaissance have necessarily partaken of both the honest and the bogus in equal amounts to preserve the balance known as modern civilization" (53).

Even more global is his advice to his daughter, Winona, advice starkly contrasting with his bitter "humans are vile" sentiments offered another young girl in *Vital Parts*. Now Reinhart focuses on the processes of life rather than judging the outcomes of those processes: "Every living thing already knows everything it needs to know: how to succeed, how to fail, how to survive, and how to perish. Sometimes we pretend we don't know, but we know all right. The older I get, the more I realize that nothing is a genuine surprise" (62).

Reinhart's new, quiet confidence stems from his finding in cooking the concrete metaphor around which to organize his philosophy. Calmly acknowledging that "the human animal, from pup to patriarch, was such a bizarre creature" and that "human relations remained a good deal less explicable than anything in atomic physics," Reinhart has forged his profound equanimity from one certain starting point: "Of all the activities of human beings, there is one thing that they alone, in all the world, do, and that is: cook the food they eat" (261). Praised for this observation by a television executive who bubbles, "Carlo, you're a philosopher," Reinhart replies, "Naw. . . . I'm better than that! I'm a cook" (262).

What Reinhart has discovered is that metaphors of nourishment, a concept indispensable for the spirit, have a physical origin, profound in its own right: "Food was a great positive, yea-saying force, the ultimate source of vitality—until a phase of the cycle was completed and oneself became food for the worms. It is only through food that we survive, and we die when we are fed on too heartily by microbes, or by the crab named cancer who eats us alive. In the emotional realm there is no more eloquent metaphor: lovers feed on one another, and passion is devouring. A philosopher lives on food for thought. One is what one eats, and eats what one is" (70). This most extended of the string of propositions spun out throughout the Reinhart series reveals that Reinhart has finally found a spot in his universe where language and concrete reality are not at odds.

Long completely at the mercy of unmerciful women, particularly his mother and his ex-wife, Reinhart can now even take in stride the news that his daughter is having a lesbian affair with a successful older businesswoman. Age has taught him that "the best defense against any moral outrage is patience: wait a moment and something will change: the outrage, he who committed it, or, most often, oneself." So long victimized by being out of step with his time, Reinhart has finally achieved the kind of understanding that is timeless.

Winona's lover (a female version of the con men who have always directed Reinhart's forays into business) contrives to lure him back into the world, first as a supermarket-product demonstrator, then as a guest "chef" for a spot appearance on a local television show, and the novel doses with the strong prospect of Reinhart's having his own show, "Chef Carlo Cooks." His apparent successes, however, are not confined to the kitchen, as Reinhart escapes the gentle and loving tyranny of his daughter, emerges unscathed from an encounter with his ex-wife, and begins a promising relationship with a young woman who seems in many ways a female version of himself—intelligent, considerate, awkward. In fact, Reinhart begins to gather around him a small band of kindred souls, hoping to buy and run a quaint small-town café. Once again the lure of business proves irresistible for Reinhart, and once again the prospect of disaster cannot be discounted, but this time the odds seem more in Reinhart's favor.

That Berger would write at least one more account of Reinhart's odyssey seemed a good bet, until fairly recently. When asked following the publication of *Reinhart's Women* whether Reinhart might appear again, Berger replied, "I won't know what becomes of him until he tells me, but I suspect that he'll be heard from again, probably when he could be said to be authentically an old man."[22] Now odds sadly seem to be against another book in the series. In August 2006 Berger acknowledged that work on a new Reinhart book was not taking off:

> As to a fifth installment of Reinhart's story, I have tried off and on to write one and have accumulated 40 or 50pp, but I inevitably lose energy after a session or two at the typewriter. In this account Reinhart has retired from his late-life career as TV chef and cookbook author, but is stimulated by the appearance of a guy who claims, perhaps fraudulently, to have been a wartime Army buddy of his but whom he cannot remember. However, this fellow has come to him with a project that has some appeal: compiling a dictionary of World War II service jargon, which Hollywood always gets egregiously wrong. As you might expect, I am fond of this language and have total recall of it. A pity I have not been able to sustain a working interest in the book, which has a great title: SINCE JESUS WAS A PFC,

> after the Army expression, which referred to how long it had been since something had happened, as in, "I haven't got any nookie since Jesus was a PFC!" (26 August 2006)

Reinhart may be Berger's greatest creation, a monument at once to the manic diversity of his twenty-three novels and to their underlying unity. Both the vitality and the vision of the Reinhart books offer ample evidence that Berger is one of America's most original and most gifted novelists: in Reinhart's singularity, Berger's readers find themselves.

Notes

Chapter 1—Understanding Thomas Berger

1. Richard Schickel, "Bitter Comedy," *Commentary,* July 1970, 80.

2. Almost all Berger's novels have seen several editions, and some, such as *Little Big Man,* have remained in print through the years, but "best-selling" status has eluded them. His best-selling novel on first publication was *The Return of Little Big Man,* at around twenty-five thousand copies, with *Arthur Rex* second at twenty thousand. Berger letter (21 June 2007). Quotations from Berger followed by a date in parentheses are from his letters to the author.

3. An abridged version of Lethem's introduction to the 2003 reprint of *Meeting Evil* was published as "Uncertainty Principle: Berger's Ambivalent Usurpations," *Village Voice Literary Supplement,* May 2003.

4. No complete bibliography of works about Berger exists. James Bense compiled a thorough bibliography through 1983: "Works by and about Thomas Berger," *Studies in American Humor* 2 (Fall 1983): 142–52. David W. Madden has compiled a valuable overview of critical response to Berger in his introduction to *Critical Essays on Thomas Berger* (New York: G. K. Hall, 1995), 1–25.

5. In 1992 Jon Wallace published *The Politics of Style: Language as Theme in the Fiction of Berger, McGuane, and McPherson.* For other critical responses, see Madden's introduction to *Critical Essays on Thomas Berger.*

6. David Streitfeld, "Berger's Story," *Washington Post Book World,* 16 September 1990, 15.

7. Quoted in Douglas Hughes, "Thomas Berger's Elan: An Interview," *Confrontation* no. 12 (Summer 1976): 24.

8. David W. Madden, "An Interview with Thomas Berger," in *Critical Essays on Thomas Berger,* 165.

9. Douglas Hughes, "Thomas Berger's Elan: An Interview," *Confrontation* 12 (Summer 1976): 24.

10. Andrew Ward, "Little Big Man's Man: An Interview," *American Heritage,* May/June 1999, 91. Available online at http://www.americanheritage.com/articles/magazine/ah/1999/3/1999_3_89.shtml (accessed 29 September 2008).

11. Referred to as "a brilliant paper" in Berger's 1951 *Intro* review, "Orwell as Essayist; Pound as Correspondent," this essay appears in Lionel Trilling, *The Liberal Imagination* (Garden City, N.Y.: Doubleday, 1950).

12. Berger details his career as a dramatist in "Trysting with Thalia," in Madden's *Critical Essays* (175–77), which also published *Other People: A Comedy in Two Acts* (179–249). Berger's *The Burglars: A Play in Two Acts* has been published in *New Letters* 55 (Fall 1988): 99–163.

13. Richard Schickel, "Interviewing Thomas Berger," *New York Times Book Review,* 6 April 1980, 22.

14. Berger remarked in a letter of 27 June 1976, "Remember that you will understand my work best when you are at your most selfish."

15. Hughes, "Elan," 27.

16. Schickel, "Interviewing Thomas Berger," 21.

17. Jonathan Lethem, "Berger's Ambivalent Usurpations," introduction to Thomas Berger's *Meeting Evil* (New York: Simon & Schuster, 2003), ix–x.

18. Mary Reefer, "The Substance of Style: An Interview with Thomas Berger," *New Letters* (Fall 1988): 93.

19. Lethem, introduction to *Meeting Evil,* x–xi.

20. Ibid., xviii.

21. Hughes, "Elan," 33.

22. Ibid.

23. Ibid., 31.

24. Ibid., 28.

25. Madden, "An Interview with Thomas Berger," 153.

26. Laurel Graeber, "The Sinister is His Hobby," *New York Times Book Review,* 12 July 1992, 7.

27. From a written interview with B. A. Nilsson, "Of Words and Letters," in *Metroland* (Albany, N.Y.), 28 February–6 March 1991, 16.

28. Michael Malone, "Berger, Burlesque, and the Yearning for Comedy," *Studies in American Humor* 2 (Spring 1983): 24. This essay is reprinted in Madden's *Critical Essays on Thomas Berger,* 92.

29. Lethem, introduction to *Meeting Evil,* xviii.

30. Madden, "An Interview with Thomas Berger," 157.

31. Ibid., 170.

32. Zulfikar Ghose, "Observations from a Correspondence: Letters from Thomas Berger," *Studies in American Humor* 2 (Spring 1983): 11–12.

33. Madden, "An Interview with Thomas Berger," 167.

34. Douglas Glover, "Caspar Milquetoast, These Are Your Lives," *New York Times Book Review,* 27 August 1989, 12.

35. Hughes, "Elan," 28.

36. Ghose, "Observations," 15.

37. Nietzsche, *Beyond Good and Evil,* 226.

38. Madden, "An Interview with Thomas Berger," 171.

39. Ibid., 157.

Chapter 2—Legendary Landscapes

1. Hughes, "Elan," 31–32.

2. For a more thorough discussion of *Little Big Man,* see chapter 3, "The Myths of the Old West," in Brooks Landon's *Thomas Berger* (Boston: G. K. Hall, 1989).

3. L. L. Lee, "American, Western, Picaresque: Thomas Berger's Little Big Man," *South Dakota Review* 4, no. 2 (1966): 35–42.

4. Fredrick W. Turner III, "The Second Decade of Little Big Man," *Nation,* 20–27 August 1977, 149.

5. Leo E. Oliva, "Thomas Berger's Little Big Man as History," *Western American Literature* (1973): 33–54. Jack's critiques of stories about the Old West include his observation that "when you run

into a story of more than three against one and one winning, then you have heard a lie" (293).

6. Henry Nash Smith, *Virgin Land: The American West as Symbol and Myth* (Cambridge: Harvard University Press, 1973), 90–111.

7. Thomas Berger, afterword to *The Pathfinder,* by James Fenimore Cooper (New York: New American Library, 1961), 435.

8. Smith, *Virgin Land,* 101.

9. Turner, "The Second Decade of Little Big Man," 150. Turner notes that Berger establishes in Jack's vision and voice "a position beyond sentimentality, beyond classic American liberalism."

10. Verlyn Klinkenborg, "Sidekick to History," *New York Times,* 9 May 1999. Online at The New York Times on the Web, http://www.nytimes.com/books/99/05/09/reviews/990509.09klinket.html (accessed 29 September 2008).

11. One can only imagine what readers made in 1967 of a publisher's blurb for Andrew Garcia's *Tough Trip through Paradise: 1878–1879.* This was purported to be a narrative of time spent among the Indians and with his Indian wives by "Squaw Kid" Andrew Garcia, recorded on "several thousand pages of legal-sized paper, both handwritten and typed" and found in 1948 by the editor, "stored in dynamite boxes, packed solid in the heavy waxed paper that powder comes in." Of course, the publisher's blurb described Garcia as "a real-life Little Big Man." Andrew Garcia, *Tough Trip through Paradise: 1878–1879,* ed. Bennett H. Stein (Boston: Houghton Mifflin, 1967).

12. "Native Americans in the Movies: A Bibliography of Materials in the UC Berkeley Library" identifies over three dozen books devoted to this subject, numerous chapters in books, over sixty journal articles, and several videorecordings of television shows and series devoted to analyzing film and television representations of American Indians. This bibliography can be found at http://www.lib.berkeley.edu/MRC/IndigenousBib.html (accessed 30 September 2008).

13. Allen Barra, *Inventing Wyatt Earp: His Life and Many Legends* (New York: Carroll & Graf, 1998).

14. Robert Rydell's *All the World's a Fair: Visions of Empire at American International Expositions, 1876–1916* (Chicago: University of Chicago Press, 1984) is the best introduction to the significance of the World's Columbian Exposition, and its view of the fair closely matches Berger's.

15. Andrew Ward, "Little Big Man's Man," *American Heritage* 50 (May/June 1999): 92. This interview is online at http://www.americanheritage.com/articles/magazine/ah/1999/3/1999_3_89.shtml (accessed 29 September 2008).

16. Ibid., 95.

17. For a more thorough discussion of *Arthur Rex,* see chapter 4, "The Matter of Britain," in Landon's *Thomas Berger* (Boston: G. K. Hall, 1989).

18. Malone, "Berger, Burlesque, and the Yearning for Comedy," 24.

19. Berger subsequently clarified this comment, explaining that in calling children "naturally vicious," he was calling them "not evil but human" (7 August 1987).

Chapter 3—The Midwestern Novels

1. D. Keith Mano, review of *Sneaky People,* "A Good Book by a Good Writer, Thomas Berger," *New York Times Book Review,* 20 April 1975, 4. Mano's review opens: "What you do, see, is go out and buy *Sneaky People.* Period. No questions asked."

2. Hughes, "Elan," 36–37.

3. Ibid.

4. Edwin McDowell, "Publishing: Pulitzer Controversies," *New York Times,* 11 May 1984, 26.

5. My understanding of the *Oresteia* has been guided by the translation and commentary of Richard Lattimore in his *Aeschylus Oresteia* (Chicago: University of Chicago Press, 1953) and by the translation and commentary of Alan Shapiro and Peter Burian in

their *Aeschylus The Oresteia* (Oxford: Oxford University Press, 2003).

6. O'Neill's play retains the three-part structure of the *Oresteia,* but almost completely ignores the concern with the public determination of guilt at the heart of Aeschylus's third play, *The Eumenides.*

7. In this respect, it is worth noting that *The Feud* is actually driven by the dictates of revenge in a manner much more reminiscent of the *Oresteia* than is *Orrie's Story.*

8. What is clear about Berger's telling of the *Oresteia* is that it will offer very different reading experiences depending on the reader's familiarity with earlier works. The reader who knows Aeschylus's three plays in the *Oresteia* will inevitably read Berger's novel in light of its faithfulness to and divergences from the original. The reader who knows *Mourning Becomes Electra* may be even more interested in seeing how Berger's Americanized reinvention of the story compares with O'Neill's. The reader who knows both Aeschylus and O'Neill will find even more to consider in *Orrie's Story.* And the reader who knows Berger's other novels will inevitably see some aspects of *Orrie's Story* in that context.

9. B. A. Nilsson, "Of Words and Letters," 16.

Chapter 4—Novels of Menace

1. Lethem, introduction to *Meeting Evil.*

2. Richard Schickel, "Interviewing Thomas Berger," 21.

3. Friedrich Nietzsche, *The Dawn,* sec. 113, cited by Walter Kaufmann, *Nietzsche: Philosopher, Psychologist, Antichrist* (New York: Meridian Books, 1965), 168.

4. Schickel, "Interviewing Thomas Berger," 21. In what seems even more specifically the tone of Berger's novel, Nietzsche states: "The striving for excellence is the striving to overwhelm one's neighbor. . . . The striving for excellence brings with it for the neighbor—to name only a few steps of this long ladder: tortures, then blows,

then terror, then anguished amazement, then wonder, then envy, then laughing, then ridicule, then derision, then scorn, then the dealings of blows, then the inflicting of tortures." A better abstract description of the action of *Neighbors* would be hard to find. (Berger does note, however, that he had not read this particular passage.)

5. The admirable qualities that generally work to the disadvantage of Berger's male characters do not seem as burdensome to his female characters, particularly Lydia, and later Molly, in *Suspects.*

6. David W. Madden, "An Interview with Thomas Berger," in Madden's *Critical Essays on Thomas Berger,* 169.

7. Berger, *The Burglars: A Play in Two Acts,* 99–163.

8. The burglars, Carl and Carol, seem to know their victims better than the victims know each other, but the converse also proves true as the victims, Faith and Adam, also have uncanny insight into the character and motives of and the relationship between the burglars. Faith not only decides she would rather be the burglar than the householder, but decides she would rather be with Carl, the original intruder, than with her husband, Adam, who, it turns out, is the kind of man, Carol, the second intruder, has been looking for. However, these new relationships quickly prove as unstable as the original ones, and Carl and Carol ultimately leave on the most amicable of terms, having ultimately assumed the roles of marriage counselors for Faith and Adam.

9. Berger has acknowledged as much. In an interview with Joanna Smith Rakoff, he noted that in writing *Best Friends* his "intention was to do something completely different," explaining that "he'd never before attempted a novel in which the main character significantly matures." Joanna Smith Rakoff, "Top Dog, Underdog," *Time Out New York,* 22–29 May 2003, 82. Berger also mentioned to Jonathan Lethem that *Best Friends* marked a breaking of new ground for him, feeling "like nothing he'd ever done before." Lethem, "Berger's Ambivalent Usurpations," xviii. When asked for further clarification of his remark to Lethem, Berger responded: "I

believe that what I meant in my comment to Lethem was that *Best Friends* is a love story, unique for me" (18 September 2007).

10. Berger readers will wonder at the date specified in this opening sentence, since most of his novels locate themselves in eras, but not in specific years. Berger explains that he so uncharacteristically set the action of *Best Friends* in 2000 because he was preparing the final manuscript for the novel just after 11 September 2001, and he "wanted to remove from the reader's mind any expectation that the characters might have a fateful appointment at the World Trade Center" (18 September 2007).

Chapter 5—Novels of Procedure and Protocol

1. Jon Wallace, "A Murderous Clarity: A Reading of Thomas Berger's *Killing Time*," in Madden's *Critical Essays on Thomas Berger*, 131.

2. Quentin Reynolds, *Courtroom* (New York: Farrar, Straus, 1950); Fredric Wertham, *The Show of Violence* (Garden City, N.Y.: Doubleday., 1949). Berger notes: "Wertham's book as I remember was of little use to me, though you may well find details in it that I used and do not recall. Reynolds's account on the other hand was exactly the journalistic kind of thing that provided me with what I needed for my fiction. Of course, when you pursue the matter of the associations between fact and fiction you must not fail to consider that what Reynolds writes is not necessarily 'fact.' The Irwin of *Courtroom* is an altogether different person from that of Wertham's book, in my judgment; and it should not astonish me to find that Detweiler is more like the patient in Dannemora than either. My Uffizi admonition to the reader was intended to suggest, in my usual convoluted manner, that fiction is not to be confused with life, because the latter is false" (27 June 1976).

3. Richard Bernstein, "Out of Kilter in a Predatory Society," *New York Times*, 13 September 1996, 33; online at http://query.nytimes.com/gst/fullpage.html?res=9903E3DD163AF930A2575AC0A960958260 accessed 30 September 2008).

4. Connie Fletcher, *What Cops Know: Cops Talk about What They Do, How They Do It, and What It Does to Them* (New York: Pocket Books, 1990).

Chapter 6—Subversions of Good Order

1. Zulfikar Ghose, review of *Adventures of the Artificial Woman, Review of Contemporary Fiction* 24 (Summer 2004): 134.

2. Hughes, "Elan," 36.

3. For example Richard Todd began his *Atlantic* review with the suspicion that "certain feminist simplicities seem to have gotten to Thomas Berger," and he felt that the book mercilessly spoofed "radical feminists by imitating and hyperbolizing their vision of society with reversed roles." Yet Lore Dickstein, reviewing the novel for *Ms.,* found nothing to offend "those of us serious about sexual politics." Claiming that to read the book solely as a comment on women's liberation or on male chauvinism was to underestimate Berger's "irresponsibility," Dickstein explained that "true to form, Berger spares no one," his "anarchic imagination exaggerating all sexual stereotypes into ludicrous postures, perhaps to show how they rob us of our freedom." Richard Todd, "God's First Mistakes," *Atlantic,* September 1973, 106–8. Lore Dickstein, review of *Regiment of Women,* by Thomas Berger, *Ms.,* August 1973, 33.

4. Leo Braudy, review of *Regiment of Women,* by Thomas Berger, *New York Times Book Review,* 13 May 1973.

5. Douglas Glover, "Caspar Milquetoast, These Are Your Lives," review of *Changing the Past, New York Times Book Review,* 27 August 1989, 12.

6. Patrick O'Donnell, "Short-Changed: Thomas Berger's *Changing the Past,*" in Madden's *Critical Essays on Thomas Berger,* 138–48. (Berger has, in a commemorative booklet privately printed in 1996 by Matthew J. Bruccoli, called *The Great Gatsby* "as nearly perfect as a novel can be, with not a word, not an emotion, not an idea in excess or lacking or misplaced or corrupted.")

7. Berger suggested this in a letter to the author, 19 February 1990.

8. Robert Louis Stevenson, "The Strange Case of Dr. Jekyll and Mr. Hyde," *The Strange Case of Dr. Jekyll and Mr. Hyde and Other Stories* (New York: Barnes & Noble Classics, 2003), 68.

9. Stevenson, "The Strange Case of Dr. Jekyll and Mr. Hyde," 69.

10. Both in interviews and in letters, Berger has made clear his exasperation on this point, at times sounding as if *Orrie's Story* was written almost as a dare to those who can only see him as a comic novelist. In a previously cited interview with B. A. Nilsson, Berger took pains to specify one intent in writing *Orrie's Story:* "I made an intentional effort to avoid anything that could be called comedy. I have never intended to be funny and have always disliked the label of 'comic novelist,' which has been applied to me by the humorless half-literates who read only to confirm received ideas. *Orrie's Story* goes out of its way to be grim" (16). Berger has even felt the need to stress this point to his publishers, as he did in a 19 July 1989 letter to Roger Donald, vice president and publisher at Little, Brown and Company: "I trust you noted that the approach is an altogether new one for me. No one can possibly see this as a comic novel, and I urge you, if you mention the work to anybody, to make that point. I must escape that designation to which I have been so inevitably condemned, with adverse consequences to my sales." And, in a 6 June 1990 letter to his agent, Don Congdon, Berger stated his case one more time: "What worries me, in addition, about the reception of *Orrie's Story* is the knee-jerk tendency on the part of New York professional readers (editors, reviewers, et al.) to assume that anything I write is satirical and thus another pretext for them to feel superior to the rest of the population. Seldom has this agreed with my intent. But to see anything amusing in *Orrie's Story* is either to be hopelessly demented or (the more likely case) deaf to anything but one's own internal monologue (as a result of the most malignant of urban diseases, moral solipsism)."

11. With specific reference to *Robert Crews,* Berger explains his narrative technique as a collaborative exercise: "I write from the character's point of view but in my own style . . . ; for me it's as if I am producing a paraphrase of what the character has told me, a more eloquent version than he or she has related to me (because I am a professional writer, and the character is not) but not corrupted by my own knowledge, tastes, or opinions" (18 May 2007).

12. In a brief interview with Laurel Graeber, "Loving the Losers," published in the *New York Times Book Review,* 6 March 1994, page 8, Berger declared himself a "lifelong fan of Robinson Crusoe," but noted that in his version "I gave Crews almost nothing to help him survive." In the original story, Berger observed: "Crusoe kept going back to the shipwreck, where he had practically a Home Depot at his disposal."

13. Jean-Jacques Rousseau, *Emile or On Education* (NuVision Publications, 2007), 158–59; online at http://www.nuvisionpublications.com/ebooksindex.hth (accessed 23 November 2008).

14. David Madden elaborates this point in his review of *Robert Crews* in *Review of Contemporary Fiction* 14 (Fall 1994): 221. "For Defoe the tale was a defense of bourgeois Protestantism, a celebration of mercantile Puritanism, and the central event in Crusoe's thirty-five year sojourn in the wilderness is his religious conversion. Crusoe sets about creating a moral replica of the world he left behind, a world whose lessons his industrious father tirelessly strived to teach him. Crews, however, has no religious conversion in the wilds and, in fact, fully realizes the moral bankruptcy of the world he has left behind."

15. Berger has mentioned another text as "one of the stimuli that evoked *Adventures of the Artificial Woman,*" Thomas Landolfi's "Gogol's Wife." Published in *Gogol's Wife and Other Stories,* trans. R. Rosenthal, J. Longgrigg, and W. Young (New York: New Directions, 1961). While the artificial woman in this delightfully odd story is more an inflatable doll than a robot, she develops autonomy

to move from being "Gogol's" slave to being his master, and, in desperation, he finally destroys her.

16. Zulfikar Ghose, review of *Adventures of the Artificial Woman, Review of Contemporary Fiction* 24 (Summer 2004): 134.

Chapter 7—The Reinhart Books

1. Diane Osen, "Interview with John Updike," National Book Foundation Archives, Author Study Guides, http://www.nationalbook.org/authorsguide_jupdike.html (accessed 30 September 2008).

2. R. V. Cassill, "Reinhart Back from Berlin, Out of Love and Ready for Freezing," *New York Times Book Review,* 29 March 1970, 27.

3. Jonathan Lethem, "Uncertainty Principle: Berger's Ambivalent Usurpations," *Village Voice Literary Supplement,* May 2003.

4. Richard Ohmann, "The Shaping of a Canon: U.S. Fiction, 1960–1975," in *Canons,* ed. Robert von Hallberg (Chicago: University of Chicago Press, 1984), 392–94.

5. Richard Schickel, "Bitter Comedy," *Commentary,* July 1970, 77.

6. Berger has mentioned his respect for several multivolume series, but doesn't see much, if anything, of them in the Reinhart books, noting, "Of Mr. Updike's works I have read only the first Rabbit," and adding, "The English-language series to which I am addicted, and have read in its entirety twice, is Anthony Powell's 12–vol *Dance to the Music of Time,* but two of the Reinharts were written before I read him" (1 September 2006).

7. Cassill, "Reinhart Back from Berlin," 4.

8. Harvey Swados, "An American in Berlin" (Review of *Crazy in Berlin*), in Madden's *Critical Essays on Thomas Berger,* 29.

9. Ibid., 29.

10. Ibid., 30.

11. Hughes, "Elan," 33.

12. Ihab Hassan, "Conscience and Incongruity: The Fiction of Thomas Berger," *Critique: Studies in Modern Fiction* 5 (1962): 4.

13. Douglas Hughes, "The Schlemiel as Humanist: Thomas Berger's Carlo Reinhart," *Cithara* 15, no. 1 (1975): 7. (Reprinted in Madden's *Critical Essays on Thomas Berger,* 45–60.)

14. Gerald Weales, "Reinhart as Hero and Clown," in Madden's *Critical Essays on Thomas Berger,* 76.

15. Ibid., 76–77.

16. Ibid., 77.

17. Ibid.

18. Thomas Berger, response in "Who Created Whom? Characters That Talk Back," *New York Times Book Review,* 31 May 1987, 36.

19. Steve Paul, "Thomas Berger Yields to Comic-Writer Image," *Kansas City Star,* 30 March 1986, 9J.

20. Harvey Swados, "An American in Berlin," *New Leader,* 15 December 1958, 24. (Reprinted in Madden's *Critical Essays on Thomas Berger.*)

21. Weales, "Reinhart as Hero and Clown," 78.

22. Jean Moore, "Author of Neighbors Says It's His Favorite," *Tampa Tribune,* 21 December 1981, 6D.

Bibliography

Works by Thomas Berger

Novels

(With the exception of *Robert Crews* and *Suspects,* all of Berger's novels have seen numerous reprints, both in the United States and in England, as mass market and trade paperbacks and even sometimes in hardback.)

Crazy in Berlin. New York: Scribners, 1958.

Reinhart in Love. New York: Scribners, 1962.

Little Big Man. New York: Dial Press, 1964. Reprint with introduction by Brooks Landon. New York: Dell, 1989.

Killing Time. New York: Dial Press, 1967.

Vital Parts. New York: Richard W. Baron, 1970.

Regiment of Women. New York: Simon & Schuster, 1973.

Sneaky People. New York: Simon & Schuster, 1975.

Who Is Teddy Villanova? New York: Delacorte Press / Seymour Lawrence, 1977.

Arthur Rex: A Legendary Novel. New York: Delacorte Press / Seymour Lawrence, 1978.

Neighbors. New York: Delacorte Press / Seymour Lawrence, 1980.

Reinhart's Women. New York: Delacorte Press / Seymour Lawrence, 1981.

The Feud. New York: Delacorte Press / Seymour Lawrence, 1983.

Nowhere. New York: Delacorte Press / Seymour Lawrence, 1985.

Being Invisible. Boston: Little, Brown, 1987.

The Houseguest. Boston: Little, Brown, 1988.

Changing the Past. Boston: Little, Brown, 1989.

Orrie's Story. Boston: Little, Brown, 1990.

Meeting Evil. Boston: Little, Brown, 1992. Reprint with introduction by Jonathan Lethem. New York: Simon & Schuster, 2003.

Robert Crews. New York: Morrow, 1994.
Suspects. New York: Morrow, 1996.
The Return of Little Big Man. Boston: Little, Brown, 1999.
Best Friends. New York: Simon & Schuster, 2003.
Adventures of the Artificial Woman. New York: Simon & Schuster, 2004.

Short Stories

Book

Granted Wishes: Three Stories. Northridge, Calif.: Lord John Press, 1984. Originally published in *Harper's,* October 1982, 52–59.

Uncollected Short Stories

"Child's Play." In *Which Grain Will Grow, Stories and Sketches of Childhood,* edited by Don M. Wolfe, 103–6. New York: New School for Social Research, Cambridge Publishing, 1950.
"Dependency of Day and Night." *Western Review* 16 (Spring 1952): 209–18.
"Professor Hyde." *Playboy,* December 1961, 88, 93, 140, 143–46.
"A Monkey of His Own." *Saturday Evening Post,* 22 May 1965, 66–67.
"Fatuous Fables." *Penthouse,* March 1973, 74, 124–25.
"Envy." *Oui* (Chicago), April 1975, 40–42, 100, 106–8.
"The Achievement of Dr. Poon." In *American Review 25,* edited by Theodore Solotaroff, 224–43. New York: Bantam, 1976.
"Tales of the Animal Crime Squad." *Playboy,* December 1980, 200–201, 216, 325–40.
"The Methuselah Factor." *Gentlemen's Quarterly,* September 1984, 266–67, 270–71, 274, 276, 278.
"Planet of the Losers." *Playboy,* November 1988, 126–27, 152, 154–56, 158–60.
"Gibberish." *Playboy,* December 1990, 140–42, 154, 218–20.
"Personal Power." *Playboy,* December 1992, 130–32, 178, 232–34, 236.

Plays

The Burglars: A Play in Two Acts. New Letters 55 (Fall 1988): 99–163.

Other People: A Comedy in Two Acts. In *Critical Essays on Thomas Berger,* edited by David W. Madden, 178–249. New York: Simon & Schuster, 1995. Also in this volume is Berger's "Trysting with Thalia," a brief account of his career as a playwright.

Uncollected Essays and Articles

Afterword to *The Pathfinder,* by James Fenimore Cooper, 429–38. New York: New American Library, 1961.

"The Family that Plays Together." *Show,* June 1962, 10–11, 14–15.

"In Quest of Miss America." *Show,* September 1962, 61, 104–6.

"New Mexico: Tom-Tom Christmas." *Show,* December 1962, 125–26.

"Jonathan Winters: Always On." *Holiday,* November 1965, 101–12.

"Thomas Berger on *Little Big Man.*" *Audience,* July–August 1972, 38–45.

"Films." *Esquire* (monthly column), April 1972–June 1973. One of these columns, "Candy Darling Is (Almost) All Girl," was reprinted in the *Esquire Anniversary Issue,* October 1973, 162, 394, 396.

"I Am Not a Movie Person." *American Film,* December 1981, 34–36.

Foreword to *German Medieval Tales,* edited by Francis G. Gentry, vii–x. New York: Continuum, 1983.

"The Justice of Ross Macdonald's Voice." In Ross Macdonald, *Inward Journey,* edited by Ralph B. Sipper, 111–13. Santa Barbara, Calif.: Cordelia Editions, 1984.

Selected Reviews by Thomas Berger

"Crisis-Morality in Fiction." Review of *The Novel of Violence in America,* by W. M. Frohock. *New Leader,* 26 August 1950, 25.

"Orwell as Essayist: Pound as Correspondent." Review of *Shooting an Elephant,* by George Orwell; *The Letters of Ezra Pound;* and *An Examination of Ezra Pound. Intro* (1951): 98–100.

"Ideology and Literature." Review of *The Age of Longing,* by Arthur Koestler, and *The Origins of Totalitarianism,* by Hannah Arendt. *Intro* (1951): 169–71.

Review of *A Woman in Berlin,* anonymous. *Socialist Call,* November 1954, 23–24.

"Back from the Pit." Review of *Human Behavior in the Concentration Camp,* by Elie A. Cohen. *Institute of Social Studies Bulletin* 3, no. 2 (1955): 22–23.

Review of *Harvest of Hate,* by Léon Poliakov. *Socialist Call,* April 1955: 22–23.

Review of *The Making of the President 1972,* by Theodore White. *New York Times Book Review,* 5 August 1973, 1, 22–23.

Interviews

Britton, Anne. "Scalping Best Seller: Thomas Berger Talks to Anne Britton in Wild West Kensington." *Books and Bookmen,* October 1965, 46–53.

Lang, Tony. "Close-Up: Thomas Berger." *Cincinnati Enquirer Magazine,* 8 October 1972, 21–24.

Rydell, Charles. "Book-Maker-of-the-Month: Thomas Berger." *Andy Warhol's Interview,* July 1975, 38–39.

Hughes, Douglas. "Thomas Berger's Elan: An Interview." *Confrontation* no. 12 (Summer 1976): 23–39. By far the most extensive and useful Berger interview before Madden's.

Schickel, Richard. "Interviewing Thomas Berger." *New York Times Book Review,* 6 April 1980. Focuses on *Neighbors* and offers a valuable update to the Hughes interview.

Knippling, James. "Thomas Berger: Reclusive Writer." *Cincinnati,* December 1981, 28, 30–31.

Moore, Jean P. "Author of *Neighbors* Says It's His Favorite . . ." *Tampa Tribune,* 21 December 1981, 1D, 6D. Reprinted in *Florida English Journal* 18 (April 1982): 4–5.

Ghose, Zulfikar. "Observations from a Correspondence: Letters from Thomas Berger." *Studies in American Humor* 2 (Spring 1983): 5–19. Illuminating excerpts from a twenty-year correspondence with writer, critic, and friend Zulfikar Ghose.

Reefer, Mary. "The Substance of Style: An Interview with Thomas Berger." *New Letters* 55 (Fall 1988): 85–98. Does not add much to other Berger interviews.

Ross, Jean W. Interview with Thomas Berger. In *Contemporary Authors, New Revision Series,* edited by Hal May and James G. Lesniak, 57–59. Detroit: Gale Research, 1990.

Nilsson, B. A. "Of Words and Letters." In *Metroland* (Albany, New York), 28 February–6 March 1991, 16. Brief interview on the occasion of the publication of *Orrie's Story.*

Graeber, Laurel. "The Sinister is His Hobby." *New York Times Book Review,* 12 July 1992, 7. Brief sidebar interview accompanying a review of *Meeting Evil.*

———. "Loving the Losers." *New York Times Book Review,* 6 March 1994, 8. Brief sidebar interview accompanying a review of *Robert Crews.*

Madden, David. "An Interview with Thomas Berger." In *Critical Essays on Thomas Berger,* edited by David Madden, 151–74. New York: G. K. Hall, 1995. The most wide-ranging and probing interview by a major Berger critic. Very useful.

Ward, Andrew. "Little Big Man's Man." *American Heritage* 50 (May–June 1999): 89–96. This interview is online at http://www.americanheritage.com/articles/magazine/ah/1999/3/1999_3_89.shtml (accessed 29 September 2008). While primarily concerned with *The Return of Little Big Man* it ranges across Berger's work.

Public Statements

"A Statement." In *Dictionary of Literary Biography Yearbook: 1980,* edited by Karen L. Rood, Jean W. Ross, and Richard Ziegfeld, 17. Detroit: Gale Research, 1981.

"Who Created Whom? Characters That Talk Back." *New York Times Book Review,* 31 May 1987, 36. Berger discusses his relationship to his characters, explaining their lack of autobiographical origin.

"Touring Western Europe, 1956." *Antaeus* no. 61 (Autumn 1988): 38. Berger's account of his return to the sites of his army service at the end of World War II. One of the few autobiographical pieces by Berger.

Manuscript Collection

Boston University Library.

Film Adaptations from Berger's Novels

Little Big Man, 1970; *The Neighbors,* 1981; *The Feud,* 1990.

Works about Thomas Berger

Books

Landon, Brooks. *Thomas Berger.* Boston: Twayne, 1989.

Madden, David W., ed., *Critical Essays on Thomas Berger.* New York: G. K. Hall, 1995.

Wallace, Jon. *The Politics of Style: Language as Theme in the Fiction of Berger, McGuane, and McPherson.* Durango, Colo.: Hollowbrook, 1992.

Special Journal Issue

Weber, Brom. "Special Issue Honoring Thomas Berger." *Studies in American Humor* 2 (Spring and Fall 1983). Weber guest edited this two-issue focus on Berger, which featured sixteen articles and offered the first sustained critical study of his fiction.

Selected Articles and Reviews

General Overviews of Berger's Writing

Landon, Brooks. "The Radical Americanist." *Nation,* 20–27 August 1977, 151–53. Praise for Berger's first eight novels; suggests that reading his celebrations of fictional forms is unsettling "since his oblique assaults on popular conceptions of rationality never advertise their complexity, while his experiments never parade themselves as such."

Lethem, Jonathan. "Berger's Ambivalent Usurpations." Introduction to Thomas Berger's *Meeting Evil.* New York: Simon & Schuster, 2003. Highly perceptive analysis of and celebration of Berger's themes, style, and importance by one of his very best readers. An abridged version of this essay appeared in *Village Voice Literary Supplement,* May 2003.

Madden, David W. Introduction to *Critical Essays on Thomas Berger,* edited by David W. Madden, 1–25. New York: G. K. Hall, 1995. The introduction to this invaluable collection of responses to Berger's fiction is an equally invaluable introduction to the critical reception Berger received during the first half of his career.

———. "The Renegade Mood in Thomas Berger's Fiction." *Studies in American Humor* 2 (Fall 1983): 130–41. An insightful and useful examination of the philosophical importance of criminals, criminality, and police officers in Berger's fiction.

Malone, Michael. "Berger, Burlesque, and the Yearning for Comedy." *Studies in American Humor* 2 (Spring 1983): 20–32. Reprinted in Madden, ed., *Critical Essays on Thomas Berger,* 89–99. A persuasive analysis of Berger's complexity that also considers why his achievements have not been better celebrated. Whatever the novel form, Berger writes comedy, as opposed to comic novels, bringing us, as does Beckett, "to confront our *metaphysical* (as opposed to our social) bewilderment."

Moore, Jean P. "Thomas Berger's 'Joyful Worship': A Study of Form and Parody." *Studies in American Humor* 2 (Spring 1983): 72–82. Berger's writing reveals his postmodern sensibility, but its most significant feature is "the revitalizing of received forms through the innovative, creative use of their conventions." Essay reflects the thesis of Moore's dissertation on Berger.

Schulz, Max F. "Thomas Berger: His World of Words, and Stereoscopes of Style." *Studies in American Humor* 2 (Fall 1983):

87–100. Focuses on the centrality of language and prose style in Berger's fiction, detailing the ways in which each of Berger's novels develops a unique style.

Wilde, Alan. "Acts of Definition, or Who Is Thomas Berger?" *Arizona Quarterly* 39 (Winter 1983): 314–15. Republished in Alan Wilde, *Middle Grounds: Studies in Contemporary American Fiction*. Philadelphia: University of Pennsylvania Press, 1987. Instructive essay on Berger's work even though several of its conclusions attempt to force a biographical reading. Wilde's phenomenology of Berger recognizes the inseparability for the author of the concepts of freedom and of self-definition, but sees in Berger's novels a "fear of otherness," which might more accurately be called a "fascination."

Bibliography

Bense, James. "Works by and about Thomas Berger." *Studies in American Humor* 2 (Fall 1983): 142–52. Reprinted and updated in *Bulletin of Bibliography* 51 (June 1994).

Articles and Major Reviews Focused on Individual Novels

The Reinhart Series

Baumbach, Jonathan. Review of *Reinhart's Women. American Book Review,* 20 March 1982, 16. Baumbach terms Berger's career one of "quiet dazzle."

Cassill, R. V. "Reinhart Back from Berlin, Out of Love and Ready for Freezing." *New York Times Book Review,* 29 March 1970. Excellent assessment of first three Reinhart books.

Cheuse, Alan. Review of *Reinhart's Women. Saturday Review,* 8 September 1981, 60.

DeMott, Benjamin. "Further Adventures of a Loser." *New York Times,* 27 September 1981. Online in *New York Times* archives; online at http://www.nytimes.com/1981/09/27/books/further adventures-of-a-loser.html (accessed 22 October 2009). Review of *Reinhart's Women* offers an overview of Berger's career, with special attention to the Reinhart books.

Hassan, Ihab. "Conscience and Incongruity: The Fiction of Thomas Berger." *Critique: Studies in Modern Fiction* 5, no. 2 (1962): 4–15. The first critical acknowledgment of Berger's complexity in *Crazy in Berlin* and *Reinhart in Love.*

Hicks, Granville. "Little Man, What Absurdity Now?" *Saturday Review,* 14 April 1962, 24. Review of *Reinhart in Love.*

Hollander, John. Review of *Vital Parts. Harper's Magazine,* April 1970, 106.

Hughes, Douglas A. "The Schlemiel as Humanist: Thomas Berger's Carlo Reinhart." *Cithara* 15, no. 1 (1975): 3–21. Reprinted in Madden, ed., *Critical Essays on Thomas Berger,* 45–60. An insightful reading of the first three Reinhart books. Reinhart, "an embodiment of those humanist values the author wishes to celebrate, clearly belongs in the tradition of the Jewish schlemiel-hero, the wise fool whose very real shortcomings are mitigated by his essential goodness."

Janssen, Ronald R. "The Voice of Our Culture: Thomas Berger's *Reinhart in Love.*" *Studies in American Humor* 2 (Fall 1983): 111–16. This essay by the first scholar to write a doctoral dissertation on Berger locates the novel's comedy in the inspection and criticism of "the values expressed in American material culture, especially as those values are promulgated by and through American commerce."

Leonard, John. "Reinhart on the Rocks." *New York Times,* 31 March 1970, 39. Review of *Vital Parts* by one of Berger's better readers.

Pinsker, Sanford. "The World According to Carl Reinhart: Thomas Berger's Comic Vision." *Studies in American Humor* 2 (Fall 1983): 101–10. Excellent analysis of the Reinhart books, placing them, along with Roth's Zuckerman series and Updike's Rabbit books, "among our literature's finest achievements. Praises

Berger's sensibility and his prose style in creating "a dense, Rabelesian [*sic*] texture, as uncompromising in its vision as it is American to its bones."

Schickel, Richard. "Bitter Comedy." *Commentary,* July 1970, 76–80. This review of *Vital Parts* offers an astute introduction to Berger's writing, positing his theme as "the devastation of the individualist ethic by the spirit of our time," and specifying Berger's basic belief that "as we lose faith in our traditional individualism we seek, at every level of life, compensatory fantasies of power, of escape, of impractical idealism." Schickel was one of the first critics to recognize Berger's uniqueness, and he remains one of the most able commentators on Berger's writing.

Simon, Myron. "*Crazy in Berlin* as Ethnic Comedy." *Studies in American Humor* 2 (Spring 1983): 33–44. Reprinted in Madden, ed., *Critical Essays on Thomas Berger,* 100–110.

Swados, Harvey. "An American in Berlin." *New Leader,* 15 December 1958, 24. Reprinted in Madden, ed., *Critical Essays on Thomas Berger,* 29–30. Unusually perceptive and prescient review of *Crazy in Berlin.*

Weales, Gerald. "Reinhart as Hero and Clown." *Hollins Critic* 20 (December 1983): 1–12. Reprinted in Madden, ed., *Critical Essays on Thomas Berger,* 76–88. Perhaps the best single essay on the Reinhart books. "The strength of the Reinhart books is that the reader keeps recognizing his similarities to the good fool, the horse's ass, when he would prefer to identify with the poet-philosopher hero that Reinhart spends so many years imagining hidden within his untidy mind and body."

Weber, Brom. "The Mode of 'Black Humor.'" In *The Comic Imagination in American Literature,* edited by Louis D. Rubin Jr., 361–71. New Brunswick, N.J.: Rutgers University Press, 1973. Identifies Berger as one of the few writers who have escaped the "decline in quality and prestige of the longstanding American black humor tradition." Places *Vital Parts* "in the great black humor tradition of Hawthorne, Melville, Faulkner."

———. Review of *Vital Parts. Saturday Review,* 21 March 1970, 42. Reprinted in Madden, ed., *Critical Essays on Thomas Berger,* 29–30. Identifies Berger as "a major American Novelist."

Little Big Man and *The Return of Little Big Man*

Betts, Richard A. "Thomas Berger's *Little Big Man:* Contemporary Picaresque." *Critique: Studies in Modern Fiction* 23 (1981–82): 85–96.

Bezanson, Mark. "Berger and Penn's West: Visions and Revisions." In *The Modern American Novel and the Movies,* edited by Gerald Perry and Roger Shatzkin, 272–81. New York: Frederick Unger, 1978. Interesting to compare with "Thomas Berger on *Little Big Man.*"

Cleary, Michael. "Finding the Center of the Earth: Satire, History, and Myth in *Little Big Man.*" *Western American Literature* 15 (1980): 195–211. Reprinted in Madden, ed., *Critical Essays on Thomas Berger,* 61–75.

Grace, Sherrill E. "Western Myths and Northern History." *Great Plains Quarterly* 3 (Summer 1983): 146–56. An excellent discussion of Jack Crabb as a "genuine fabulator," a character "who knows how to exploit and manipulate language and rhetorical style." Jack's self-consciously crafted story is twentieth-century captivity narrative that "explores all the white psychological fears and taboos" of early captivity narratives, "while at the same time exploiting the ritual and mythic pattern of all such narratives."

Gurian, Jay. "Style in the Literary Desert: *Little Big Man.*" *Western American Literature* 3 (1969): 285–96. Noting that Berger "never sacrifices his imagination to realism," Gurian argues that *Little Big Man* "is a great novel because it portrays western 'society' in the nineteenth century as it really was—violent, yes, but also absurd, melodramatic, incongruous."

Hitt, Jim. *The American West from Fiction (1823–1976) into Film (1909–1986).* Jefferson, N.C., & London: McFarland, 1990. 102–7.

Klinkenborg, Verlyn. "Sidekick to History." *New York Times,* 9 May 1999. Online at *The New York Times on the Web,* http://www.nytimes.com/books/99/05/09/reviews/990509.09klinket.html (accessed 29 September 2008). Review of *The Return of Little Big Man.*

Landon, Brooks. "The Measure of *Little Big Man.*" *Studies in American Fiction* 17, no. 2 (1989): 131–42. Overlaps Landon's introduction to *Twenty-fifth Anniversary Edition of Thomas Berger's Little Big Man.* New York: Dell, 1989. xi–xviii.

Lee, L. L. "American, Western, Picaresque: Thomas Berger's *Little Big Man.*" *South Dakota Review* 4, no. 2 (1966): 35–42. The picaresque form of *Little Big Man* allows the author to explore western myth without becoming its sentimental victim. Berger's theme is that "the truly worthy man is the individual," meaning "to have the courage and strength to live one's own life."

Oliva, Leo E. "Thomas Berger's *Little Big Man* as History." *Western American Literature* 8 (1973): 33–54. Thoroughly documents the historical accuracy of details in *Little Big Man* (finding only one chronological incongruity), while praising the creative skill with which Berger assembled those details.

Royot, Daniel. "Aspects of the American Picaresque in *Little Big Man.*" In *Les Americanistes: New French Criticism on Modern American Fiction,* edited by Ira D. Johnson and Christiane Johnson, 37–52. Port Washington, N.Y.: Kennikat Press, 1978. French concepts of the picaresque need to be modified to understand how "Crabb's unique experience withstands efforts toward generalization," and how his adventures "teach that reality *is* at best seen as someone's make-believe."

Sinowitz, Michael Leigh. "The Western as Postmodern Satiric History: Thomas Berger's *Little Big Man.*" *CLIO: A Journal of Literature, History, and the Philosophy of History* 28 (January 1999): 129–48. Title says it all.

Turner, Frederick W., III. "Melville and Thomas Berger: The Novelist as Cultural Anthropologist." *Centennial Review* 13 (1969):

101–21. Compares the project of *Little Big Man* with that of Melville's *Israel Potter.*

———. "The Second Decade of *Little Big Man.*" *Nation,* 20–27 August 1977, 149–51. Celebrates *Little Big Man as* a "seminal event in what must now seem the most significant cultural and literary trend of the last decade: the attempt on many fronts to develop structures, styles, ways of thinking that are beyond any version of ethnocentrism."

Turner, John W. "*Little Big Man.* The Novel and the Film: A Study of Narrative Structure." *Literature / Film Quarterly* 5 (1977): 154–63. Compare with Bezanson and with "Thomas Berger on *Little Big Man.*"

Wallace, Jon. "The Implied Author as Protagonist: A Reading of *Little Big Man.*" *Western American Literature* 22 (February 1988): 291–99. Excellent focus on the form of *Little Big Man.* By attending to the implied author behind Snell and Crabb, "we discover not only another voice in Berger's novel . . . but also another story that is told in terms of style rather than plot."

Berger's Other Novels

Bernstein, Richard. "Out of Kilter in a Predatory Society." *New York Times,* 13 September 1996, 33. Online at http://query.nytimes.com/gst/fullpage.html?res=9903E3DD163AF930A2575AC0A960958260 accessed 30 September 2008). Review of *Suspects.*

Braudy, Leo. Review of *Regiment of Women. New York Times Book Review,* 13 May 1973, 6–7. Perceptive review that sees beyond the topical subject matter into Berger's larger concerns.

Davenport, Guy. "Masters of Time and Place." *National Review* 19 (1967): 1283. Review of *Killing Time* that recognizes Joe Detweiler as "one of the most complex characters in modern fiction."

———. "Tough Characters, Solid Novels." *National Review* 17 (1965): 66–70. Review of *Little Big Man* and glance at Berger's early career by an able commentator on Berger's fiction.

Dickstein, Lore. Review of *Regiment of Women,* by Thomas Berger. *Ms.,* August 1973, 32–34. Reprinted in Madden, ed., *Critical Essays on Thomas Berger,* 34–35. Evenhanded feminist review.

Eder, Richard. "Dangerous Liaisons." *New York Times,* 10 September 2007. Review of *Best Friends.*

Edwards, Thomas R. "Domestic Guerrillas." *New York Times Book Review,* 6 April 1980. Review of *Neighbors* makes a strong case for Berger's importance in American literature, calling our failure to read and study Berger "a national disgrace."

Ghose, Zulfikar. Review of *Adventures of the Artificial Woman. Review of Contemporary Fiction* 24 (Summer 2004): 134. Brief but trenchant.

Glover, Douglas. "Caspar Milquetoast, These Are Your Lives." *New York Times Book Review,* 27 August 1989, 12. Review of *Changing the Past.*

Herman, Harold J. "Teaching White, Stewart, and Berger." In *Approaches to Teaching the Arthurian Tradition,* edited by Maureen Fries and Jeanie Watson, 113–17. New York: MLA, 1992. Points to some of Berger's divergences in *Arthur Rex* from other contemporary Arthurian tales.

Jankofsky, Klaus P. "Sir Gawaine at Liberty Castle: Thomas Berger's Comic Didacticism in *Arthur Rex: A Legendary Novel.*" In *Gawain: A Casebook,* edited and with an introduction by Raymond H. Thompson and Keith Busby, 319–36. New York: Routledge, 2006.

Jones, Louis B. "Evil Incarnate Is a Guy Named Richie." *New York Times Book Review,* 12 July 1992, 7.

Landon, Brooks. "Language and the Subversion of Good Order in Thomas Berger's *Regiment of Women.*" *Philological Quarterly* 62 (1983): 21–30.

———. "Thomas Berger's Arthur Rex." In *Arthur through the Ages,* edited by Valerie Lagorio and Mildred Leake Day, 240–54. New York: Garland, 1990.

———. "The Whole Kit and Caboodle: Language as Irony in Thomas Berger's *Neighbors* and *Sneaky People.*" *Studies in American Humor* 2 (Spring 1983): 61–71.

Lehmann, Chris. "Tom Perotta Hails Suburban Sendup *Neighbors.*" You Must Read This, NPR, 6 June 2007. Novelist Perotta offers high praise for *Neighbors,* calling Berger "the funniest serious writer in America."

Madden, David W. Review of *Best Friends. Review of Contemporary Fiction* 23 (Fall 2003): 135. Brief but insightful review by a scholar well versed in Berger's writing.

———. "Thomas Berger's Comic-Absurd Vision in *Who Is Teddy Villanova?*" *Armchair Detective* (1981): 37–43. Compares TV with Chandler's *Farewell, My Lovely;* unlike Chandler, Berger has his protagonist expose not hidden truth, but the elusiveness of truth.

Malone, Michael. "American Literature's Little Big Man." *Nation,* 3 May 1980, 535–37. An important review essay, describing *Neighbors* as a "flawlessly crafted morality play," and judging Berger "the real thing: a major Major Writer." After stating that "no one at work in this country writes better than he does—and precious few write anywhere near as well," Malone explains some of the reasons for Berger's relative lack of fame. He identifies Berger's three basic themes as a "war with time," a "yearning for human rightness," and "a baffled love of women in uneasy tension with idealistic aspirations about manliness and realistic despair about sexual politics."

Mano, D. Keith. "A Good Book by a Good Writer, Thomas Berger." *New York Times Book Review,* 20 April 1975, 4–5. Exuberantly perceptive review of *Sneaky People,* with special attention to the style of its narrative.

Marx, Bill. "It's All Greek: Berger Perfects the Slow Burn." *Boston Phoenix Literary Section,* October 1990, 6. Reprinted in Madden, ed., *Critical Essays on Thomas Berger,* 41–44. Review of *Orrie's Story.*

Maslin, Janet. "She's Too Good to Be True: Sexy and Battery-Operated." *New York Times,* Books of the Times, 29 April 2004, 8. Review of *Adventures of the Artificial Woman* finds the author "in high spirits, and in a high-concept storytelling realm."

Michaels, Leonard. "If Hammett and Chandler Were Written by Perelman." *New York Times Book Review,* 20 March 1977, 1, 26. Reprinted in Madden, ed., *Critical Essays on Thomas Berger,* 36–37. Review of *Who Is Teddy Villanova?*

Mitchell, Burroughs. *The Education of an Editor.* Garden City, N.Y.: Doubleday, 1980. 141–45. Brief but interesting details about working with Berger early in his career.

O'Donnell, Patrick. "Short-Changed: Thomas Berger's *Changing the Past.*" In Madden, ed., *Critical Essays on Thomas Berger,* 138–48. New York: G. K. Hall, 1995.

Prose, Francine. "Outnumbered by Jerks." *New York Times Books Review,* 12 April 1987, 9. Review of *Being Invisible* that praises Berger's cranky sensibility.

Queenan, Joe. "Follies." *New York Times Book Review,* 29 September 1996, 19. Review of *Suspects.*

Rakoff, Joanne Smith. "Top Dog, Underdog." *Time Out New York,* 22–29 May 2003, 81–82. Review of *Best Friends* with comments by Berger and an overview of Berger's career.

Romano, John. "Camelot and All That." *New York Times Book Review,* 12 November 1978. Review of *Arthur Rex* in which Romano identifies as the wry paradox at the book's heart the belief that "doing good in a world that is mostly bad can have bizarre or disastrous consequences." Praises Berger's power "to be both farcical and moving at once" and concludes that *Arthur Rex* is "the Arthur book for our time."

Rowe, John Carlos. "Alien Encounter: Thomas Berger's *Neighbors* as a Critique of Existential Humanism." *Studies in American Humor* 2 (Spring 1983): 45–60. Reprinted in Madden, ed., *Critical Essays on Thomas Berger,* 111–24. One of the most provocative studies of Berger.

Rudd, Jay. "Thomas Berger's *Arthur Rex:* Galahad and Earthly Power." *Critique: Studies in Contemporary Fiction* 25 (January 1984): 92–100.

Streitfeld, David. "Berger's Story." *Washington Post Book World,* 16 September 1990, 15. Review of *Orrie's Story.*

Stypes, Aaron. "Thomas Berger and Sheer Incongruity." *South Dakota Review* 32 (January 1994): 34–43. Breezy overview of Berger's writing by a critic determined to see Berger as a comic writer or satirist.

Thompson, Raymond H. "Humor and Irony in Modern Arthurian Fantasy: Thomas Berger's *Arthur Rex.*" *Kansas Quarterly* 16 (July 1984): 45–49.

———. *The Return from Avalon: A Study of the Arthurian Legend in Modern Fiction.* Westport, Conn.: Greenwood, 1985. See pages 155–61. *Arthur Rex* is "in many ways the most impressive" of contemporary Arthurian ironic fantasies.

Trachtenberg. Stanley. "Berger and Barth: The Comedy of Decomposition." In *Comic Relief: Humor in Contemporary American Literature,* edited by Sarah Blacher Cohen, 45–69. Urbana: University of Illinois Press, 1978. Useful not for its comparison of Berger with Barth as much as for its recognition of larger patterns in Berger's fiction.

Tyler, Anne. "Home Folks at One Another's Throats." *New York Times Book Review,* 8 May 1983, 1, 24. Reprinted in Madden, ed., *Critical Essays on Thomas Berger,* 38–40. Review of *The Feud.*

Wallace, Jon. "Laughter as Self-Defence in *Who Is Teddy Villanova?*" *Studies in American Humor* 5 (Spring 1986): 40.

———. "A Murderous Clarity: An Intertextual Reading of Thomas Berger's *Killing Time.*" *Philological Quarterly* 68 (Winter 1989): 101–14. Reprinted in Madden, ed., *Critical Essays on Thomas Berger,* 125–37. Superb analysis of philosophical implications of Berger's use of sources in *Killing Time.*

Index